CW01346189

THE BRITISH SCHOOL OF
ARCHAEOLOGY AT ATHENS

Supplementary Volume No. 20

EXCAVATIONS IN CHIOS
1952–1955
BYZANTINE EMPORIO

EXCAVATIONS IN CHIOS 1952–1955

BYZANTINE EMPORIO

by
MICHAEL BALLANCE
JOHN BOARDMAN
SPENCER CORBETT
SINCLAIR HOOD

SUPPLEMENTARY VOLUME NO. 20

Published by
THE BRITISH SCHOOL OF ARCHAEOLOGY AT ATHENS
THAMES AND HUDSON
1989

© The British School of Archaeology at Athens
and individual authors 1989

ISBN 0 500 96023 2

Typeset by Oxbow Books
at Oxford University Computing Service
Printed in Great Britain at the Alden Press, Oxford

To the Proedros and People of Piryi,
who provided the foreman and the work force
for the excavations at Emporio

Contents

Preface and Acknowledgements	vii
Abbreviations	ix
Introduction (Sinclair Hood)	1
Chapter 1. The Early Christian Basilica Church Complex	11
1. The Christian Church at Emporio (Spencer Corbett)	11
2. Comments on the Church Complex (Sinclair Hood)	28
3. Analysis of Coins from the Church Complex (Sinclair Hood)	33
4. Sections through the Church Complex (Spencer Corbett and Sinclair Hood)	35
5. Index to Finds from the Basilica Church Complex Area	46
Chapter 2. The Settlement and Fortress	47
1. The Sea Shore Trials (Sinclair Hood)	47
2. The Byzantine Fortress (Michael Ballance)	49
3. Analysis of Coins from Settlement and Fortress (Sinclair Hood)	82
4. Index to Principal Findspots in the Fortress (John Boardman)	84
Chapter 3. The Finds (John Boardman)	86
1. Introduction	86
2. The Pottery	88
3. Other Materials	122
4. The Coins	139
Chapter 4. Tombs at Emporio and Dotia (Sinclair Hood)	143

Preface

Sinclair Hood

This is the fourth and last volume of final reports on the excavations by the British School at Athens at Emporio on the south coast of Chios between 1952 and 1955. The first volume (*Greek Emporio*) by John Boardman was published in 1967, the two volumes of *Prehistoric Emporio* by Sinclair Hood in 1981 and 1982. This fourth volume deals with the Late Roman, Byzantine and later mediaeval finds from the excavations. Preliminary notices of the work in the Early Christian basilica church complex and in the Byzantine fortress have appeared in *JHS* lxxiv (1954) 163 and *AR* 1954, 22f.

The excavations at Emporio were made possible by the generosity of citizens of Chios (see *Greek Emporio* v; *Prehistoric Emporio* i, xi). The prehistoric site there was discovered by Sinclair Hood in June, 1952, and soundings were made later that year into deposits of an Early Bronze Age destruction assignable to the time of the First City of Troy (Emporio prehistoric Period IV). Excavations were begun on a larger scale in 1953 and continued until 1955.

As part of the programme of work in 1953 a curved piece of walling in open ground about 100m north-west of the main area (A) of the prehistoric excavations (*Prehistoric Emporio* i 86 fig. 47) was examined by Anthony Baynes. This proved to belong to a circular baptistry with a marble-lined cruciform font. Further soundings showed that the baptistry was attached to an Early Christian basilica church. Spencer Corbett, then Librarian of the British School at Rome, accepted an invitation to continue the exploration of the basilica church complex in the following year (1954). Geraldine Talbot assisted in this work. Sinclair Hood drew the archaeological sections and studied the stratigraphy.

Between 1953 and 1955 the Early Byzantine fortified settlement on the Acropolis hill overlooking the sites of the main prehistoric excavations and the basilica church complex was explored under the direction of John Boardman (1953) and Michael Ballance (1954–55). The fortifications may have been constructed in the early part of the reign of Constans II (641–68) against the Arab threat. The settlement within them was evidently destroyed by the Arabs shortly before the attack on Constantinople which began in 674. This destruction horizon in the fortress is Period I. The basilica church complex was also destroyed in Period I, and traces of a Period I destruction were noted in soundings (Sea Shore Trials) in what appears to have been an area of open settlement north of the harbour (FIG. 1 A–E).

There were at least two phases of subsequent reoccupation (Period II) in the fortress. During the first of these, which ended in the early ninth century, parts of the basilica church complex seem to have been restored to use. Later phases of the Period II reoccupation of the fortress appear to have come to an end before the close of the eleventh century and perhaps a good deal earlier. Glazed pottery of the eleventh century was found in a grave by the chapel on the Acropolis hill, but the chapel and the graves round it may date from a time after the fortress had been abandoned and settlement on the Acropolis hill had ceased.

For a map of Chios showing the position of Emporio in the south of the island see *Prehistoric Emporio* i 3 fig. 1. A map of South Chios is published in *Greek Emporio* xii fig. 1. The map drawn by Michael Ventris (*Greek Emporio* xiii fig. 2) covers the area of Emporio with the valley behind it and the Archaic Greek city on Profetes Elias north of the harbour. The relationship of the Basilica Church complex to the Greek Sanctuary by the harbour and the main prehistoric excavations is illustrated by the plan of the area below the Acropolis hill to the west in *Prehistoric Emporio* i 87 fig. 48.

DRAWINGS I–X are loose fold-outs in the flap at the back of the volume. In the catalogues of pottery, other finds and coins, the abbreviation Bas is used for the basilica church complex, and SS for the Sea Shore Trials in the area of open settlement north of the harbour.

Acknowledgements

We are deeply indebted to the late Dr Philip Argenti and Mr George Choremis, and to all the many other donors, citizens of Chios, who by their generosity made the work at Emporio possible.

We would also like to take this opportunity of thanking all those who helped with the excavations at Emporio, both those whose names appear in this and the previous volumes of reports, and those who have not been mentioned by name.

Professor Cyril Mango kindly read the first draft of the Introduction, corrected errors in it, and suggested references for the background of the period. We are much obliged to him. Any errors that remain are there through our fault.

Professor Martin Harrison, who as a student of the British School at Athens helped with the excavations at Emporio, most generously agreed to read the draft of the report on the Early Christian basilica complex, and also looked at a later version of the Introduction. We are grateful to him for helpful suggestions and references.

The map of the area on FIG. 1 was traced by Mrs Patricia Jacobs from the original drawing by the late Dr Michael Ventris. Mrs Jacobs also made the tracings of the tombs. Mr William Taylor drew the map on FIG. 2, and traced the plans and elevations of the fortress and all the archaeological sections. The basilica plans and drawings apart from the archaeological sections are the work of Mr Spencer Corbett.

We are grateful to Mrs Vasso Pennas for work on the Byzantine coins, and for attempting to find the three missing coins from beneath the north wall of the basilica church in Chios Museum.

Abbreviations

The following abbreviations are used in addition to those current in *BSA*:

Ahrweiler 1966	Hélène Ahrweiler, *Byzance et la Mer* (Paris, 1966)
Antoniadis-Bibicou 1966	Hélène Antoniadis-Bibicou, *Études d'Histoire Maritime de Byzance: à propos du 'Thème des Caravisiens'* (Paris, 1966)
Aupert 1980	P. Aupert, 'Céramique Slave à Argos (585 Ap. J.-C.)', in Études Argiennes (*BCH* Supplément vi) (Athens, 1980) 373–394
Bersu 1938	G. Bersu, 'A 6th century German Settlement of *foederati*: Golemanovo Kale, near Sadowetz in Bulgaria', *Antiquity* xii (1938) 31–43
Chabot 1903	*Corpus Scriptorum Christianorum Orientalium: Scriptores Syri* ser. 3 tom. 4.1 Chronicon Miscellaneum ad AD 724 Pertinens: ed. E. W. Brooks, interpretatus est I. B. Chabot (Paris, 1903) 61–119
Charanis 1945	P. Charanis, 'On the Social Structure of the Later Roman Empire', *Byzantion* xvii (1944–45) 39–57
Charanis 1947	P. Charanis, 'On the Question of the Hellenization of Sicily and Southern Italy during the Middle Ages', *American Historical Review* lii (1946–47) 74–86
Charanis 1950	P. Charanis, 'The Chronicle of Monemvasia and the Question of the Slavonic Settlements in Greece', *DOPapers* v (1950) 139–166
Charanis 1953	P. Charanis, 'On the Slavic settlement in the Peloponnesus', *BZ* xlvi (1953) 91–103
Charanis 1955	P. Charanis, 'The Significance of Coins as Evidence for the History of Athens and Corinth in the Seventh and Eighth Centuries, *Historia* iv (1955) 163–172
Christidis 1981	V. Christidis, 'The raids of the Moslems of Crete in the Aegean sea, Piracy and Conquest', *Byzantion* li (1981) 76–111
Conze 1912	A. Conze, *Altertümer von Pergamon* Bd 1 Text 1 *Stadt und Landschaft* (Berlin, 1912)
Diehl 1896	Ch. Diehl, 'L'origine du régime des thèmes dans l'empire byzantin', in *Études d'histoire du moyen age dédiées à Gabriel Monod* (Paris, 1896) 47–60
Felten 1975	Florens Felten, 'Die christliche Siedlung', in H. Walter (ed.), *Alt Ägina* Bd I, 2 (Mainz, 1975) 55–78
Foss 1975	C. Foss, 'The Persians in Asia Minor and the end of Antiquity', *English Historical Review* xc (1975) 721–747
Foss 1976	C. Foss, *Byzantine and Turkish Sardis* (Harvard, 1976)
Foss 1977	C. Foss, 'Late Antique and Byzantine Ankara', *DOPapers* xxxi (1977) 27–87
Foss and Winfield 1986	C. Foss and D. Winfield, *Byzantine Fortifications. An Introduction* (Pretoria: University of South Africa, 1986)

Gagniers 1985	J. des Gagniers, *Soloi — Dix campagnes de fouilles (1964–1974)* (Sainte-Foy, 1985)
Gelzer 1899	H. Gelzer, *Die Genesis der Byzantinischen Themenverfassung* (Leipzig, 1899)
Greek Emporio	J. Boardman, *Excavations in Chios 1952–1955, Greek Emporio* (London, 1967)
Haldon 1979	J. F. Haldon, *Recruitment and Conscription in the Byzantine Army c. 550–950. A Study on the Origins of the Stratiotika Ktemata* (Österreichische Ak. der Wiss., Phil.- Hist.-Kl., Sitzungsberichte 357) (Wien, 1979)
Humann 1904	C. Humann, *Magnesia am Mäander* (Berlin, 1904)
Huxley 1977	G. L. Huxley, 'The Second Dark Age of the Peloponnese', Λακωνικες Σπουδες iii (Athens, 1977) 84–110
Huxley 1986	G. L. Huxley, *Why did the Byzantine Empire not fall to the Arabs?* (Inaugural Lecture by George Huxley, Director of Gennadius Library, in the American School of Classical Studies at Athens) (Athens 22. x. 1986)
Karayannopulos 1959	J. Karayannopulos, *Die Enstehung der byzantinischen Themenordnung* (Munich: Beck, 1959)
Kythera	J. N. Coldstream and G. L. Huxley, *Kythera* (London, 1972)
Lawrence 1983	A. W. Lawrence, 'A Skeletal History of Byzantine Fortification', *BSA* lxxviii (1983) 171–227
Lemerle 1954	P. Lemerle, 'Invasions et migrations dans les Balkans depuis la fin de l'époque romaine jusqu' au VIIIe siècle', *Revue Historique* vol. 211 (1954) 265–308
Lemerle 1963	P. Lemerle, 'La chronique improprement dite de Monemvasie: le contexte historique et légendaire', *REByz* xxi (1963) 5–49
Lemerle 1981	P. Lemerle, *Les plus anciens recueils des Miracles de Saint Démétrius et la pénétration des Slaves dans les Balkans* i *Le Texte*, ii *Commentaire* (Paris 1979, 1981)
LRP	J. W. Hayes, *Late Roman Pottery* (London, 1972)
Lewis 1951	A. R. Lewis, *Naval Power and Trade in the Mediterranean A.D. 500–1100* (Princeton, 1951)
Lilie 1984	R.-J. Lilie, 'Die zweihundertjärige Reform. Zu den Anfängen der Themenorganisation im 7. und 8. Jahrhundert', *Byzantinoslavica* xlv (1984) 27–39, 190–201
Mango 1980	C. Mango, *Byzantium. The Empire of New Rome* (London, 1980)
Metcalf 1962 (1)	D. M. Metcalf, 'The Slavonic Threat to Greece circa 580: some Evidence from Athens', *Hesperia* xxxi (1963) 134–157
Metcalf 1962 (2)	D. M. Metcalf, 'The Aegean Coastlands under threat: Some Coins and Coin Hoards from the Reign of Heraclius', *BSA* lvii (1962) 14–23
Miles 1964	G. C. Miles, 'Byzantium and the Arabs: Relations in Crete and the Aegean Area, *DOPapers* xviii (1964) 1–32
Müller-Wiener 1986	W. Müller-Wiener, 'Von der Polis zum Kastron', *Gymnasium* xciii (1986) 435–475
Obolensky 1971	D. Obolensky, *The Byzantine Commonwealth: Eastern Europe, 500–1453* (London, 1971)

Ostrogorsky 1942	G. Ostrogorsky, 'Agrarian conditions in the Byzantine Empire in the Middle Ages', in J. H. Clapham and Eileen Power (edd.), *The Cambridge Economic History of Europe from the decline of the Roman Empire* i *The Agrarian Life of the Middle Ages* (Cambridge, 1942) 194–223
Ostrogorsky 1953	G. Ostrogorsky, 'Sur la date de la composition du livre des thèmes et sur l'époque de la constitution des premiers thèmes d'Asie Mineure (A propos de la nouvelle édition du 'De Thematibus' de A. Pertusi)', *Byzantion* xxiii (1953 pub. 1954) 31–66
Ostrogorsky 1963	G. Ostrogorsky, *Geschichte des Byzantinischen Staates* (*Handbuch der Altertumswissenschaft* xx. 1. 2) (Munich, 1963)
Pertusi 1952	A. Pertusi, *Costantino Porfirogenito: De Thematibus* (Citta del Vaticano, 1952)
Picard 1979	O. Picard, 'Trésors et circulation monétaire à Thasos du IVe au VIIe siècle après J.-C.', in *Thasiaca* (*BCH* Supplément v) (Athens, 1979) 411–454
Popovic 1978	V. Popovic, 'La descente des Koutrigours, des Slaves et des Avars vers la mer Égée: le témoinage de l'archéologie', *CRAI* 1978, 596–648
Prehistoric Emporio	S. Hood, *Excavations in Chios 1938–1955, Prehistoric Emporio and Ayio Gala* i, ii (London, 1981, 1982)
Schneider 1929	A. M. Schneider, 'Samos in frühchristlicher und byzantinischer Zeit', *AM* liv (1929) 96–141
Setton 1954	K. M. Setton, 'On the raids of the Moslems in the Aegean in the Ninth and Tenth Centuries and their alleged occupation of Athens', *AJA* lviii (1954) 311–319
Tomlinson and Fossey 1970	R. A. Tomlinson and J. M. Fossey, 'Ancient Remains on Mount Mavrovouni, South Boeotia', *BSA* lxv (1970) 243–263
Tsakos 1979	K. Tsakos, *Symbole sten Palaiochristianike kai Proïme Byzantine Mnemeiographia tes Samou AE* 1979 Parart. 11–25.
Vryonis 1981	S. Vryonis, 'Michael W. Weithmann, *Die slavische Bevölkerung auf der griechischen Halbinsel* (1978)', *Balkan Studies* xxii (1981) 405–439
Waage	F. O. Waage, *Antioch-on-the-Orontes* IV 1 (Princeton, 1948)
Welkov 1935	I. Welkov, 'Eine Gotenfestung bei Sadowetz (Nordbulgarien)', *Germania* xix (1935) 149–158
Wiseman 1978	J. Wiseman, 'Stobi in Jugoslavian Macedonia: Archaeological Excavations and Research, 1977–78', *Journal of Field Archaeology* v (1978) 391–429
Wittek 1932	P. Wittek, 'Zur Geschichte Angoras im Mittelalter', in T. Menzel (ed.), *Festschrift für Georg Jacob* (Leipzig, 1932) 329–354
Yannopoulos 1980	P. A. Yannopoulos, 'La Pénétration Slave en Argolide', in *Études Argiennes* (*BCH* Supplément vi) (Athens, 1980) 323–371

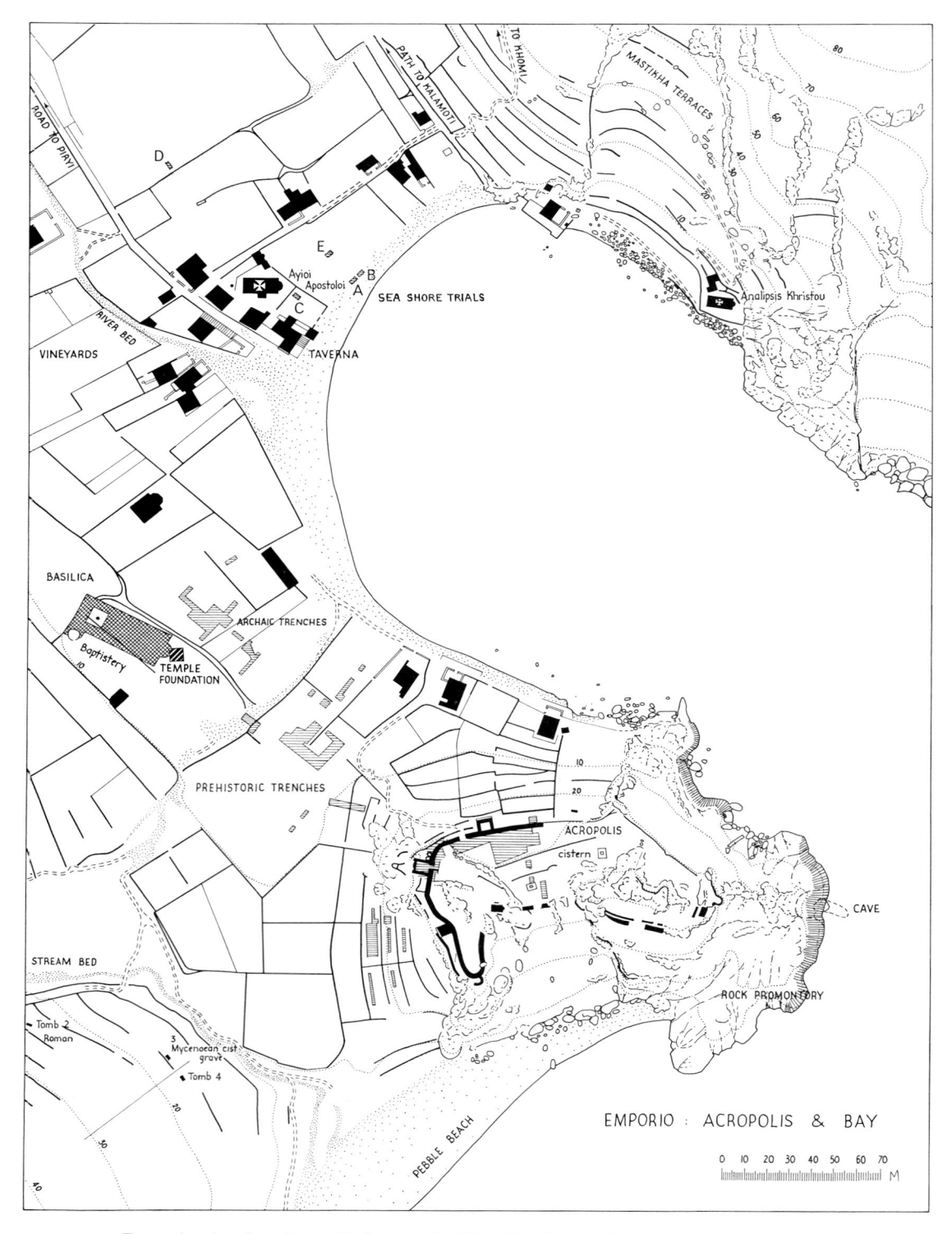

FIG. 1. Emporio, showing Acropolis fortress, basilica church complex, and Sea Shore Trials (A–E).

Introduction

Sinclair Hood

There was evidence for continuous occupation on a small scale at Emporio through the early Roman period, and probably from the 8th century BC or earlier, as Boardman notes (p. 86). Whether there was settlement on a really substantial scale anywhere in the region, however, between the time of the abandonment of the town on the slopes of Profetes Elias *c.* 600 BC and the 6th century AD when the Early Christian basilica church complex was built, appears to be doubtful. Boardman (*Greek Emporio* 249) has observed that it is reasonable to assume that after the town on the slopes of Profetes Elias was abandoned the main centre of occupation in the region was down by the harbour. But five small soundings (Sea Shore Trials) made in 1954 behind the houses at the north inner end of the harbour, north of the bed of the stream which flowed into the bay of Emporio from the north-west (FIG. 1 A–E), failed to reveal any traces of occupation earlier than Late Roman or Early Byzantine. These soundings, however, were too restricted in number and in size to allow conclusions which are in any way definitive.

Pottery from surface levels on the Acropolis hill overlooking the harbour suggested continuous occupation of some kind there into Hellenistic times (*Greek Emporio* 61). But no Early Roman pottery was identified from the Acropolis, although it was attested in the Sanctuary area by the harbour below it. Boardman, however, notes (p. 86) that the earliest Late Roman pottery from the Acropolis seems to be of the fifth century AD, and suggests that there must have been a considerable occupation there before the hill was fortified in the seventh century; but no occupation deposits and no walls or floors were recognised dating from this time. In fact no traces of buildings of any period were identified on the Acropolis between the latest Mycenaean assignable to the eleventh century BC and Early Byzantine of the seventh century AD. The recovery of a fragment of a plaque of *lapis lacedaemonius* (F141) is suggestive, but is not enough on its own to prove that a sumptuous public building or villa existed on the Acropolis before the construction of the fortress.

The Harbour Sanctuary at the foot of the Acropolis hill evidently continued to flourish, however, throughout Greek and into Roman times. Pottery ranging from the fifth century BC to the first AD was found in different places on the site of the earlier Greek sanctuary, although nowhere in contexts indicating clear building or occupation levels (*Greek Emporio* 83ff.). The altar that may have belonged to the fifth century temple (*Greek Emporio* 78f.) and of which pieces were eventually incorporated into the basilica church and baptistry, was still standing and being inscribed as late as the third century AD (*BSA* lix (1964) 34–6 no. 28). Many other stones and architectural pieces used by the builders of the church complex towards the end of the sixth century AD appeared to come from Classical, Hellenistic and Roman structures which might have been connected with the sanctuary. The base of a large rectangular building of the Early Roman period was evidently adopted as a platform for the nave and aisles of the basilica itself. The cistern on the south-east edge of the Harbour Sanctuary area may also have been Early Roman, dating perhaps from the first century AD (*Greek Emporio* 60, 84, 52 fig. 28: trench A. Cf. *Prehistoric Emporio* i 146 Area C.2: trench EE; 86f. figs. 47, 48).

The fact that the Harbour Sanctuary at Emporio continued in existence throughout the Hellenistic and Roman periods does not necessarily imply that a large settlement existed in the neighbourhood then. At Kato Fana along the coast to the west of Emporio the important sanctuary of Apollo Phanaios flourished from Early Greek into Roman times, but no traces of a major settlement have yet been identified near it. The building of a basilica church, however, with a baptistry attached at Emporio suggests the existence of a reasonably large population for which it was catering by that time, and the archaeological evidence, such as it is, from the five Sea Shore Trials (FIG. 1 A–E) indicates settlement in the flat ground beyond the north end of the bay in the Late Roman and Early Byzantine periods. There are even hints of a marked increase of population in the region of Emporio in the sixth century AD when the church complex was built. In addition to the admittedly tenuous evidence from Emporio itself, Boardman has drawn attention to the traces of Late Roman or Early Byzantine occupation assignable to the sixth and seventh centuries elsewhere in the area around, notably on the sites of what appear to have been farmsteads (p. 87).

The large built tomb above Vroulidhia bay at the western end of the Dotia plain (see p. 144) may date from the sixth century: it would suggest the comparative prosperity of the area at the time it was constructed. This impression would be heightened if, as seems likely, the stones which covered the tomb chamber were roofing slabs of a type used for monumental buildings like churches between the fifth and seventh centuries, although no building for which such roofing slabs might have been intended has yet been identified in the area.

In the immediate neighbourhood of Emporio itself only one tomb was discovered belonging to the Early Byzantine period contemporary with the basilica church complex and with the fortress on the Acropolis hill (p. 143 tomb 2). But very few graves of any period of antiquity were found during the course of the excavations (cf. *Prehistoric Emporio* i 150–3): this Early Byzantine tomb was in fact the only one noted dating from a time between the sixth and fifth centuries BC (*Greek Emporio* 97f.) and the early Middle Ages (tenth or eleventh century AD) (see p. 80).

If there was an increase of population in the region of Emporio in the Late Roman or Early Byzantine period, it could reflect the coming of refugees who had escaped from some part of the Balkan peninsula, ravaged by Goths and Huns at the end of the fourth and in the early fifth century, and from the time of Justinian (527–65) onwards subjected to massive raids by the Bulgars (Kotrigurs) and later by the Avars and Slavs (Lemerle 1954; 1981. Obolensky 1971. Popovic 1978. Mango 1980, 22–5).

In 540 the Bulgars (Kotrigurs) sacked Potidaia in Chalcidice and raided as far south as the Isthmus of Corinth, taking it is said over 100,000 prisoners. The Slavs appear to have moved into the Balkans in large numbers in the following decade, and may have begun to establish permanent settlements in some remote and mountainous areas there at this time (Lemerle 1954, 287. Cf. Popovic 1978, 631f.). Place names listed by Procopius suggest that they had become settled especially in the region between Niš and Sofia before the end of Justinian's reign in 565 (Mango 1980, 22).

Coin hoards indicate that there were other raids and invasions of the Balkans in the period after 562 in addition to those attested by the scanty historical records (Popovic 1978, 612, 616). A hoard of coins found in the area of the city of Thasos may reflect some early threat by Slav or Avars to this offshore island. The latest datable coins are assigned to 571/2 shortly before a major descent into the Balkans by the Avars under their ruler Baian in 573 or 574; but Picard (1979, 450) believes that the hoard may have been buried somewhat later at the time of the Slav invasion of *c.* 578–80.

Several coin hoards from Athens appear to reflect a Slav incursion around 580 or not much later (Charanis 1955. Metcalf 1962 (1)). This may have been connected with the Slav invasion of the Peloponnese which was followed by the establishment of Slav settlements there. It was during this period that the Avars took Sirmium (582) and organised their Slav subject-allies in a vigorous but unsuccessful siege of Salonika. Charanis (1947) has suggested that the influx of large numbers of refugees from the southern part of the Balkan peninsula especially after the Slav/Avar invasions in the early years of Maurice (582–602) may have been responsible for the hellenisation of Italy and Sicily for which there is evidence at this time.

The Slavs seem to have overrun Corinth (with the probable exception of the fortress on Acrocorinth) in the winter of 584/5, and subsequently occupied Argos in the spring perhaps of 585 (Yannopoulos 1980). Corinth and Argos were soon restored to Byzantine control; but the central and western parts of the Peloponnese were evidently abandoned to the Slavs. The first permanent Slav settlements there are dated by the Chronicle of Monemvasia to 587/8 (Charanis 1953. Aupert 1980. Yannopoulos 1980. Vryonis 1981). The testimony of the Chronicle about the Slav occupation of the Peloponnese and the refugee movements from it is now widely accepted as reliable in its main outlines (Charanis 1950. Lemerle 1963. Huxley 1977, 86–92). The Chronicle gives details of how the inhabitants of the Peloponnese took refuge from the Slavs in the mountains, or escaped to Italy and to Monemvasia and islands in the Aegean like Aegina. The settlement founded by refugees from Corinth on Aegina has been reasonably identified with the Byzantine town established about this time on the Kolonna hill there (Felten 1975, 77).

The evidence for an increase of population in the region of Emporio appears to go back earlier than this, and the basilica church complex may date from the end of the third quarter of the sixth century, before *c.* 575. There must have been extensive movements of refugees, however, from various parts of the Balkan peninsula including the north of Greece before the Slav break-through into the Peloponnese in the 580s. The scanty historical sources, supplemented by the lives of saints and letters, only afford glimpses of these against the background of constant raids and invasions, accompanied by the destruction of settlements and the leading away of large numbers of people into captivity. Those who could do so had every incentive to escape to places of relative safety, whether fortresses like Salonika or Monemvasia, or islands overseas.

The fortress on the Acropolis hill at Emporio was constructed in the time of Heraclius (610–41) or of his successor Constans II (641–68). The pottery from the hill suggests that there was occupation of some kind there, however, from the fifth century AD onwards. The earliest pottery recovered from the Sea Shore Trials (FIG. 1 A–E) at the north end of the bay similarly dates from the fifth or early sixth century. This may have been the main area of settlement in the region of Emporio throughout the Early Byzantine period. Occupation evidently continued here after the erection of the fortress, and was only brought to an end for a time when the fortress itself was destroyed by the Arabs *c.* 670.

The building of such a fortress at Emporio is unlikely to reflect the spontaneous and unaided efforts of the local population. The elaborate character of the defences suggests an initiative on the part of the regional or even central authorities. The remarkable variety in the style of construction of the defence walls may seem to belie this idea, but is simply due to the fact that large squared blocks of local white stone were taken from some earlier building for the main wall on the north side, while for that on the west rough boulders from the Acropolis hill itself were used: the defence wall here owing its primitive almost Cyclopean appearance to this.

The reasons for the construction of a fortress at Emporio and the question of who garrisoned

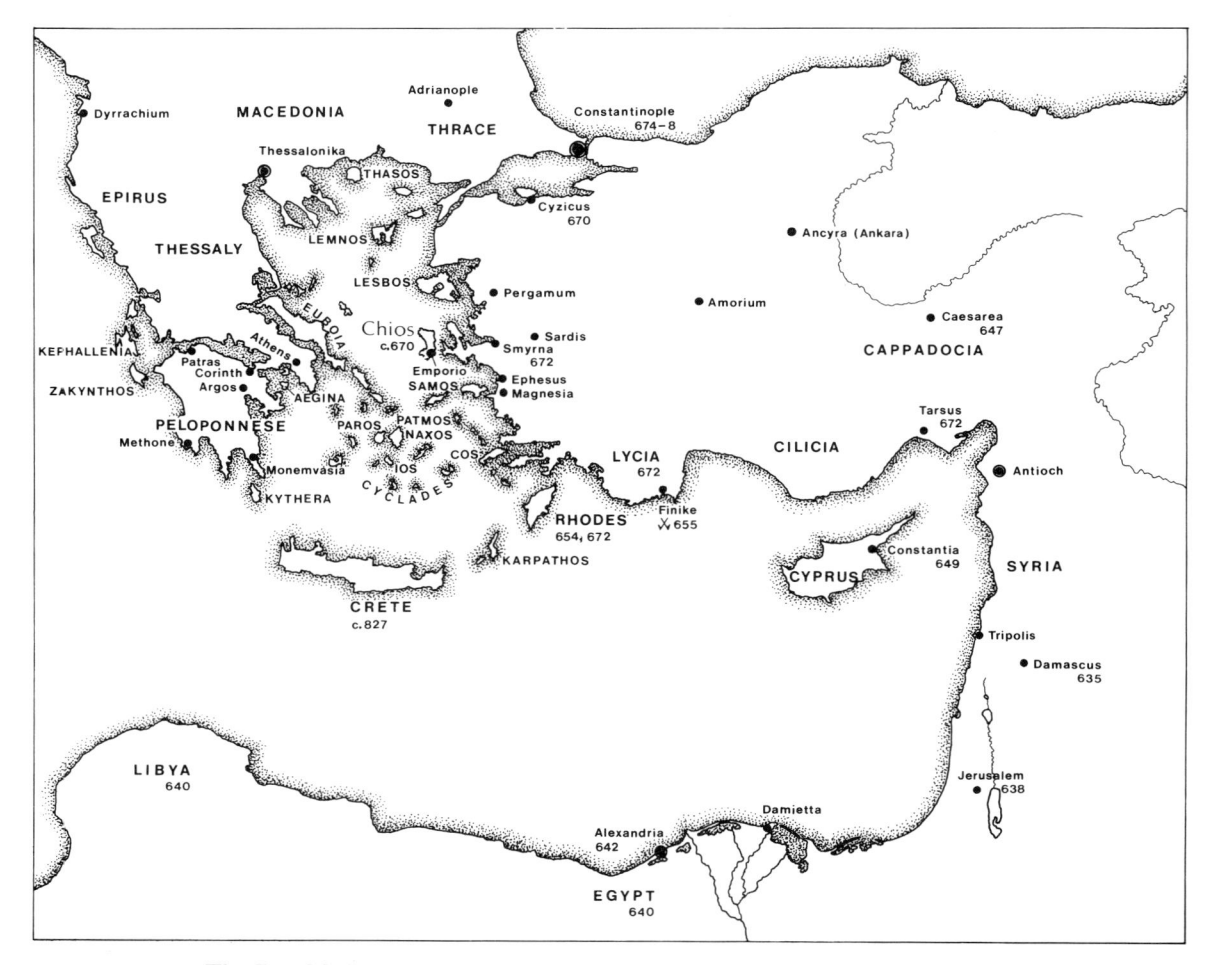

FIG. 2. The East Mediterranean in the late 7th century AD, with dates of main Arab thrusts.

it have to be considered against the background of the time. Boardman (p. 122) notes that the place was as much a fortified town as a military camp in the last few years of its existence, and it may have been so from the start. Fishing tackle and tools are much in evidence among the finds from the Arab destruction level of c. 670, and there are indications of retail trade in the shape of steelyards, balances and weights. Room IX looks as if it might even have been a shop. A graffito (FIG. 44, ii) on the shoulder of a pithos marks John the Boatswain as its owner. At the same time there are highly suggestive resemblances between the fortress at Emporio and somewhat earlier fortresses in the Balkans which appear to have been occupied by frontier troops (limitanei), like Sadovsko Kale and Golemanovo Kale described below.

From the end of the sixth century onwards, with the Slav and Avar penetration of the Balkans and the great invasions of the eastern provinces, first by the Persians and later by the Arabs, every part of the Byzantine Empire became in effect a frontier. The fluid situation created by these raids and invasions led, apparently by stages, to a complete reorganisation of the system of provincial government with the establishment of provinces of a new type known as themes (a term originally applied to military units) in which the military commander of the region was supreme over the civil administration as well. The uniting of civil and military powers in the hands of one official was nothing new. Justinian (527–65) had combined civil with military authority in this way on a large scale in the eastern provinces and especially in Anatolia (Karayannopulos 1959, 59ff.). The constant warfare in every part of the Empire in the seventh century can only have served to confirm the practice.

The earliest themes were large, and relatively few in number, like the army commands of the previous Masters of Soldiers (magistri militum) from which they appear to have evolved. Heraclius (610–41) may have established the first large themes in Anatolia at the time of the Persian war whch ended in 629. But the system was only extended it seems by stages, and was finally regularised at the end of the seventh century or the beginning of the eighth (Diehl 1896 is still basic. Gelzer 1899. Charanis 1945. Pertusi 1952. Ostrogorsky 1942, 196; 1953; 1963, 80. Karayannopulos 1959 with references. Ahrweiler 1966, 21f. Antoniadis-Bibicou 1966, 47–61. Obolensky 1971, 75. Mango 1980, 45–7. Lilie 1984).

Another important change which it has been suggested took place during this period was the extension of the traditional Late Roman system of frontier troops (limitanei) holding land which they cultivated in return for military service to every part of the Empire. Men from conquered provinces may have received land in exchange for military service in this way (Charanis 1945, 48f.). Such a development would have given the soldiers a vested interest in the defence of the territory in which they were based: the soldiers were in any case no longer for the most part foreign mercenaries, but native subjects of the Empire. The scanty records of the seventh to ninth centuries throw no certain light on this development, and there is dispute as to whether it took place at all (e.g., Haldon 1979). But in the conditions of the time, with every province effectively a frontier, it seems reasonable to believe that it did. The character of the fortress at Emporio itself suggests that it may have been garrisoned on such a basis.

It has also been suggested that against the background of destruction and movements of population caused by the invasions, the Late Roman system of big estates worked by peasants tied to the land like serfs may have largely disintegrated, leading to the predominance in what was left of the Empire of a free peasantry, which socially and economically merged into the class of soldier-peasants owing military service (Ostrogorsky 1942).

Various small fortresses of this general period resemble that at Emporio. The fort of Sadovsko Kale for instance on the river Vit in northern Bulgaria *c.* 40km south of Pleven and well south of the Danube shows instructive similarities, including an outer wall (*proteichisma*), a main tower (corresponding to the North-west Tower at Emporio), and a row of rooms (or cottages as Lawrence calls them) built against the inner face of the main defence wall (Lawrence 1983, 19of. fig. 9. Welkov 1935). This fort seems to have been manned by a garrison of Goths serving as *limitanei*, and was destroyed by the Avars during the reign of Maurice (582–602), probably about 584/5 at the time of the onslaught which opened the Peloponnese to their Slav subject-allies (Popovic 1978, 619).

Even more comparable with Emporio is the fortress of Golemanovo Kale across the river Vit from Sadovsko Kale (Bersu 1938). This was built in the time of Justinian (527–65) on the site of an earlier Roman settlement, which had been deserted after a destruction by fire in the fifth century. Bersu had the impression that Golemanovo Kale was garrisoned by Germans like Sadovsko Kale; but he emphasised that it was essentially a fortified village inhabited by peasants, although they were peasants who probably had the status of *foederati* (Bersu 1938, 42). Such fortified villages, as Bersu emphasised, could not have come into being simply through the initiative of the local population: their establishment must reflect the deliberate policy of the government. The fortress at Golemanovo Kale was eventually overwhelmed by the Avars around 600, shortly before or perhaps at the time when the Danube frontier was finally abandoned by the Byzantine authorities.

There was an open settlement near the fortified village at Golemanovo Kale, and this was destroyed by fire at the same time around 600 or not much later. The inhabitants of open settlements like this or the one in the area of the Sea Shore Trials (FIG. 1 A–E) at Emporio were no doubt able to seek refuge in the neighbouring fortresses in times of danger.

The area enclosed by the inner defence walls at Golemanovo Kale was about the same size as at Emporio. The line of the defences was similarly irregular in shape, adapted to the contours of the ground. There was a main tower, corresponding to the North-west Tower at Emporio, and an additional defence wall (*proteichisma*) was built just outside the main wall on the weakest (north) side. Some distance beyond this was a third defence wall not attested at Emporio.

Some of the houses and other structures at Golemanovo Kale were built along the inside of the main defence wall as at Sadovsko Kale and Emporio. This system is said to be usual in Byzantine fortification (Bersu 1938, 38); but the idea of building a row of rooms against the inside of a defence wall is found in all ages: Tsakos (1979, 13f. note 1) has collected many examples in connection with such an arrangement in the remarkable defended enclosure of Kastro tou Lazarou on top of Mt Lazaros in Samos.

The single defence wall at Kastro tou Lazarou was between 1.70 and 2.00m thick, and like the buildings enclosed by it was constructed without any use of mortar, which was only employed it seems for the small church (Tsakos 1979). Tsakos notes that this is not the only case where defence walls were constructed without mortar in the Early Byzantine period, citing a small fort on Mt Mavrovouni in southern Boeotia, dating perhaps from the time of Justinian (527–65) (Tomlinson and Fossey 1970, 261–3).

The defence wall at Kastro tou Lazarou encloses an area of *c.* 380 × 120 m, some seven or eight times larger than the space within the fortress at Emporio, and it has every appearance of being intended as the place of refuge for a considerable population. Surface pottery and a single coin of Constans II (641–68) indicate that the occupation of the Kastro dates from the period of the Arab attacks which led to the assault on Constantinople between 674 and 678. Tsakos (1979, 19) appears to believe that the Kastro was occupied throughout the period of the assault on Constantinople, and was only abandoned after peace was made as a consequence of the Arab defeat in 678. On this view the Kastro might have replaced the tunnel of the Eupalinos aqueduct as a place of refuge for the inhabitants of the main centre of Samos (*AA* 1973, 72–89, 401–16; 1975, 19–35).

Rhodes is known to have been occupied by the Arabs from 673 until after the death of Muawiya following the defeat of 678. There is a hint in the literature that Samos was similarly occupied for a time (Schneider 1929, 100 citing Khalkokondyles ed. Bonn 143). If there was an Arab occupation of Samos it was no doubt short-lived like that of Rhodes: the German excavators have suggested a period of about ten years for it from *c.* 668 to 678 (*AA* 1975, 35). It seems more likely, however, that in the case of islands like Chios and Samos the Arabs during this period were content to storm the coastal towns and fortresses like that at Emporio, but refrained from leaving garrisons, which they only did at a few main bases occupied in force, like Cyzicus, used against Constantinople, and Rhodes, which was a convenient intermediary station for ships coming from Syria or Egypt (cf. Lawrence 1983, 201).

The fortress at Emporio cannot have been built before the time of Heraclius (610–41). The latest datable coin of his from below the floors of buildings inside the fortress is C31 of 616/7. The Persian wars, lasting from 605 to 629, might have been the occasion for building such a fortress. Persian armies reached the Bosphorus more than once, taking Chalcedon opposite Constantinople in 615, and besieging it again in 626 (Foss 1975). In 622 or 623 the Persians are said to have overrun Rhodes and led away many captives including the Byzantine general (Foss 1975, 725 note 1, 744, citing the chronicle in Chabot 1903, 113. Cf. Metcalf 1962 (2) 14). A few years later about 627/8 they are thought to have attacked Samos: the inhabitants of the chief city of the island may have first used the tunnel of the Eupalinos aqueduct as a refuge on this occasion (*AA* 1975, 35).

Another incentive for building a fortress at Emporio during this period might have been the threat from Slav sea-raiders. Around 615 or not much later, at the time when they attempted to capture Salonika, the Slavs are reported to have taken to the sea in dug-out log boats, raiding and destroying far and wide throughout the Aegean including the Cyclades and parts of Asia Minor (Lemerle 1954, 295f.; 1981, 85ff. Yannopoulos 1980, 340, 362, 369. The doubts of Vryonis 1981, 422, about the feasability of such dug-out pirate voyages seem unjustified). Coins suggest that the city on the island of Thasos was destroyed in 619 or soon afterwards, apparently as the result of a Slav raid, which was followed by a long period of abandonment until the twelfth or thirteenth century (Picard 1979, 452). In 623 the Slavs even succeeded in reaching Crete in the course of these sea raids (Obolensky 1971, 54). The small fortified settlement at Kastri on Kythera (where the latest datable coins were assignable to 615/6) may have been abandoned as the result of Slav pressure at this time (*Kythera* 44f. Huxley 1977, 99).

It seems more likely, however, that the fortress at Emporio was built in response to the Arab threat. Lawrence (1983, 200–4) describes the scenario, and sets the destruction (and by implication the construction) of the Emporio fortress under the heading of 'Small-Scale Work Against the Arabs, Mid Seventh — Early Eighth Centuries'. The Arabs under the Caliph Omar began the invasion of the Empire in 634, and completed the conquest of Egypt in 642. In September 642 Byzantine troops withdrew from Alexandria to Rhodes.

The Arabs did not become a threat by sea, however, until Muawiya, the governor of Syria, began constructing a fleet soon after the death of Omar in 644. In 649 the first recorded Arab sea expedition attacked Cyprus and stormed the capital Constantia (Salamis) (Gagniers 1985, 123). In 654 Muawiya ravaged the island of Rhodes and took Cos. In the following year 655 the Byzantine fleet under the Emperor Constans II was defeated off Phoinike on the coast of Lycia. There was then a temporary respite from the Arab threat owing to the civil war between Muawiya and Ali after the murder of the Caliph Othman in June 656. This allowed Constans II to turn his attention to the west: he eventually settled in Sicily where he was assassinated in 668.

The construction of the fortress at Emporio may date from this period of manifest threat from the Arabs at sea in the reign of Constans II (641–68). While the harbour at Emporio was no doubt used upon occasion by Byzantine warships, a village fortress like this is unlikely to have been built in connection with the fleet which Constans II organised against the Arabs in the 650s. The decision to have a fortress here probably reflects the importance of the mastic crop of this part of southern Chios. The bay at Emporio may have been the main harbour from which the valuable mastic gum was exported from Chios in ancient times.

There seems to have been a good deal of fortress building against the Arabs during the reign of Constans II. The inner citadel at Ankara seems to date from this time (Wittek 1932, 330f. Foss 1975, 736; 1977, 74f.; 1986, 133f. Lawrence 1983, 204). Foss (1977, 74f.) would place the building of the citadel walls in the period 656–61 after the Arab capture of Ankara in 654. More interesting from the point of view of what happened at Emporio is the evidence for the presence of military detachments at Sardis around 660 when a new highway was built through the centre of the city destroyed by the Persians *c.* 616: it has been suggested that the fortress on the Acropolis was probably erected on this occasion (Foss 1976, 57–9. Foss and Winfield 1986, 131f.). Other Byzantine fortresses in western Anatolia, at Ephesus, Magnesia on the Maeander and Pergamum, may go back to the time of Constans II (Foss 1975, 742. Lawrence 1983, 202f. Foss and Winfield 1986, 132f.). Humann (1904, 2) assigned that at Magnesia to the age of Heraclius, but without citing evidence; while Conze (1912, 305) connected the one at Pergamum with an attack by the Arabs in 716. There was an earlier Arab capture of Pergamum, however, in 664 (Müller-Wiener 1986, 452. Cf. Conze 1912, 81 note 1).

It seems possible, although not certain, that two coins of Constans II (C41, C46) came from below floors of the fortress at Emporio: the later of these (C41) is datable to 645/6. If it was built in the early 650s after the Arab threat by sea had become critical the fortress would only have had a life span of some fifteen to twenty years before it was destroyed in the events which culminated in the five-year assault on Constantinople (674–8). Lawrence (1983, 200) formed the impression that the Emporio fortress was destroyed by the Arabs not long after it was built, and the archaeological evidence does not seem against this view. The latest datable coins of Constans II from the fortress were C41 of 645/6 and C44 with a range of 642–8. But two of the three coins of Constans II found in the area of the basilica church complex are assignable to his later years, C47 to 655/6–657/8, and C48 to 659/60.

A solitary coin (C49) of Constantine IV (668–85) who was Emperor during the period of the Arab attacks on Constantinople from 674 to 678 may be significant for the date of destruction of the fortress. This came from sounding C of the Sea Shore Trials (FIG. 1), and it was apparently found in association with pottery assignable to the period of the fortress destruction. The coin cannot be earlier than 668, and it may have been minted in 673, the year when Rhodes was occupied by the Arabs, and only a year before the attacks on Constantinople began. Possibly therefore the fortress, the basilica church complex, and the settlement area with the Sea Shore Trials north of the harbour, all suffered destruction at the hands of the Arabs upon the same occasion when this coin (C49) of Constantine IV was lost.

The fortress at Emporio, lying on the direct sea-route between the Arab base in Rhodes and the forward base at Cyzicus, is unlikely to have survived until the attack on Constantinople began in the spring of 674. The latest possible date for its destruction would seem to be the winter of 673/4. It might have been destroyed earlier, however, in 672 when the Arabs occupied parts of the coast of Cilicia and Lycia and took Smyrna on the mainland not far from Chios, or in 670 when they first gained possession of Cyzicus, or slightly before then as suggested by Ostrogorsky (1963, 103). Arab troops appear to have spent the winter of 666/7 in Pergamum and Ephesus with a cavalry depot at Malagina close to Nicaea (Huxley 1986).

Leo III (717–41) defeated the Arabs besieging Constantinople in 718, and some thirty years later in 747 a great Arab fleet was destroyed off Cyprus. From then onwards for half a century or more the Byzantines were in effective command of the sea (Lewis 1951, 66–70). At some point the fortress at Emporio was reoccupied and its defences were restored to inaugurate Period II. The area of the Sea Shore Trials north of the harbour also appears to have been resettled, and resettlement may have begun here before the restoration of the fortress. Parts of the basilica church complex, including the baptistry and its anteroom, were brought into use again at this time. Boardman (p. 114) notes that little pottery of this Period II reoccupation was recovered from the basilica area, and the only published vases are a couple from the anteroom to the baptistry (285, 287). The narthex, however, also appears to have been a focus of activity during this period, and a church of reduced dimensions may have occupied the former south aisle of the basilica or part of the nave.

The first phase of reoccupation of the fortress in Period II seems to have come to an end early in the ninth century. Two coins, one (C50) of Nikephoros I (803–11) and the other of Leo V (813–20), were found in debris above the earliest Period II floors in the fortress. To judge from the pottery, and in the absence of any coin evidence, the final destruction of the restored parts of the former basilica church complex might date from the same period. The baptistry at any rate appears to have been destroyed by fire, but no signs of a fire destruction in Period II were noted in the fortress.

The opening decades of the ninth century were marked by intensive Arab aggression in Greek waters (Setton 1954). Some of the islands, including large ones like Kythera, seem to have been abandoned by their inhabitants (*Kythera* 45). In the 820s Crete was conquered by an army of Spanish Arabs from Cordova who had established themselves at Alexandria. They were in fact descendants of Celto-Romans who had been born Moslems. These Cretan Arabs immediately became active in the Aegean. About 830 they are said to have seized Aegina, and may have remained in occupation of the island (Christidis 1981, 88, 96, 99f.). The Byzantine settlement on the Kolonna hill appears to have been destroyed by fire about this time (Felten 1975, 77f.). This may have been the occasion when the grandparents of St Luke the Steiriot fled from Aegina which was their native island (Miles 1964, 3).

It has been suggested that Cretan Arabs gained control of Cos for a time before the end of the reign of Michael II (820–29) (Christidis 1981, 91). Around 830 they destroyed a Byzantine fleet near Thasos and afterwards ravaged the Cyclades. Samos may also have suffered at the hands of the Arabs during this period (Schneider 1929, 101, citing Theophanes Continuatus iii.39 (ed. Bonn 1938 p. 137)). The end of the first phase of Period II reoccupation in the fortress and the final destruction and abandonment of the basilica church complex at Emporio are perhaps to be linked with this activity of the Cretan Arabs by sea in the years around 830.

Rather shadowy traces were noted of a further phase of reoccupation on the Acropolis hill at Emporio after the horizon of destruction or abandonment in the early ninth century. It is not clear when this reoccupation began, and there was no evidence as to how long it lasted. Whether the defences of the fortress were reactivated during this period is uncertain, but it seems likely that they were in view of the troubled state of the Aegean in the late ninth and early tenth centuries (see Christidis 1981, 92–7). There does not appear to have been any attempt to restore parts of the basilica church complex for use during this later phase of reoccupation on the Acropolis.

In the ninth century Chios seems to have been an independent maritime command like Cyprus and Crete (Ahrweiler 1966, 86, 101). For a time after this it was apparently in the theme of the Aegean Sea of which the city of Chios may have been the capital (Pertusi 1952, 83, 154f. Ahrweiler 1966, 108, 132 note 5). At the end of the tenth century, after Byzantine victories over the Arabs, Chios became a theme in its own right under a strategos (Ahrweiler 1966, 100f., 108, 130f., 133).

The small chapel by the Postern Gate of the fortress might have been built to serve the community which inhabited the Acropolis hill during the latest phase of reoccupation there. Glazed pottery (nos. 288–290) from one of the graves (Tomb III) connected with the chapel appears to date from the eleventh century and perhaps from the first half of it. This is in harmony with the calibrated radiocarbon dates for lumps of charcoal obtained from the bottom of the cistern in trench C of 1954: AD 1027 ± 32 with 5568 half-life, or 999 with 5730 half-life, which with MASCA calibration is *c.* 1040, but which with the Stuiver and Pearson calibration now standard hits a series of wiggles allowing a date over a wide range *c.* 1040–1160 (*AJA* lxv (1961) 367. *Radiocarbon* iv (1962) 152; xxviii (1986) No. 2B Calibration Issue 805–38).

Only one other fragment of glazed pottery (no. 291) was recognised from the Acropolis apart from what was found in Tomb III by the chapel. It is therefore possible that the inhabitants had moved down from the Acropolis hill to live by the harbour some time before the chapel was built. This would have been a reasonable step to take after the restoration of comparative peace to the Aegean following the reconquest of Crete from the Arabs in 960/1. But the Sea Shore Trials (FIG. 1 A–E) revealed no signs of occupation in that area as late as this.

Towards the end of the eleventh century after the battle of Manzikert (1071) the Seljuk Turks occupied Chios for a time (Ahrweiler 1966, 184, 208 note 4). In the couple of centuries which succeeded the Latin conquest of Constantinople in 1204 Chios was ravaged upon occasion and changed hands several times, but eventually came under Genoese control which lasted until the island was incorporated in the Ottoman Empire in 1566.

There was no evidence from our excavations for occupation anywhere in the region of Emporio during the Middle Ages between the eleventh and the fifteenth centuries. The surviving population of the area may have withdrawn during this period to inhabit the site of the now deserted inland village with defence walls and central tower at Dotia. It would be interesting if excavations could establish the date when occupation began there.

The bay at Emporio must have remained in use as a harbour for the region, however, and a few people may have continued to live by it at any rate during the summer months. Coins suggest that the chapel at the south-east corner of the former basilica church flourished in the fifteenth and sixteenth centuries. It seems just possible that the tombstone of a priest who built a church in the ruins of the ancient city of Emporio (published by Forrest, *BSA* lix (1964) 37 no. 33) refers to this chapel, but it may date from a century or so later.

The graves by the chapel and the coins from the area round it suggest the existence of a more or less permanent population at Emporio in the fifteenth and sixteenth centuries. Walls to the west and north of the chapel assignable to the same period may be those of contemporary houses. From that time onwards until the present day there was probably always a scatter of houses by the bay which forms the harbour, although the cemetery by the chapel appears to have gone out of use in favour of burial at Pirgi, the village some 5 km inland, in whose territory Emporio lies.

In the thirty years or more which have elapsed since the time of our excavations in the early 1950s improved access by road and recognition of the attractions of Emporio as a summer resort with excellent bathing have encouraged much new building in the area.

Chapter 1
The Early Christian Basilica Church Complex

1. The Christian Church at Emporio
Spencer Corbett
(DRAWINGS I–III, PLATES I–II)

General Description
The Christian church at Emporio stood about 120m west of the harbour, at a place where the gently sloping ground begins to ascend more steeply towards the heights to the south-west. Before the excavations of 1953–5 the remains of the church lay almost entirely below ground; only a small part of the baptistry wall, incorporated in a field boundary, suggested the presence of an ancient building. The area is divided into two parts by a field terrace which runs diagonally across the site. North of the terrace wall little remains but foundations and fragments of pavement. To the south, where the terrace retains a greater depth of soil, some walls of the church and of its adjoining rooms stand more than two metres high.

In most respects the church has a normal plan, comprising an axially laid-out atrium, narthex and assembly hall (FIGS. 3, 4; DRAWINGS I–II). A circular baptistry with a large anteroom and at least two other rooms lie to the south. The assembly hall appears to have been a straight-forward Christian basilica with a single apse at the east end and with aisles separated from the nave by colonnades of eight columns. Presumably the nave was lit by clerestory windows. The narthex was a narrow chamber set at right-angles across the west end of the basilica; its entrance was at the north end and it had an exedra at the opposite end; in the east wall the usual three doorways led into the nave and aisles of the basilica. Two doorways in the west wall of the narthex gave access to the atrium, an open court with stoae on its north, west and south sides. The baptistry lay south of the atrium, together with other rooms of uncertain function. The doorway at the north end of the narthex appears to have been the main entrance to the church; indeed it is possible that it was the only entrance.

Materials
Probably in the second quarter of the fifth century BC an apsidal Ionic temple, with its tetrastyle portico facing east, had been erected a few feet to the east of the ground where the

church was subsequently built. It is described in *Greek Emporio* 68–81. Part of the temple foundation remains *in situ*, serving to support the extremity of the church apse; it consists of carefully dressed blocks of white limestone, originally clamped together by wooden clamps fitting into dove-tail mortices. Many other limestone blocks pillaged from the temple by the builders of the church are identifiable in the church masonry, notably in the nave floor (PLATE 2 (*a*)), and there are also a number of worked marble blocks from the temple superstructure. Apart from this re-used material the structure of the church consists principally of three kinds of stone: a) a hard, crystalline material not unlike Roman *selce*, but almost white; b) a hard dark grey stone resembling basalt; c) grey and pink Chian marble, probably from the quarry at Latome near Chios town. Various other marbles occur as fittings.

The walls of the church are built of random rubble set in mortar, with larger and more rectangular blocks at the angles. Stones forming doorways etc. were cut accurately, but with a roughly dressed surface. Any finely tooled stones found in the structure probably came from older buildings. Inside the church the uneven rubble wall-faces were concealed by plaster, some of which survives. We do not know whether the exterior was plastered or if the rubble was exposed.

The apses and the baptistry were vaulted. Elsewhere the church had tile-covered roofs, witness many fragments of terracotta roof tile spread over the site.

The flanking aisles of the basilica and also the narthex had mosaic pavements ornamented with simple patterns. In the atrium and the ante-room to the baptistry the pavements were of black and white beach-pebbles arranged to form interlacing circles and squares (PLATES 8 (*a*), (*b*); 9 (*a*)). The baptistry floor was of unpolished green marble. Somewhat incongruously the nave of the basilica, where the pavement would ordinarily be at least as elaborate as elsewhere, was paved with white stone blocks, many of them disfigured by the dove-tail mortices which had been cut for their previous use in the fifth-century temple foundations (PLATE 2 (*a*)). To explain the incongruity it has been suggested that the nave floor was meant to be covered by rugs, as in many mosques.

The Basilica

At the beginning of their work the builders of the church prepared a perfectly level and rectangular platform (ABCD on FIG. 4) outlined by strong walls of carefully dressed stone blocks, some if not all taken from earlier structures (PLATE 3 (*a*), (*b*)). During our excavations the character of the platform masonry was seen to differ markedly from the other foundations of the church (e.g. PLATE 9 (*f*)); the blocks were more neatly cut and more accurately laid. This led to the suggestion that the platform might remain from some antecedent use, and although this was afterwards questioned it is now agreed that the platform does in fact appear to be the base of a building of the Early Roman period.

The outline of platform ABCD was identified in several places. The whole of the east side was revealed and a large part of the north side. The surface of the north-east corner block was taken as *datum* for the various levels noted on the general plan (DRAWING I); the north-west corner is at precisely the same level. Part of the west side of the platform was seen in a trench dug at the north end of the narthex, and its south side was seen in a deep cross-section cut through the south wall of the basilica, some 5m east of the south-east corner (DRAWING I). The platform is 25.85m long and 16.60m wide, dimensions which are repeated in the perimeter walls of the basilica. The platform retaining wall is at its highest at the north-east corner (B on FIG. 4), where it stands 0.70m above the gently sloping ground. Here there are three courses of

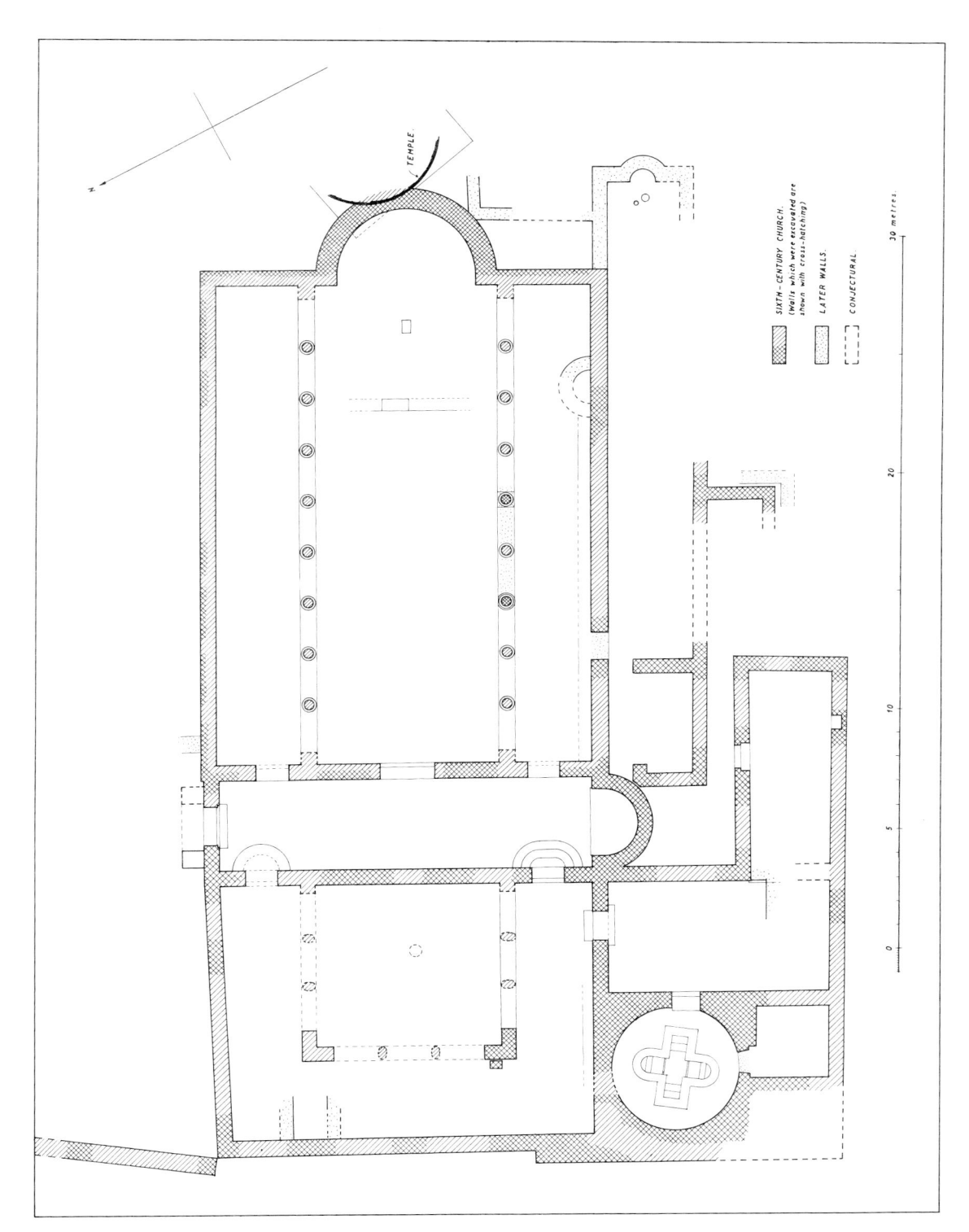

FIG. 3. Simplified plan of basilica church complex.

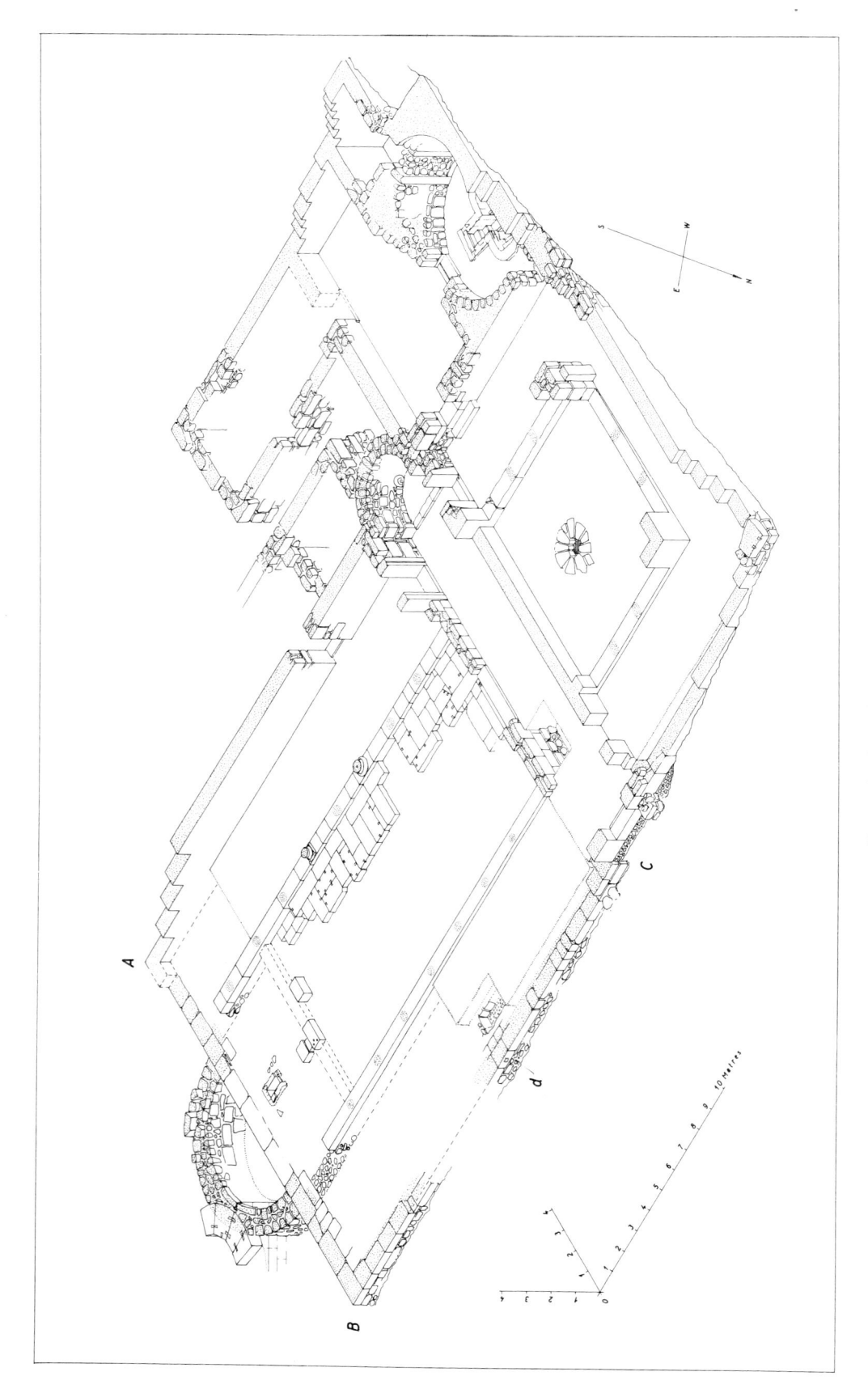

FIG. 4. Isometric view of basilica church complex.

masonry, but westwards towards C and northwards towards A the lower courses diminish in thickness, conforming with the gradual ascent of the terrain. At C the top course rests directly on the earth. Generally the lower courses consist of rather roughly finished stones, but the top course is consistently made of large, well-squared blocks carefully set to form a perfectly straight and horizontal margin, the latter emphasised by a drafted line on some blocks, 0.03m from the edge. Within the line of perimeter blocks, a second row of flat-topped stones at the same level gives the platform retaining wall a horizontal upper surface up to 1.30m wide. Some of the perimeter blocks are of Chian marble, others are of white *selce*. A number have projecting bosses; and one of these exposed in the north outer face of trench G comprises an inverted statue-base with an inscription dating probably from the last third of the sixth century B.C. (*BSA* lviii (1963) 54 no. 3. *Greek Emporio* 63 pl. 72 no. 22) (PLATE 7 (*b*)). Three copper coins were found beneath this when it was lifted for removal to the museum in Chios town at the end of the excavations.

The four perimeter walls of the basilica coincide precisely with the outline of the platform. The apse projects beyond the line of the east side, and the narthex and the atrium extend to the west. Although the rubble footings of the apse are not bonded with the masonry of the east side of the platform there can be little doubt that the apse was contemplated from the beginning. In quarrying stone from the fifth-century temple the church builders were careful to leave *in situ* the part of the early building which would be useful as underpinning of the apse.

Since the destruction of the church, the land has tended to revert to its natural contours with the result that the north-east corner of the building is the most razed; here nothing remains of the structure above the platform. At the north-west corner the upper structure is represented by two stone blocks. Further south, beside the central doorway of the basilica, two courses of masonry survive, and at the south-west corner of the basilica the walls stand more than two and a quarter metres high, being protected by the much greater depth of soil retained by the modern field terrace. The basilica walls are constructed with outer and inner faces of more or less accurately set rubble enclosing a core of small chips and fragments, all bound in lime mortar.

Upon the surface of the platform and within the lower courses of the basilica walls the substructure of the nave and aisle pavements was built up with packed earth and stones carefully laid in distinct strata (FIG. 6). The nave was separated from the aisles by the stylobates, which stood 0.11m above floor-level and consisted of carefully squared blocks of dark grey stone; beneath them is a stereobate of rubble set in mortar. The nave pavement (PLATE 2 (*a*)) is composed of thick white stone blocks taken from the temple foundations. The uneven texture of the present surface doubtless results from exposure to weather following the ruin of the church. The levelling of the heavy blocks in the church floor was effected by stone chips inserted in the earth fill; one chip appears in the foreground of the photograph (PLATE 2 (*a*)). Because of the sloping terrain the only paving stones to remain in position are those in the south-west part of the nave. The slabs which lie just inside the central doorway are of marble. From the relative levels of the marble threshold stone and the adjacent slabs it is certain that the nave floor had no decorative covering such as mosaic. FIG. 6 is a composite drawing taken in general along the line of section E–F in trench G; but members which are missing on that line are supplied from data obtained in other trenches, and are distinguished in the drawing by their pecked outline. The three courses of the platform wall retain a terrace of earth which extends as far as the nave colonnade where, at the same level, a zone of cobbles set in mortar is presumably the footing for the colonnade stereobate. (This feature was seen in the east trench (D) in the area of the north aisle, where higher members of stereobate have gone.) On the north

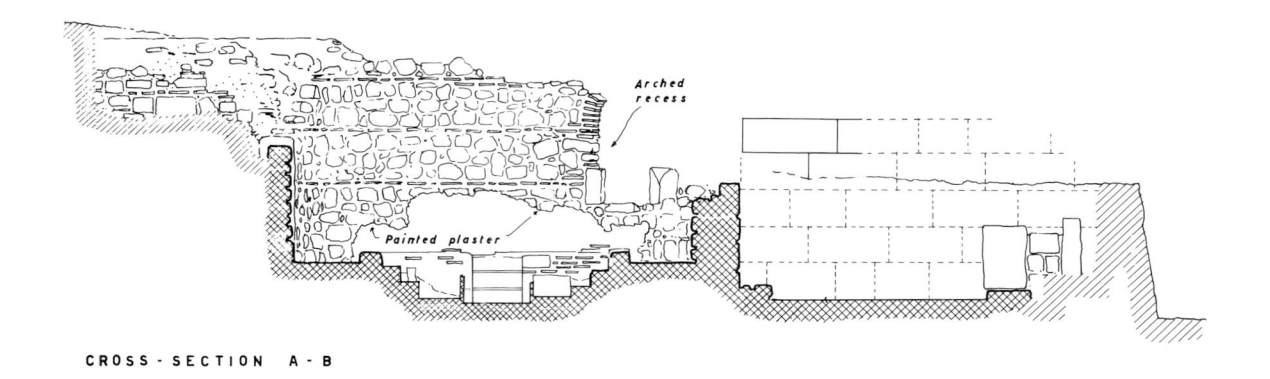

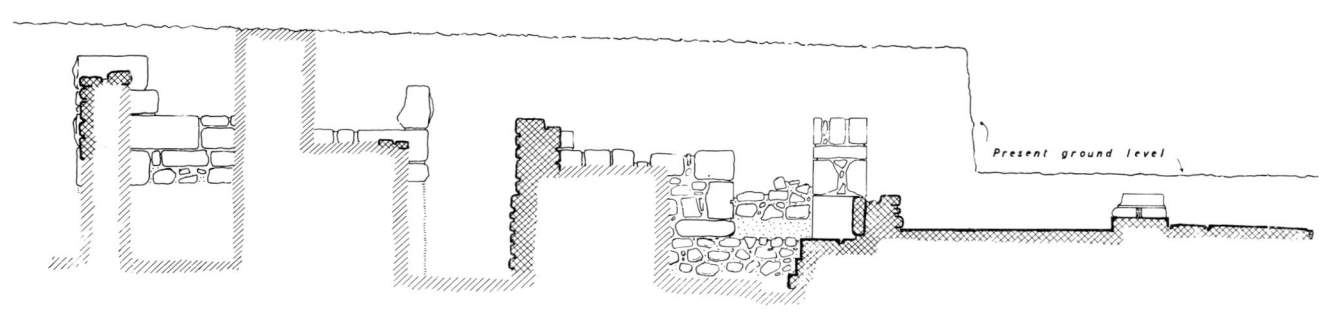

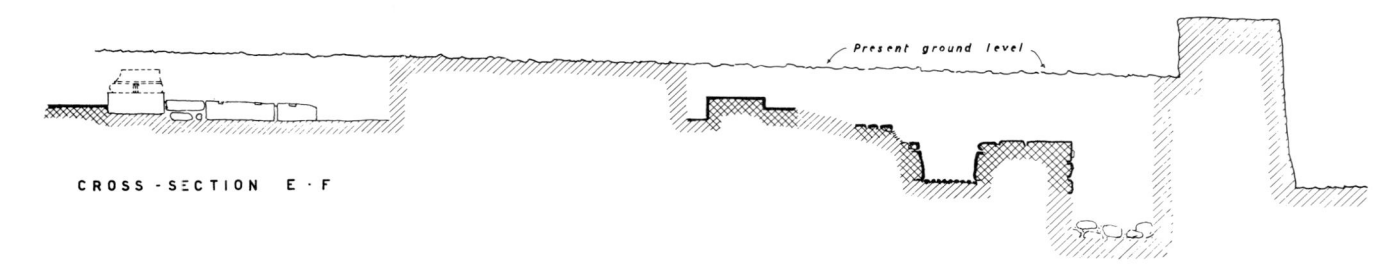

FIG. 5. Architectural sections.

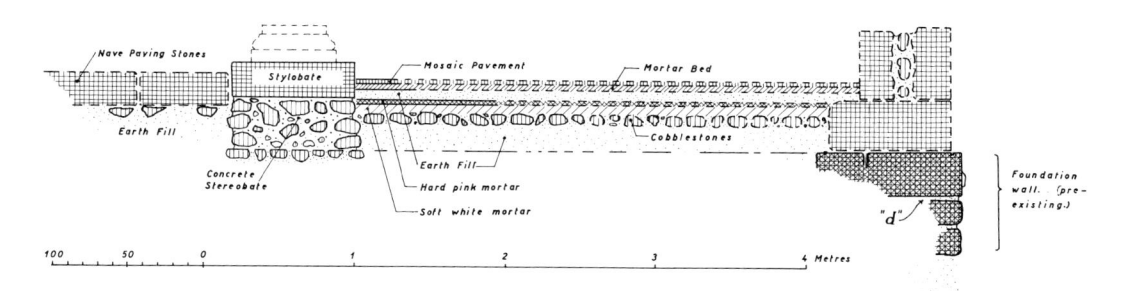

FIG. 6. Architectural section through north aisle on line E–F. Parts drawn with broken outline are not in position, but are supplied by analogy from other areas of the church.

side of the aisle, above the top course of the platform wall, the base of the basilica wall is shown; first a horizontal footing stone and then the vertical inner and outer facing stones of the wall itself, as discovered elsewhere in the building.

The mosaics of the aisle pavements (PLATES 2 (*b*); 4 (*b*)) are set in a bed of hard white cement which lies on top of a double stratum of fine hard, buff-coloured, clay-like earth, well packed (FIG. 14 Section 4. PLATE 7 (*b*)). Beneath was a thin layer of pink cement composed of broken potsherd (*opus signinum*), presumably a barrier against moisture which might otherwise weaken the mosaics. Further down was a thick layer of poor quality mortar mixed with earth, and below that was a carefully laid course of cobblestones. The aisle mosaics are of rather coarse quality, most tesserae being unshaped and separated from one another by a high proportion of bedding material. For red, pieces of terracotta were used. Black was derived from the basalt-like stone mentioned above. White, which predominates, is made of white marble, and colours such as violet, pink and brown were obtained from selected pieces of Latome marble. In the south aisle about half the original area of mosaic survives; in the north aisle only a minute portion was recovered.

The Apse   (PLATE 4 (*a*))

The apse foundation is built of a miscellany of large stones roughly bound by mortar. Many stones come from earlier buildings including parts of two volute capitals from the fifth-century temple. In radius the curve of the apse is nearly equal to that of the temple, and marble facing stones from the temple fit neatly in the apse wall. The most easterly part of the apse rests on the temple foundations, evidently preserved for that purpose. FIG. 7 shows the correspondence between the two foundations but for clarity omits, in the southern segment, the uppermost surviving stones of the apse. Here the apse wall is 0.90m thick and consists of the usual inner and outer skins of large, roughly shaped blocks enclosing a mortar-bound rubble core (PLATE 4 (*a*)). The buff-coloured clay-like earth noted under the nave and aisle pavements was also seen in the apse; being of a light colour it shows clearly in PLATE 4 (*a*), where its cross-section appears in the baulk which was allowed to remain on the centre-line (cf. FIG. 16 Section 8 level (4)). The chisel-shaped outline of the clay suggests that the darker earth to the east (FIG. 16 Section 8 level (5)) may remain from the base of a synthronos. Five Roman coins varying in date from the first to third centuries AD were found in the darker earth just underneath the tapering part of the clay (FIG. 16 Section 8 level (7)). Presumably this darker earth was brought from elsewhere when the site was being levelled to receive the apse pavement.

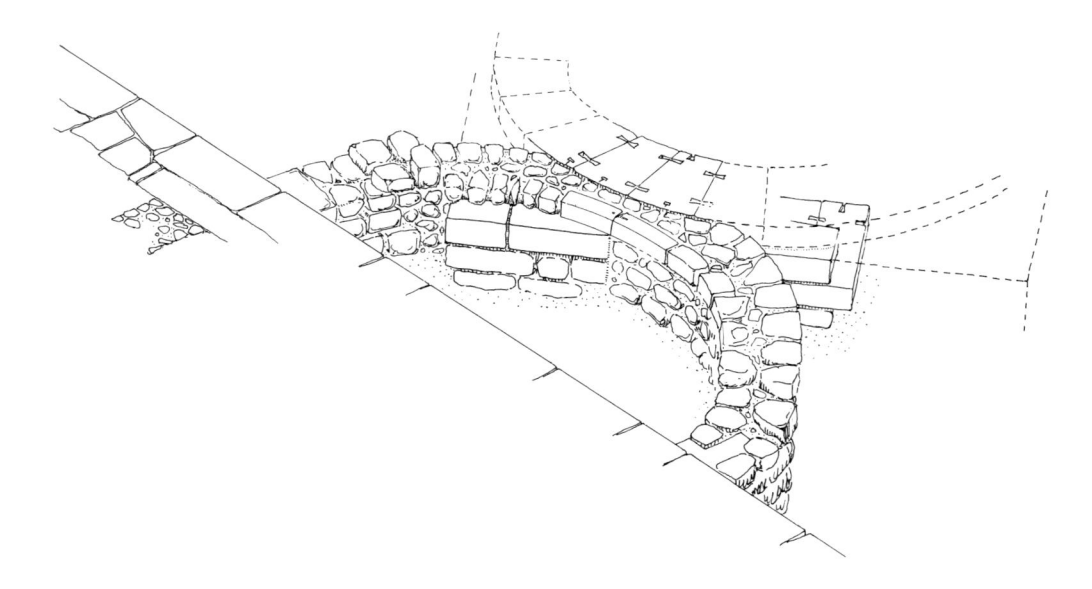

FIG. 7. Relationship between apse of basilica church and that of Greek temple (to right).

The apse roof was a half-dome of brick laid in horizontal courses. This was deduced from a fragment of interior plaster which had the imprint of three bricks on its reverse face; it was found inside the apse, together with much broken mortar and grit. The bricks had gone, probably having been salvaged after the ruin of the church. Careful search yielded no mosaic tesserae.

Colonnades

The stylobate of the south colonnade was cleared for almost its whole length. It comprises a row of well squared grey stone blocks which rise a little over 0.10m above the adjoining pavements. Two column bases were found *in situ* and the positions of four other columns were shown by traces of bedding mortar. Evidently there were eight columns, the bases which survive being the third and fifth from the west. The rectangular piers which often terminate the colonnades of a basilica have gone, but if the columns were regularly spaced, such piers would have projected about 0.40m from the east and west walls; alternatively there might have been half-columns. The surviving bases are not alike, though both are of grey Chios marble. The larger (FIG. 8, PLATE 1 (*e*), (*f*)) has torus, astragal and apophyge carved in one piece and is evidently spoil from the fifth-century temple. Both upper and lower surfaces have central dowel-holes and the upper surface has a channel for the lead which originally encased the dowel; there is also a mason's mark E. (A fragment of a second base with the same profile was found, loose, during the excavations.) The base was held in position on the south stylobate by a late wall which partly enveloped it (PLATE 2 (*b*)). Two rough recesses hacked through the torus and astragal appear to have been formed to accommodate vertical screens. However, as no other traces of screens were found on the stylobate or on the other surviving column base, it seems probable that these secondary screens were a late feature of the temple to which the base had originally

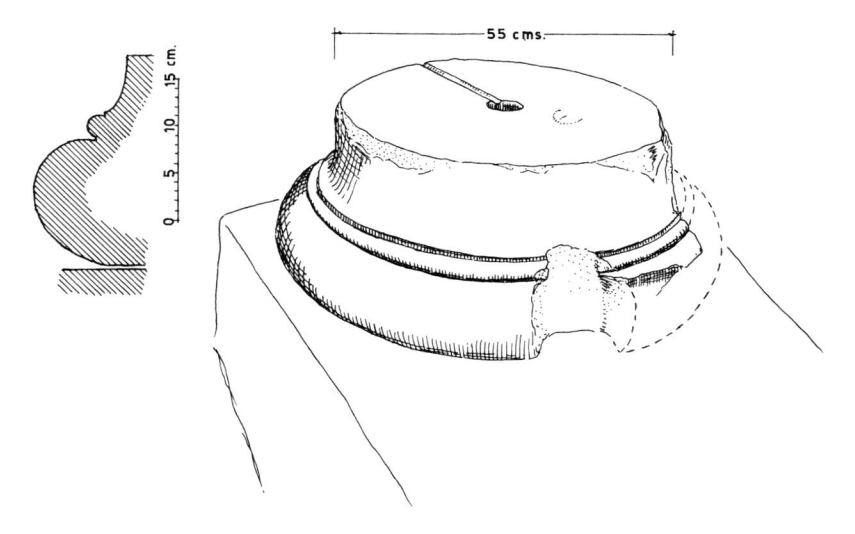

FIG. 8. Column base from Greek temple reused in centre of south stylobate.

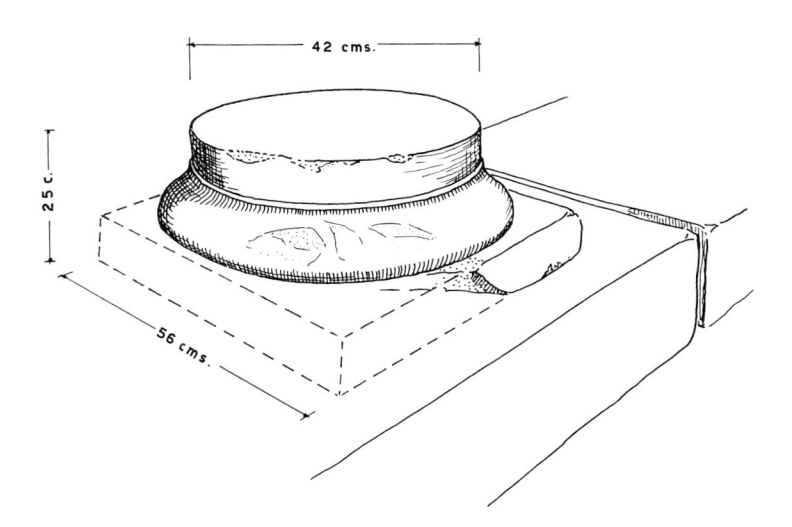

FIG. 9. Earlier column base reused at east end of south stylobate.

belonged. The smaller base (FIG. 9) has a rectangular die surmounted by a torus of cyma profile and then a short cylindrical section, evidently part of the shaft. No dowel-hole appears on the exposed surface. Whether this was originally a base or a capital is uncertain. Of the north stylobate only one block was found (in trench G, PLATE 7 (*b*)), its surface exactly level with that to the south; elsewhere the north stylobate was attested by its robbers' trench. Several fragments of grey and pink Chian marble column shafts were found in the excavations. They were unfluted and of about the same diameter as the top of the base which we presume to come from the temple.

The Bema

Not enough is left of the nave pavement to afford any clear idea of the arrangement of altar, ambon, screens and other furniture of the basilica. Nevertheless, one important feature came to light at the centre of the area where the bema must once have been: a small rectangular recess, sunk below the level of the former paving stones of the axis of the nave and two metres west of the chord of the apse (PLATE 5 (*a*)). Presumably it was made to contain a relic, possibly the bones or ashes of the church's founder, and it is probable that the altar stood over it. The recess is lined with miscellaneous bricks and stones. To south and east there remain a few levelling stones from the former bema pavement, and it may be that the lid of the recess was level with the floor. The earth excavated from the recess contained much broken glass, possibly fragments of hanging lamp-bowls.

The position of the bema railing is suggested by a stone of the nave floor which remains in position three metres west of the reliquary (PLATE 5 (*b*)). It is worn smooth by use and upon its upper surface are four rough grooves, a mortice and three shallow circular sockets of varying size. The sockets are not large enough to be dowel-holes for an upright post, but they could be bolt sockets or hinge sockets associated with a metal gate at the entrance to the bema.

The bema floor has gone, but part of its substructure remains. A layer of large roughly shaped flagstones lies about 0.30m below the socketed stone described in the preceding paragraph and immediately to the east. Since the pavement substructure of the bema differs from that of the nave, we presume that the pavement also differed, but we have no other knowledge of it.

The screens which enclose the bema are probably represented by the single fragment of a large white marble slab, discovered in the fill of the baptistry in 1953 (PLATE 6 (*b*)). As well as can be deduced from the fragment, the slab was decorated with a large cross in relief, surrounded by a plain border with a cyma moulding. On the top edge of the slab (assuming it was set vertically) and immediately above the cross is a saucer-like depression, 0.02m deep and 0.10m in diameter. It may perhaps have been a lamp. A similar feature occurs in the single chancel slab to remain in the church which was formed inside the Erectheion at Athens (J. M. Paton *The Erechtheum* (1927) figs. 207, 210: the feature is not mentioned in the text).

A piece of small white column shaft, 0.18m in diameter, with a cross embossed on one side was found in the fill of the baptistry in 1953; it might be one of the supports of an altar (PLATE 6 (*a*)). Another find of 1953 was a pyramidal dosseret block, 0.43m wide, 0.70m long and 0.17m thick (PLATE 6 (*c*)). A neatly carved cross was embossed on one narrow side and the long sides had deep upright grooves; it probably came from the head of a pillar set between two arched windows. It was found lying upside down in the south aisle.

Entrances to the Basilica

The threshold stone of the central doorway at the west end of the nave remains *in situ*, a large block of Chian grey marble 2.60m long and 0.75m wide (PLATE 7 (*a*)). It has mortices for two successive sets of doors. First, a wide opening which had door leaves fixed by vertical lugs which revolved in circular sockets; second, a narrower opening with a wooden frame from which, presumably, the door leaves were suspended on metal hinges. The round sockets of the original doors are seen near the ends of the stone. The wooden frame of the second arrangement is deduced from two square sockets which lie a little closer together than the round sockets; presumably they steadied the lower ends of wooden posts. Three small square sockets near the middle were evidently for metal bolts. Certain toolings on the surface of the threshold suggest that it had been used elsewhere before being brought to the church.

The west doorway of the south aisle has a plain threshold. The jambs, standing nearly two metres high, are orthostats with mouldings of two fasciae on the west side, but without rebates. The corresponding doorway in the north aisle has gone, the wall being destroyed below threshold level.

The east wall of the basilica has gone, and there is nothing to show whether there were doorways at the east end of the aisles. A small doorway in the south wall of the south aisle had been blocked up and its threshold and jamb-stones removed, leaving a gap in the original masonry about 1.20m wide.

Narthex

The carefully built platform retaining wall which forms the base of the north wall of the basilica does not extend beyond the end of the aisle; further west, the narthex and atrium walls have footings of large rubble stones bedded in mortar. In elevation the end of the narthex was set slightly to the south, so that the north-west corner of the basilica was emphasised by an offset. The principal entrance to the church was a doorway just over 1.50m wide centrally placed in the north end of the narthex; its threshold and the base of its western jamb remain in position (FIG. 10. PLATE 7 (*c*)). The jamb stone is a block of Chian marble with the south-east corner rebated for the door and countersunk at the foot of the rebate to hold the pivot of the door leaf. The threshold, also of marble, 0.37m thick, 0.65m wide and 1.55m long, has sinkings for a secondary door frame similar to those noted in the central doorway of the basilica.

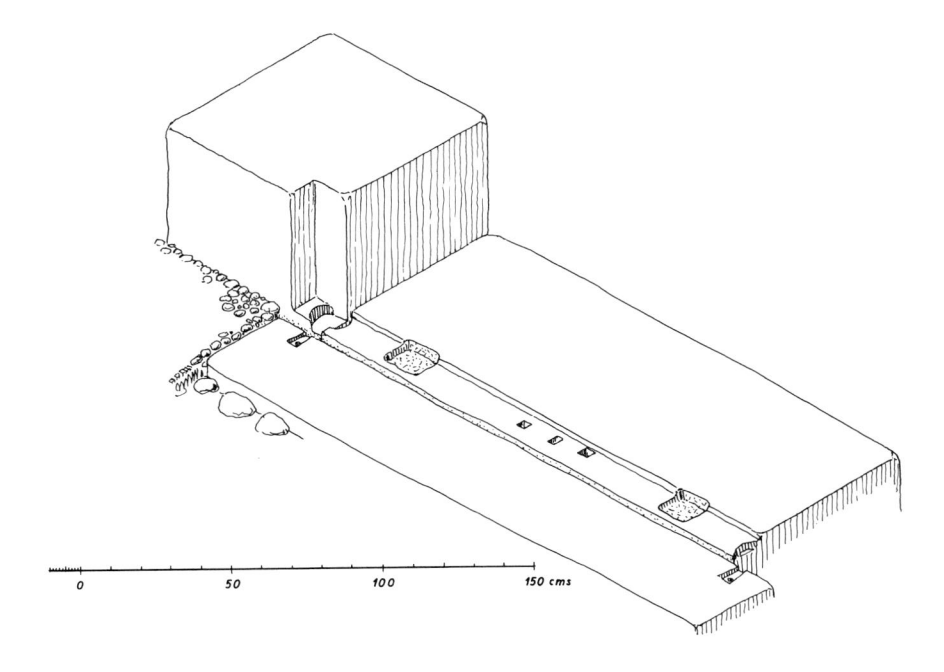

FIG. 10. Threshold and door-jamb of north entrance to narthex.

Two doorways in the west side of the narthex led into the north and south stoae of the atrium. Conforming with the rise in the ground level at the west end of the church, the pebble floor of the north stoa (just seen in the foreground of PLATE 7 (*c*)) lay 0.53m higher than the narthex floor, necessitating two steps inside the narthex. The lower step remains and is, in fact, the only evidence of a former doorway, the wall above that level having gone. The step is roughly semicircular and is made of grey marble blocks pillaged from a curved building of greater radius than the step, possibly the fifth-century temple. The corresponding doorway to the south stoa of the atrium is well preserved by the deep soil retained by the field terrace. It is approached by three curved steps instead of two because the south stoa lies higher than that to the north (PLATE 9 (*c*)). PLATE 9 (*b*) shows the south doorway as viewed from the west during the excavations. Just visible beyond the threshold is the upper of the three steps going down to the narthex (at that time unexcavated).

At the south end, almost the whole width of the narthex is taken up by a semicircular exedra with a floor raised 0.10m above that of the narthex (PLATES 8 (*c*); 9 (*a*)). The rubble masonry seen in the photograph was of course hidden originally by plaster, fragments of which remained at the base. PLATE 8 (*c*) shows part of an Ionic capital, pillaged from the fifth-century temple and used as rubble. The exedra floor was covered with mosaics forming a simple fish-scale pattern.

The narthex is paved with mosaics similar to those of the basilica (PLATE 8 (*d*)); but they are less carefully bedded and rest directly on a stratum of cobble stones without any *opus signinum*. The mosaic patterns run up to the curved steps of the atrium doorway almost as though the mosaics continued underneath, but removal of one marble block showed that the mosaics do not extend below the steps. Hence the continuity of the mosaic patterns along the west wall of the narthex proves that there was no central doorway from the narthex to the atrium even though the narthex wall has been demolished at that point to a level below that of a threshold stone.

Atrium

The atrium lies west of the narthex, its north and south walls nearly in line with the side walls of the basilica. The court, presumably unroofed, had stoae to north, south and west; there was none on the east side, perhaps because there was a window there to light the narthex. A corner pier remains *in situ* at the junction of the south and west stoae; it stands almost a metre high, but when excavated was surrounded by loose fallen masonry which precluded full clearance. A monolith about 0.90m high adjacent to the west face of the corner pier may be the eastern abutment of an arch which spanned the west stoa. A stylobate was exposed, running eastwards from the corner pier to the narthex, but no evidence for columns could be obtained, either in the centre or at the places where two equally spaced supports would have been. Nevertheless we assume that there was a colonnade and the assumption was borne out by the discovery, near the middle of the south stoa, of broken and incomplete fragments of two similar but distinct column-shafts, each shaft comprising a pair of half-columns attached to a rectangular pier (FIG. 11. PLATES 8 (*b*)–(*d*); 9 (*e*)). Columns of similar form occur in the nave of the church at Olympia (Curtius and Adler, *Olympia* ii 93–105 pls. 67–70). Together with the shafts in the south stoa was a matching capital of Doric form. Such columns are commonly used in Byzantine buildings as intermediate supports in multiple windows, the flat sides being suitable for the attachment of lattices or shutters. If these fragments come from the atrium colonnades it would seem that the stoae had screened fronts.

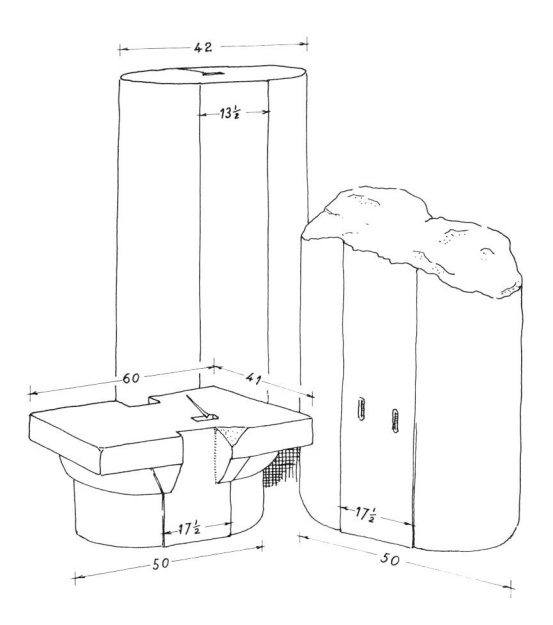

FIG. 11. Column shafts and capital from south stoa of atrium.

The stoae were paved with black and white pebble mosaics set in white mortar and neatly arranged in geometrical patterns (PLATE 9 (*b*)). Doubtless the pebbles came from the near-by beach where vast quantities of both kinds abound. Much of the pavement remains at the west end of the south stoa; a very small area of the same material was excavated in the north stoa, but was beyond preservation.

A well, still used, occupies a position near the middle of the atrium. The present well-head is, of course, at a level far above the original atrium floor, but the focal position of the well suggests that it was originally dug in connection with the church.

Baptistry

An opening to the south near the south-east corner of the atrium leads up two steps into a large rectangular chamber which we have called the ante-room to the baptistry; it seems likely that it was built as a school-room for catechumens. The floor is paved with black and white pebbles arranged in a pattern of interlacing circles and squares (PLATE 8 (*a*), (*b*)). In the east wall of the ante-room is an opening to a range of buildings which stood parallel with the basilica. Full excavation was not possible, but such trenches as could be dug revealed the east end of the range, and a doorway in the north wall which gave access to a narrow place beside the basilica; here various walls were found, possibly earlier than the church buildings.

An opening on the west side of the ante-room led into the baptistry. The rebated threshold is *in situ*, and also the lower part of the jambs, which are not rebated. A large lintel of grey Chian marble, 1.84m long, found in the debris about a metre east of the opening, presumably spanned it (FIG. 12. PLATE 10 (*c*)). Numerous large blocks of tumbled masonry in this part of the site indicate that the church was severely damaged by earthquake. The moulded face of the lintel is

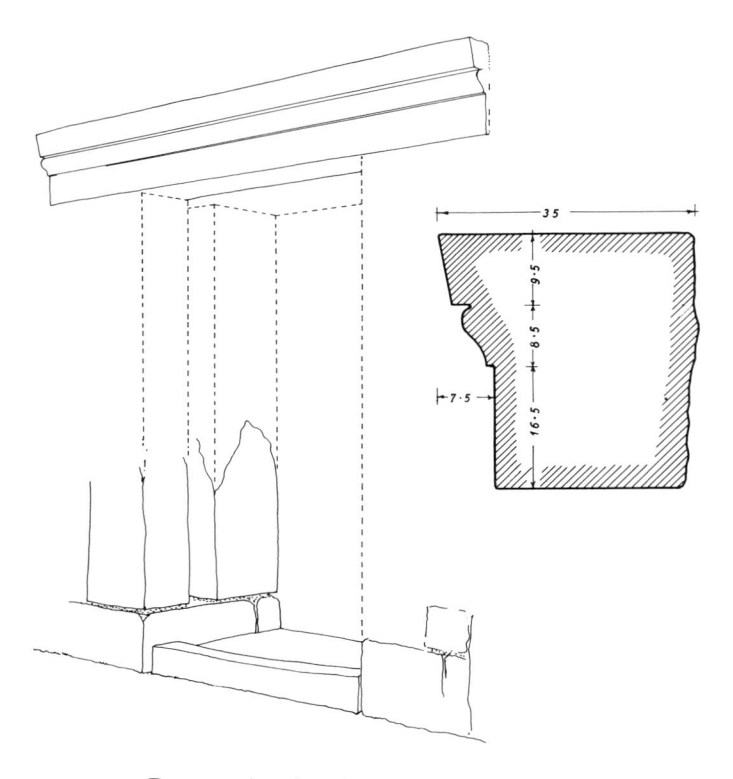

FIG. 12. Doorway into baptistry with cross-section of lintel.

covered with roughly executed inscriptions and graffiti (W. G. Forrest, *BSA* lix (1964) 35f. no. 28 (c)).

For some unexplained reason the entrance to the baptistry was placed about half a metre south of the normal axis of the circular chamber. In consequence, so that the steps going down into the font might come opposite the entrance, the font itself is set off-axis. It is a cruciform basin sunk in the baptistry floor and enclosed in brick walls which rise as parapets a little above floor level. The whole basin is lined with thin sheets of Proconnesian marble (PLATE 10 (*a*)). Of the four arms, those to west and east are rectangular and contain steps whereby the person baptised first descended into the water and then emerged; those to north and south are apse-shaped and contain features resembling steps, but more probably seats for the officiating clergy (PLATE 10 (*b*)). The pavement in front of each seat is level with the floor of the font, but there were marble screens to retain the water. Thus the priests could stand on the same level as the catechumen and take up the baptismal water without stooping, themselves remaining dry while the catechumen stood up to his knees in water or, perhaps, knelt down for total immersion.

An opening on the south of the baptistry gave access to a small rectangular chamber, probably some kind of sacristy. This opening also is off the normal axis, but the anomaly is probably due to this part of the church being set deeply into the hillside so that expense was spared by placing the sacristy as far to the east as possible. The vacant corner to the west is virgin rock.

The sacristy, like the ante-room, was filled with broken masonry, evidently thrown down in an earthquake. Nevertheless, the baptistry continued in use after the two adjoining rooms had been thus made unusable, the openings to the sacristy and ante-room being walled up and a new entrance to the baptistry being roughly cut through the wall which separates it from the atrium. The plaster facing on the baptistry wall, crudely painted to resemble marble, must date from after the earthquake since the same plaster extended across the masonry which sealed the original entrance (PLATES 10 (c); 11 (a), (b)).

There is a small arched recess in the north-west quarter of the baptistry wall about 0.80m above the floor (PLATES 10 (c); 11 (a)). The baptistry may have had windows above the level of the adjoining roofs, or there may have been an oculus in the dome.

Around the font, the circular chamber is paved with large sheets of cippollino marble, split in its laminations, neatly jointed and carefully cut to fit the lobes of the font. Over most of the area the cippollino remains in position, but in the south-east quarter it is replaced by a rough patchwork of stone slabs; these include one which was formerly a perforated drain-cover and another with a cross carved on the surface. Probably the original floor was damaged by the collapse of the roof in the earthquake which wrecked the sacristy, and the crude repairs seen in PLATE 10 (a) are contemporary with the blocking of the doorways and the 'marbled' plasterwork on the walls (PLATE 11 (a), (b)).

Stratification

DRAWING III (a) shows the stratification of the ground on the south side of the basilica as revealed in trenches dug on the line C–D of the plan at DRAWING II. The south aisle of the basilica appears to the right in the drawing with its south wall superimposed on the structure of the underlying platform (E) in the same way as the east, north and west walls were superimposed on platform walls AB, BC and CD (FIG. 4). Wall E stands on natural rock, as also does a parallel wall (F), a little over three metres to the south. Both E and F are bedded in a layer of hard red earth (12)–(13) which yielded Hellenistic and Roman pottery. The layer probably existed before wall F was built. The triangular stratum of thick reddish earth (11) which lies on top of (12) on the south side of F is probably the result of soil washing down the hillside and piling up against the wall. Thus F, whether by accident or design, became a terrace supporting the soil on its southern or up-hill side and preventing the accumulation of hillside wash in the space between itself and wall E.

Layer (10), overlying (11) and (12), is a very distinctive stratum composed of the debris of a friable, sandy kind of rock which occurs in the vicinity. It formed the earth surface when the east wing of the baptistry complex (walls G and H) was built. Layer (10) must have been in existence for a considerable length of time when the baptistry wing was built as it would need years of consolidation before such material could sustain the weight of a wall; it cannot be spoil from the excavation of trenches for the building of the basilica and its annexes. As layer (10) rests against the upper and thinner part of wall F we know that that too antedates G and H.

The masonry of walls G and H has exactly the same character as the narthex and atrium walls and there is no reason to think that the building to the east of the ante-room is later than the rest of the church. We assume that walls G and H are contemporary with the basilica.

The ground surface when the church was built thus appears to have followed the top of stratum (10) as far as wall F and to have dropped to the top of stratum (12) in the space between walls F and E. The builders of the church seem to have allowed wall F to remain in position as a terrace between the south aisle of the basilica and the east wing of the baptistry complex.

The line of cross-section C–D passes through a small doorway in the south wall of the basilica with the result that the wall itself does not show on DRAWING III (a); only the later blockings of the doorway, J and K, appear. The threshold stone of the former doorway may perhaps be recognised in a large stone which now forms the south face of blocking J. When the church was built, the ground-level outside the small south doorway was raised to correspond with the aisle floor, and layer (9) therefore is contemporary with the church. Above is layer (8), a thin stratum of grit and sand, possibly the substructure of a former pavement. Layer (9) yielded a coin (C15) of A.D. 564–5, but we presume that it was taken down to that level during the excavation and should properly be assigned to layer (8).

Concerning the later history of the church something may be gleaned from the stratification above layer (8). It appears that the south doorway was closed, or perhaps made into a window, when a stone bench (J) was built, on top of the mosaic floor, along the side of the south aisle. Layer (6) is soil which accumulated against the basilica wall just below the sill of the presumed window. The next event seems to be the very serious damage, if not almost complete destruction of the building, presumably by earthquake. This occasioned the masses of fallen masonry found south and east of the baptistry and also the heavy deposit of similar material which appears as layer (5) in the figure. Layer (3) is a second stratum of ruin debris which occurs in the south aisle of the basilica and also outside the south wall; it includes great quantities of broken roof tile. Taken in conjunction with wall L (a very feeble structure erected on top of the south colonnade stylobate, between the two surviving bases) stratum (3) indicates reoccupation of the church after its first ruin. It seems that part of the south aisle was cleared of debris and re-roofed, possibly to make a smaller church. The ruins of the original church were piled up on the south side of the aisle wall and threatened to pour through the window, but were prevented from doing so by a flimsy wall (K), actually based on the debris which it was designed to exclude. In time this feeble blocking also collapsed and quantities of broken tiles (3) appeared on the aisle floor.

Conclusions

The church is exactly what one would expect to find in a small but prosperous Aegean town during or soon after the reign of Justinian. Many features are closely paralleled in the church of Gul Bagtsche (Gülbahçe) near Izmir which must be roughly contemporary (*BZ* x (1901) 568–573). It is unlucky that the eastern parts of the aisles are so much destroyed that we are uncertain if there were doorways there, or not. In any case it seems unlikely that there were side chapels.

The exedra at the south end of the narthex is interesting. It corresponds very closely with the description of a special kind of Diakonikon mentioned in *Testamentum Domini*, a fourth or early fifth-century writing which includes a chapter describing the correct plan for a church. It says 'Let the diakonikon be to the right of the right hand entry, to the purpose that the eucharists, or offerings that are offered, may be seen. Let there be a forecourt with a portico running round to this diakonikon'.

Standing opposite the entrance to the church, the narthex exedra at Emporio could hardly be used more appropriately than as a place for the display of the gifts which people provided for the maintenance of the church and its ministers. Located as it is, to the right of the right hand entrance, with a portico (of the atrium) running round to it, one is almost tempted to assert that this exedra was consciously provided to meet the requirements of the *Testamentum Domini*. It suggests that the liturgical practice of displaying the eucharistic gifts near the church door survived into the sixth century. Other examples of this kind of diakonikon are found at Epidaurus, Nikopolis, Gul Bagtsche, Apollonia of Cyrenaica, and perhaps even in Rome where the eighth-century church of San Saba, built by refugees from Jerusalem, still includes an apsed exedra at the left-hand end of the narthex.

A noteworthy variation from the ordinary plan of an early Christian church is seen, at Emporio, in there being no western gateway to the atrium. Admittedly the place in question was not fully excavated, but the rise in terrain makes it almost impossible for there to have been an entrance in the west wall. Thus the atrium was entered from the narthex instead of vice-versa, and the stoa-surrounded court appears to have lost its original function.

The church is not precisely dated, but coins found at or near the foundations suggest that it was not built before the time of Justin II (565–78). That it is not much later than that period is shown by the substantial quality of the masonry and by the simple basilical plan. If prothesis and diakonikon chapels ever flanked the central bema, they must have been rudimentary ones, consisting merely of altars placed at the ends of the aisles. The continuity of the south colonnade stylobate to within 1.50m of the east wall shows that there were no side-chapels, isolated by cross-walls, as in later Byzantine churches. Such chapels, often domed and apsed, are thought to have been introduced in consequence of a liturgical innovation, the Great Entrance, which probably dates from Justin II's reign. Having no side-chapels, the church at Emporio seems to have been built before the Great Entrance was widely used. The third quarter of the sixth century is suggested as a likely date.

2. Comments on the Church Complex
Sinclair Hood

In the course of preparing the report of the church complex for publication some discrepancies have emerged between the architectural study by SC and the interpretation of the archaeological sections by SH. Some of these discrepancies are explicit in a comparison of Section C–D (DRAWING III (a)) composed by SC and Sections 1 and 2 (DRAWING III (b) and FIG. 13) which, like the other archaeological sections (3–10), are the work of SH. Attention is drawn to these discrepancies, since they are not uninstructive, and serve to emphasise if nothing else that observation of the relationships in archaeological sections is not necessarily infallible. The main outlines of the history of the church complex, however, are not at issue.

The date of the construction of the church complex is relatively well fixed by the general character of the arrangements in it and by the coin evidence to the third quarter of the sixth century AD as SC has shown. There seems little doubt that the builders of the church used an earlier Roman structure of the first century AD as a basis for the main body of their Basilica, including the Nave and Aisles, but without the Apse and Narthex. This was the impression at the time of the excavations (cf. *Greek Emporio* 60, 84f.). The study of the architecture by SC confirmed it as correct. It was questioned, however, by SH on the grounds that it conflicted with observations made in studying the archaeological sections. But such discrepancies as there are seem likely for the most part to reflect false interpretations of the sections involved.

When the inscribed Archaic statue base reused in the wall forming the north side of the Basilica in trench G (FIG. 14 Section 4) was removed for transport to Chios Museum three bronze coins were found beneath it. These had evidently been placed here in the wall at the time it was built. The coins appeared to be late Greek or early Roman in character, but they have unfortunately escaped identification since they were deposited in Chios Museum. A fourth coin (C1), however, which had evidently been incorporated in the north face of the wall below the inscribed statue base, is dated to the first century BC or AD.

Early Roman pottery (1–3) was found in a pit to the east of the Basilica, and a little Early and Middle Roman (13, 20) was recovered from below the floors of the Basilica complex together with some Late Roman Phocaean Red Slip Ware (25, 33, 37, 55). None of the later varieties of Phocaean Red Slip Ware, however, and no examples of other Early Byzantine fine wares of the kind in evidence above floors of the Period I destruction in the fortress came from such a context, although they were well represented in the area of the Basilica church complex.

An apse was added at the east end of the Early Roman structure when it was converted to serve as the basis for the outer walls of the Basilica. This Apse was not bonded with the earlier wall on which it abutted, and it differed from it in construction. When studying Section 8 (FIG. 16) SH had the impression that the foundation trench for the Apse was dug from the same level (top of level (8)) as that for the wall of the Early Roman structure to the west. It seems more likely, however, that the apse foundations were in fact sunk from the top of level (7). Pottery assignable to the second-third centuries AD (nos. 5–12), together with a small group of Early Roman lamps (nos. 292–6, 309) and several Roman coins including C3 and C5, was recovered from level (7), or from what appeared to be the equivalent deposit in trench RR in the northern part of the space enclosed by the Apse. The coins might have been lost or discarded outside the east end of the Early Roman building during the period when it was in use.

Harrison has noted that the sheets of Proconnesian marble lining the font and the cippollino slabs of the Baptistry floor were presumably taken from some earlier building in the area. It is tempting to think that they might have come from the Early Roman structure which the builders of the Basilica used as a basis. Boardman has suggested that some blocks of a poorly executed entablature with triglyph frieze, probably Early Roman in date, might have belonged to this structure; but no other stone architectural members could be assigned with confidence to it (*Greek Emporio* 85). No floors that certainly belonged to it were recognised in the excavations. The cobbles of level (6f) above level (7) in trench G (FIG. 14 Section 4) below the North Aisle of the Basilica might represent such a floor; and the cobbles exposed at the bottom of the later grave some 0.40m below the tops of these are another possibility, unless they went with an even earlier structure on the site.

In the south-east angle of the Basilica in trench X (FIG. 15 Section 6) possible earlier floors were identified below what appears to have been the make-up for the mosaic pavement of the South Aisle: level (4e), a thin layer of pink cement, and level (4f) below it, might have been such floors. Pottery described as Early Roman seems to have been recovered from level (5) which may represent debris from digging the foundation trench for the south wall of the Early Roman structure used as a base for the south wall of the Basilica. The line of stones (l in Section 6) running from north to south at the west side of trench X must belong to some still older building.

No traces of earlier floors or structures, however, were observed in trenches L or M in the southern part of the Nave. The sounding in L was carried down to a depth of over a metre below the tops of the massive blocks of the Nave pavement until the natural rock, which sloped from south to north here, was reached at a point below the north edge of the South Stylobate. No sign of any earlier floor or occupation surface was detected in this sounding, and the pottery from it was said to be assignable to early perhaps in Period I, the time of Justinian I or earlier. This might suggest the presence of a fill dumped as make-up below the massive blocks which appear to have served as a base for the Nave pavement. The sounding in M (FIG. 14 Section 5) further to the east revealed a comparable situation. This was carried down to the rock at a depth of 2.25m or more from the surface through Bronze Age deposits some 1.25m deep without any hint of a post-Bronze Age floor or occupation surface which had preceded the construction of the Early Christian Basilica.

The floors of the Aisles of the Basilica and of the Narthex were paved with mosaics, those of the Stoae round the Atrium and of the Anteroom to the Baptistry with pebble mosaics. The Baptistry itself in its original state had been paved with large slabs of marble. In the Nave of the Basilica a few massive blocks of stone taken from some earlier building remained in position. SC has argued that the tops of these blocks served as the floor of the Nave, in spite of the clamp holes visible in them, being covered perhaps by carpets (see his restored section, FIG. 6). But A.H.S. Megaw has suggested that the blocks are more likely to have formed the base for a floor composed of marble slabs (as in the Baptistry) or of bits of cut marble forming patterns (*opus sectile*). FIG. 6 shows the tops of the blocks in the Nave as somewhat higher than the mosaic pavement in the South Aisle. But the levels on the plan (DRAWING 1) suggest that they were slightly lower: 0.50m above Datum being marked for the top of one of the blocks in the Nave, and 0.54m for the South Aisle mosaics.

The Narthex, and the Atrium which was surrounded by Stoae on three sides, together with the Baptistry and the Anteroom to the east of it, all appear to have been built at the same time as the Basilica. The main entrance to the basilica complex appears to have been through the north end of the Narthex. This is unusual, but Harrison has brought to our attention a sixth century episcopal basilica complex at Stobi entered through a doorway in this position (Wiseman 1978, 396 fig. 4). A sounding below the floor level in the southeastern part of the Baptistry revealed that the cruciform font had been sunk into an irregular cutting in the soft greenish yellow rock. The space behind the font had been refilled with rock debris and with stones roughly cemented into place.

The rock debris of Section 1 level (10) (DRAWING III (b)) is similar to the rock of the Baptistry area. The bottom of Wall G is sunk into the top of this rock debris. SC has emphasised that a considerable time must have elapsed after this debris was deposited to allow it to settle before Wall G was built in the top of it. The implication of this appears to be that, if the debris came from cuttings in the rock for the Baptistry and font, Wall G (and by extension Wall H to the south of it and the out-building to which they belonged) must have been erected some considerable time after the main body of the church complex although still within Period I.

Period I

Unstratified pottery from the area of the Basilica church complex includes some Early Roman and much Late Roman and Early Byzantine ranging in date from the 5th century to the time of the Period I destruction of the fortress around 670. The only complete vase, a large bowl (79) of Phocaean Red Slip Ware, seems assignable to the late 6th century: it may have been buried when the church was built.

The main church complex seems to date from the third quarter of the sixth century. It was constructed some time before the fortress on the Acropolis hill, but appears to have remained in use throughout the life of the fortress in Period I. It can hardly have escaped damage when the fortress was destroyed by the Arabs around 670. Pottery assignable to Period I like that from the main destruction level of the fortress was recovered from various parts of the church complex. Clear evidence for destruction by fire in Period I was noted in the space immediately south of the South Aisle of the Basilica in trench T. A lamp (322) from the Period I destruction deposit here (FIG. 13 Section 2 level (5c)) was made from the same mould as two fragmentary lamps from the Acropolis. The evidence for a final destruction by fire in the Baptistry, however, must date from Period II, if, as seems highly probable, it was in use again then. Similarly the burnt layer reported in trench BB north of the Baptistry at the west end of the South Stoa of the Atrium may be debris of a Period II destruction.

Four coins of Heraclius were found in the church complex (C30, C34, C35, C37), and another (C26) came from the area near it. Three coins of Constans II (C40, C47, C48) were similarly recovered from the area round the church. Two of these were the latest of his reign identified from any part of the excavations: C47 dated to 655/6–657/8, and C48 to 659/60. All of these coins of Heraclius and Constans II might have been lost at the time of a destruction of the church complex in Period I around AD 670. Only one of them, however, is from a safe context of the Period I destruction. This is C30 of Heraclius from ruin debris of the Period I destruction by fire in trench T (FIG. 13 Section 2 level (5c)). Two of the other three coins of Heraclius were found in debris above the level of what appear to have been later (Period II) floors: one (C35) about a metre above the original Period I floor in the south-east corner of the Stoa of the Atrium just south of the door leading from it into the Narthex, the other (C37) about 0.40m above the original floor in the Anteroom to the Baptistry.

It seems reasonable to assume that the destruction accompanied by fire in the Basilica church complex in Period I was contemporary with the Period I destruction of the fortress, and that the agents of destruction in both cases were the Arabs. In marked contrast, however, to the situation in the fortress, very few finds which had obviously been involved in the Period I destruction were recovered from the church complex. Some of the relatively few and rather unexciting objects of bronze and iron, for instance, appear to be earlier or later in date (see Index to Finds, below). The church buildings may also have suffered damage as a result of one or more earthquakes, either before the time of the Arab destructions around 670 or afterwards. SC has indicated the evidence for earthquake damage in the Baptistry and adjacent areas of the church complex in particular.

Period II

There was no doubt an interval of time after the Arab destruction around 670 during which both the fortress and the church complex were abandoned. But when the fortress was reoccupied to inaugurate Period II there it seems clear that parts of the church complex were also brought back into use.

Pottery assignable to Period II of the fortress was reported from every part of the Narthex (trenches E, N, P and EE), and from the north-west corner of trench J immediately beyond the north end of the Narthex outside the original entrance porch of the church. Pottery from the Anteroom to the Baptistry was assigned to Period I, but also, although rather dubiously, to Period II. Traces of a later cement or plaster floor were detected in the north-west corner of the Anteroom at a height of *c.* 0.10m above the top of the original pebble mosaic (PLATE 8 (*a*)). This later floor appears to date from a time after the pebble mosaic there had suffered a good deal of damage. The only Period II vases published from the church complex, a cooking pot (285) and a mug (287), both came from above the level of this later floor in the Anteroom. The pottery assigned to Period II in trench EE at the south end of the Narthex was described as coming from a level which began some 0.15–0.30m above that of the original mosaic floor. In the apsed Diakonikon the mosaic floor raised 0.10m above that of the adjacent Narthex had later been covered with cement which was only removed with difficulty during the course of the excavations to reveal the well-preserved mosaics below. This cement floor and the later floors in the Narthex and the Anteroom to the Baptistry presumably date from Period II.

The Baptistry appears to have been restored to use in Period II. In its original state in Period I the Baptistry may have been roofed with a vault as SC has indicated. But no evidence for the existence of a vault was noted when the Baptistry was cleared of debris in 1953. Patches of charred wood were observed for a depth of *c.* 0.50m above the floor on the south side of the circular chamber, and a deposit of burnt matter about 0.05m deep mixed with earth, stones and a few tiles, was recorded immediately above the floor in this area. Stones, tiles and plaster were reported in the fill above. This suggests that, although it may have once been vaulted, the Baptistry was roofed with timber and tiles at the time of the final destruction which appears to have been accompanied by fire.

The Baptistry had certainly undergone many other alterations before that time. These alterations, as SC has noted, included the blocking of the south door leading into the Sacristy (trench Y) and the opening of another door on the north side into the South Stoa of the Atrium. A niche in the wall of the Baptistry just to the west of this new door was blocked at some point with large stones and earth, and the surviving wall plaster (painted in red, black, grey and pale green on a white ground to imitate the veining of coloured marble) runs across the blocking of this niche. The floor of the Baptistry was found in very poor condition, and it had been rather roughly patched before the time of the final destruction there as SC describes.

The original paving was bedded on a layer of hard pink cement *c.* 0.05–0.06m thick. This was replaced by hard sandy brown clay in the areas where the floor had been repaired.

SC has suggested that in the last stages of the life of the Baptistry the doorway leading from it into the Anteroom was blocked. But no traces of a later blocking wall were noted in the doorway at the time of the excavations in 1953, and the Anteroom like the Baptistry appears to have been in use in Period II. There were no signs of later blocking walls in the doorways leading from the Anteroom into the South Stoa of the Atrium and from there into the Narthex. This implies that there was open access during Period II throughout this part of the church complex after the spaces to the south and west (e.g., trench Y and trench T) had been abandoned.

Parts of the Stoae round the Atrium, however, may have been left choked with debris after the Period I destruction. Pottery of Period I was noted in Trench HH on the south edge of the North Stoa of the Atrium. But the burnt layer in trench BB at the west end of the South Stoa just outside the Baptistry may reflect a fire destruction in Period II like that which appears to have finally destroyed the Baptistry itself. This burnt layer with large fallen stones was recorded as some 0.75m thick continuing down to a depth of 1.25m from the surface. Period I pottery was reported as coming from the level beneath it.

A dense layer of roofing tiles which must reflect a destruction covered the original mosaic pavement or what was left of it in the South Aisle. Large parts of the mosaic pavement had in fact disappeared by the time of this destruction, and SC had the impression that it must date from Period II. But the stratigraphy as observed in Section 2 (FIG. 13) suggested to SH that the ruin debris here should be assigned to Period I. No traces of any later blocking wall, however, were noted in the well-preserved doorway leading from the South Aisle into the Narthex. This is in harmony with the idea that the west end of the South Aisle was accessible from the Narthex during Period II when the Narthex is known to have been in use. The stretch of poorly built wall which overlaps the top of the South Stylobate between the two surviving column bases might have belonged to a church of Period II constructed in the South Aisle of the former Basilica as SC has suggested.

No pottery appears to have been recorded from the excavation of the main part of the South Aisle which comes into Sections 1 and 2 (trenches T Ext and M). Pottery from the east end of the South Aisle, however, in trench F (and also in trench X (Section 6) where it was associated with fallen tile) seemed assignable to Period I. But this part of the Basilica had been much destroyed and nothing of the mosaic pavement remained in position, although two large fragments of it from the south edge of trench R (just to the north of the point where the South Stylobate had been robbed away) suggest that it must have continued to the east end of the South Aisle. The whole of this end of the Basilica might have been abandoned after the Period I destruction, being left in ruins and plundered for stone when the western and central parts of the South Aisle were cleared for reuse in Period II.

In the absence of relevant coins the only evidence for the end of the Period II reuse of parts of the church complex is the pottery from the ruins. The end may have coincided with the end of the first phase of the Period II reoccupation of the fortress site on the Acropolis hill early in the ninth century AD, or it may have come later.

Late Mediaeval Chapel and Cemetery

There may have been an interval of time after the end of the Period II reuse of parts of the church complex during which it was entirely abandoned and the Chapel on the Acropolis hill served as a place of worship for the community that lived at Emporio. In the late Middle Ages, however, a Chapel was built outside the south-east corner of the ruins of the former basilica church. Walls belonging to dependent structures or to separate houses were associated with this Chapel along with graves which coins suggested must date from the fifteenth/sixteenth centuries AD.

One of these late graves was noted at the east end of the South Aisle in the north-east corner of trench X, and others came to light at the east end of the North Aisle in trench C and just outside the Basilica to the north of this in trench GG. There may have been similar graves inside the apse of the Basilica in trench RR (see FIG. 16 Section 8, level (8)), and several were found outside the apse to the east in trench B (FIG. 16 Section 9. PLATE 11 (*c*), (*d*)). A pair of bronze earrings (?) (F 136) was recovered from the deeper of the two graves (2a) visible in Section 9 (FIG. 16).

Part of what appeared to be a grave was exposed in trench G in the North Aisle of the former Basilica (FIG. 14 Section 4). When the section was being studied it looked as if the grave here must have preceded the laying down of the fill (level (7c)) below the mosaic floor of the North Aisle. It seems likely, however, that this was a false observation and that the grave in fact dated from the fifteenth/sixteenth centuries like the others in the area.

3. Analysis of Coins from the Church Complex
Sinclair Hood

Twenty four identifiable coins of the Byzantine period or earlier were recovered from the church complex or the area round it. To these must be added three coins discovered below the inscribed Archaic statue base (*Greek Emporio* 186 no. 22) in trench G on the north side of the Basilica when this was removed to Chios Museum. These 27 coins are additional to the Classical and Hellenistic coins already published in *Greek Emporio* 229 nos. 432–442. Four of these earlier coins (nos. 433, 435, 440–1) were from the area of the Basilica; two came from beneath the foundations of the north wall, and one (no. 439) from near the apse.

The builders of the Basilica appear to have used an older (Early Roman) building as a basis for the Nave and Aisles, adding an apse at the east end (cf. *Greek Emporio* 85). The two coins from below the foundations of the wall used as a base for the north wall of the Basilica are assignable to the third century BC and ?Hellenistic (*Greek Emporio* 229 nos. 437, 442). A coin (C1) built into the foundations of this wall on the north side below the Archaic statue base in trench G is datable to the 1st century BC or AD. This is in harmony with the Early Roman date suggested for the original building. A more precise dating for it may become possible if the three coins found below the Archaic statue base can be identified in Chios Museum.

SC has assigned the construction of the Basilica and its appendages to the third quarter of the sixth century AD, and probably not before the time of Justin II (565–78). The coin evidence seems in harmony with this, with a concentration of coins from the area of the church complex in the reigns of Justin I (C13, C14), Justinian I (C15, C16, both relatively late in his reign), and Justin II (C18–20). One of the coins of Justin II (C18) seems to have been struck early in his reign (566/7?), and the other two may be of similar date but are very worn. These 7 coins and 4 earlier ones of the end of the fifth or beginning of the sixth century AD (C8–11) could all have been lost at the time the church complex was built.

Only two coins were certainly stratified below floors of the original church complex: these were C15 from trench T (FIG. 13 Section 2) and C22 from trench MM (FIG. 13 Section 3). Others, however, like C18 and C19, may have come from below floors. The large group of coins from a deep level just beyond the north wall of the Basilica in trenches JJa and JJb must surely have been lost or discarded at the time it was built. Six coins in all were recovered here, mostly in the western part of JJa at depths of between 1.17 and 1.42m from the surface: these were C8, C9, C11, C14, and two which were undecipherable. The two coins from a depth of 1.15m below the surface at the west end of JJb were C13 and C16. The depths at which these coins were found roughly correspond to that of level (5) in trench G (FIG. 14 Section 4) some five metres to the east of the spot from which the coins in trench JJb came. This appeared to be a deposit with building debris from the construction of the Basilica.

There is a gap of nearly fifty years in the series of coins from the area of the church complex between the latest of Justin II, dating apparently from the early part of his reign (566/7?), and the earliest of Heraclius (C26) dated 610–613 (?). This and three coins of Constans II (C40, C47, C48, dated 642/3, 655/6–657/8, and 659/60) came from trench C Extension beyond the north-east corner of the Basilica. They were presumably lost at the time of the main destruction of the church complex in Period I like four other coins of Heraclius (C30, C34, C35, C37) found in its ruins.

One of these coins of Heraclius (C30) was in debris assignable to the Period I destruction in trench T south of the Basilica (FIG. 13 Section 2 level (5c)). C34 came from a depth of 1.25m from the surface in a trial made in 1953 in the region of trench MM. C35 and C37 were both found near the Baptistry: C35 in the south-east corner of the Stoa of the Atrium, about 0.25m west of the south jamb of the doorway into the Narthex, and a metre above the original pebble mosaic floor; C37 in the Anteroom, about 1.50m from the north wall and 0.75m from the east wall, and 0.50m above the original floor. While both these coins are likely to have been lost at the time of the period I destruction, they were not from undisturbed ruin debris like C30, and came from deposits above the level of floors or surfaces which appear to have been in use in Period II.

Pottery assignable to Period II was recovered from parts of the church complex, especially from the area of the Narthex; but no coins were found to match the two (C50, C51) of early ninth century date from the fortress. Coins of this period, however, tend to be scarcely represented on provincial sites.

4. Sections through the Church Complex

Spencer Corbett and Sinclair Hood

Section C–D (DRAWING III (a)) represents an interpretation by Spencer Corbett of the evidence derived from the archaeological Sections 1 and 2 drawn by Sinclair Hood. The interpretation given in Sections 1 and 2 (DRAWING III (b) and FIG. 13) differs in some details from that in Section C–D.

The levels on Sections 1 and 2 are numbered on the same system as those on Section C–D to make comparisons easier.

DRAWING III (a). Section C–D (SC) combining Sections 1 and 2 (SH) (DRAWING III (b) and FIG. 13)

Levels

(1) Surface.
(2) Red earth with many stones, deposited after the final destruction of the church complex.
(3) Ruin debris of the secondary church complex (Period II).
(4) Debris from the collapse of the original church complex, washed down from the higher part of the site.
(5) Ruin debris from the collapse of the original church complex (Period I).
(6) Soil which accumulated against the blocking of the doorway east of Wall H while the original church complex was in use (Period I).
(7) Sandy fill deposited at the time of the construction of the original church complex (Period (I).
(8a) Thin layer of grit and sand, possibly substructure of a former pavement.
(8b) Debris laid down during the construction of the original church complex (Period I).
(9) Fill deposited at the time of the construction of the original church complex (Period I).
(10) Rock debris.
(11) Soil washed up against Wall F.
(12) and (13) Hard red earth with some large stones. Hellenistic pottery.

DRAWING III (b). Section 1: trenches TT, VV, V and T (west side)

The levels are numbered on the same system as those in Section C–D (DRAWING III (a)).

Levels

(1) Surface.
(2) Reddish clay, in trenches TT and VV.
(2a) Red clay with abundant stones, north of Wall H, apparently the same as (2).
(4) Washed down ruin debris of the Period I destruction.
(4b) As (4) with large stones, north of Wall K above (5d).
(5) Crumbly reddish south of Wall H: with lumps of cement in trench TT, with stones and tile in trench VV. Apparently level of the Period I destruction.
(5a) Period I destruction between Walls H and G.
(5b) Period I destruction between Walls G and F. The fragment of a 6th century lamp (no. 339) came from this deposit.
(5d) Period I (or II) destruction, with abundant tiles, above partly destroyed mosaic floor of South Aisle.
(6) Red clay with small stones, apparently accumulated during Period I against the south face of Wall H and the blocking wall (D) to the east of it with its bottom at h–h.
(7) Clean sand, apparently make-up for a floor of Period I north of Wall H.
(8) Sandy reddish with lumps of cement below (7), apparently building debris of Period I. This deposit overlapped the footings of the wall (I) which ran from north to south linking Walls G and H.

(8a) Crumbly reddish with lumps of cement and very little tile. Probably the same as (8) beyond the limits of the church complex to the south. Wall D running from west to east from the corner formed by Walls H and E had its bottom (h–h) sunk into the top of (8a): it appears to have been built during Period I to block a doorway or north-south passage leading out of the church complex on this side.

(10) Greenish yellow debris of the friable sandy rock of the area. The top of this deposit formed the surface when Walls G and H were built. A foundation trench (FT) was noted on the south side of Wall H dug through (10) and into (12) below it. The deposit (10) may represent spoil from the excavations made for the Baptistry complex immediately to the west. Scraps of pottery assignable to Period I were reported from it. SC has emphasised, however, that a considerable interval of time must have elapsed between the deposition of (10) and the building of a wall like G resting on top of it. Wall G and the complex south of the main body of the church were in any case built before the end of Period I.

(11) Thick reddish clay above (12) between Walls F and G. This seemed to overlap the offset on the south side of Wall F. The lower part of the south face of Wall F below the offset (k–k) presented a rough and irregular face of stone and concrete as if it had been built in a foundation trench cut into levels (12) and (13). The large stone at the bottom of (11) may have been left by the builders of the church complex as surplus to their needs.

(12) Hard red clay, with some large stones in the top in trench TT. Hellenistic pottery was recovered from this level, together with the lamp no. 300 assigned to the 1st century AD.

(13) Sandy dark red-brown clay with stones. As (12), but mixed with rock debris, and with large stones at the bottom above the native rock in trench TT. Hellenistic pottery was recovered from this level. A coin (C18) of Justin II dated 566–7 (?) was recorded from the bottom of this level in the north-west corner of trench VV: it may have been lost at the time of the construction of the church complex, but had presumably fallen from a higher level ((7), (8) or (10)).

In trench LL to the west of trench V, with the westwards continuations of Walls F and G, pottery of the Period I destruction was found in a deposit about 0.30m thick above a white cement floor at a depth of *c.* 1.30m from the surface. This floor was above a fill with pottery described as '(?) Early Roman'. The fill here may correspond to level (12) in Section 1 from which the pottery was said to be Hellenistic.

In trench NN immediately to the west of trench LL a pebble floor, apparently a southward continuation of the pebble mosaic floor of the Anteroom to the Baptistry, was reached at a depth of 1.25m from the surface. A wall running from west to east in the south-east corner of the trench with the bottom only 0.70m below the surface appeared to be much later, contemporary perhaps with the Late Mediaeval Chapel to the east.

FIG. 13. Section 2: trenches V and T (east side)

The levels are numbered on the same system as those in Section C–D (DRAWING III (a))

Levels

(1) Surface.
(1a) Reddish clay.
(2a) Red clay with abundant stones.
(3) Reddish clay with specks of white, stone and tile, only noted in trench T. A line of black (a, a, a) visible in places in the top of this deposit may represent a former surface level. The deposit might have formed after the Period II destruction, as suggested in Section C–D (DRAWING III (a)), but this is uncertain: it could be much later.
(4a) Hard light reddish brown speckled with white: apparently washed down ruin debris of the Period I destruction. Presumably the equivalent of (4) in Section 1.
(4b) Washed down ruin debris of the Period I (?) destruction. Reddish with large stones, tiles and lumps of cement.
(5b) Period I destruction south of Wall F.
(5c) Period I destruction between Wall F and the tile wall (e–e). Light brown with abundant cement lumps and stones; much tile and carbonised wood at the south end. The evidence strongly suggests that the Period I destruction of this part of the church complex was accompanied by fire. Coins, C20 of Justin II (565–78) and C30 of Heraclius dated 614/5, were recovered from the ruin debris. The lamps 322–3 appear to come from this deposit along with the bronze hook from a weighing machine (F 105).
(5d) Period I (or II) destruction, with abundant tiles, above the partly destroyed mosaic floor of the South Aisle.
(6) Gritty brown earth, with patches of sand (g) in places in the top of the deposit, and a group of paving stones (h, h) in position above it immediately north of Wall F. Evidently make-up for the floor associated with Wall F and the tile wall (e–e). In existence at the time of the Period I destruction.

(8) Thin layer of grit and sand, with a patch of cement (b) on top of it. Possibly the make-up for an earlier floor or pavement associated with the tile wall (e–e). A skirt of cement (c) at the bottom of the deposit abuts against the south face of the stone (d) which forms the base of the tile wall (e–e).

(8b) Brown with stone chips, small stones and specks of cement, running over the top of Wall E and apparently continuing below the stone (d) at the base of the tile wall (e–e).

(9) Crumbly red clay, which appeared to run over the top of Wall E and continue beneath (8b) and the stone (d). Probably an artificial fill dumped here in the course of building the church complex. It overlapped the footings of Wall E, but the foundations of Wall F were sunk into it. A coin (C15) of Justinian I datable 564–5 was recorded from this deposit; but the pottery which appears to have been associated with it is described as Late Roman (late 5th century AD).

(10) As Section 1 level (10).

(11) As Section 1 level (11).

(11a) Gritty brown earth with stone chips, cement lumps and patches of small stones. Building debris which may date from the time of the construction of the Basilica. The coin C19 assigned to the late 6th century AD appears to have come from this level.

(13a) Brown clay with stones. Probably the same as (12) or (13) in Section 1.

(14) Yellowish brown rock debris mixed with earth. Perhaps a patch of much earlier deposit. Possible Archaic sherds were reported from it.

Notes on Sections 1 and 2

The whole of the church complex was evidently constructed before the destruction which ended Period I. It seems likely, however, that work was begun on the Basilica itself first, even if, which is by no means certain, the other elements of the complex were all part of the original design.

If the stratigraphy of Sections 1 and 2 was correctly observed and recorded the sequence would appear to have been:

(1) Wall E used as the foundation for the south wall of the Basilica may have belonged to an earlier (Early Roman) rectangular building the same size and shape as the Nave and Aisles. There was originally an open doorway through the south wall (K) of the Basilica erected on top of Wall E: the stone block (d) used as a base for the later tile wall (e–e) blocking this doorway in Section 2 may be its upturned threshold as SC suggests.

(2) The building debris (11a) in Section 2 was deposited to overlie the footings of the foundation Wall E.

(3) The fill (9) in Section 2 was deposited to run over the top of the foundation Wall E.

(4) Wall F was built with foundations sunk into the fill (9) on the north as visible in Section 2. In the light of this evidence it is difficult to regard the lower part of Wall F as an earlier wall incorporated in the church complex. The doorway through the south wall (K) of the Basilica may have been closed with the construction of the tile wall (e–e) at this time or later in Period I.

(5) Deposits (11) and (10) formed against the south face of Wall F, overlapping the offset here. If (10) is rock debris from cuttings made for the Baptistry complex it would indicate that the Baptistry was built at this stage and not earlier.

(6) Walls G and H built with their foundations sunk into the top of deposit (10) or through it.

Stages 3–6 may have been part of the original plan for the church complex and may simply reflect the order in which the work was done. On the other hand the fact that the foundations of Wall G are built in the top of the deposit (10) might indicate that stage 6 was separated from stage 5 by a considerable interval of time: SC has emphasised that it is difficult to imagine a wall like this being constructed on top of a recent fill owing to the risk of subsidence.

There is no evidence to show at what stage the doorway through the south wall (K) of the Basilica was blocked with the tile wall (e–e), but it must have been some time before the Period I destruction.

The bench (J) was built on top of the mosaic pavement of the South Aisle against a cement face on the north side of the block (d) which formed the base of the tile wall (e–e). The bench may date from Period II if, as SC has suggested, the South Aisle was cleared of debris and reused then.

There is some uncertainty as to whether the tile debris above the mosaic pavement in the South Aisle (level (5d)) belongs to the main Period I destruction or to a subsequent one in Period II. SC has assigned it to Period II, and has interpreted the stone (k) with a bit of tile wall above it in Section 2 as the south face of a wall built over the Period I ruin debris (level (5c)) and holding back level (4a) washed down from the slope above.

In drawing Section 2, however, SH had the impression that the stone (k) with the bit of tile wall above it was really just a piece of the tile wall (e–e) which had toppled southwards into the debris represented by level (4a) some time after the Period I destruction. Moreover level (4) in Section 1 corresponding to level (4a) of Section 2 appeared to run over the tops of the south wall (K) of the Basilica and merge with (4b) above the tile ruin debris (5d) in the South Aisle. If these observations were correct they would suggest that (5d) was ruin debris of the major destruction which overtook the church complex in Period I.

The much dilapidated state of the mosaic pavement of the South Aisle below the tile debris (5d) might appear to favour the idea of a later destruction. The mosaics of the Narthex, where there was abundant evidence from pottery for occupation in Period II, were in a similarly ruinous state. But there was evidence that in Period II the Narthex mosaics, or what was left of them, were covered with a layer of debris and that the floor or surface then in use was at a higher level. The existence of a later floor assignable perhaps to Period II was relatively clear in the Anteroom to the Baptistry (PLATE 8:1). The pebble mosaics of the original floor below this had been much destroyed like the mosaics in the Narthex and the South Aisle. In the Baptistry, however, the original marble slab floor, although damaged and patched in places, appears to have been exposed throughout Period II. The South Aisle might also therefore have been cleared down to the level of the original mosaic floor for reuse then.

An argument in favour of this idea is the fact that no traces of a blocking wall were noted in the relatively well preserved doorway between the South Aisle and the Narthex. If the South Aisle was left choked with debris after the destruction in Period I, a blocking wall would have been needed to keep it back from the Narthex which was certainly a centre of activity in Period II.

SC has suggested that the rude wall built overlapping the top of the South Stylobate of the Basilica between the two surviving column bases (PLATE 2: 1, 2) may date from Period II when the South Aisle was cleared for reuse. On this view it might have formed the north wall of a small Period II church which occupied the western part of the original South Aisle.

On the other side it may be argued that (1) there was no evidence from coins or pottery for assigning the tile ruin debris of level (5d) to Period II rather than to Period I; (2) no evidence was noted to suggest that the tile ruin debris (5d) overlapped the crude wall on the line of the South Stylobate or was subsequent to the time of its construction; (3) this wall may be much later, dating perhaps from the time of the Late Mediaeval Chapel when other buildings are known to have existed in the area.

FIG. 13. Section 3: trench MM (west side)

In this Section, only just over seven metres to the east of Section 1 on the west side of trench V, the stratigraphic situation is entirely different. What appears to be the floor level of Period I (above (7)) is c. 0.20m lower than the Period I floor between Walls F and G in Section 1. Between 0.25m and 0.30m above it (over (6)) is a floor associated with Walls A1 and B dating from the period of the Late Mediaeval Chapel (15th–16th centuries AD).

Levels

(1) Surface.
(2) Red clay with some small stones.
(3) Red clay with stones: some tile at the bottom.
(4) Red clay with tile. Patches of black at the north end of the trench may be remains of decayed vegetation.
(5) Hard gritty reddish flecked with white: large lumps of cement, occasional stones, and scraps of charcoal. Ruin debris of the Late Mediaeval occupation of the site. Patches of hard sand mark a floor at the bottom of this deposit. A lead statuette of the Virgin (a) (F 137) was recovered from it, together with two coins of the fifteenth/sixteenth centuries AD (C54, C55): one of these came from immediately above the floor, the other from the continuation of the deposit north of Wall A1. The fragmentary Late Roman lamp (338) was also found in this deposit.
(6) Dark gritty reddish flecked with white: small lumps of cement and occasional stones. Ruin debris of the Period I destruction. A thin layer of hard sand, with stone slabs in one place (b) in the top of it, marks a floor at the bottom of (6). A coin (C10) of Anastasius I (491–518) was recovered from this deposit. A wide foundation trench seems to have been cut into it for the later Wall B, but Wall A1 was apparently built on top of it.
(7) Dark reddish flecked with white: stones, cement lumps and charcoal. Apparently building debris from the construction of the church complex. A very worn coin (C22) assignable to the 6th century AD seems to have come from this deposit.
(8) Dark sticky red clay. Possibly an artificial fill dumped here during the construction of the church complex as suggested for level (9) in Section 2. No foundation trenches seem to have been dug through this deposit for Walls A2 or C, which is consistent with the idea that they were built before it was formed.

FIG. 14. Section 4: trench G (west side)

Levels

(1) Surface.
(2) Brown with small stones.
(3) Reddish brown with white specks, lumps of concrete, and stone chips. Accumulation after the plundering of the ruins of the church complex for stone (cf. level (6) in Section 5, and level (2) in Sections 6 and 8).
(3a) Robber trench of the North Stylobate of the Basilica.
(4) Hard gritty light brown with specks of white, shading to dark brown at the north end of the trench. The top of this deposit appears to be a former ground surface.
(5) Brown with cement lumps: apparently building debris from the construction of the Basilica.
(6) Make-up for mosaic pavement of the North Aisle, including possible earlier floors. From top to bottom: (a) white cement, (b) yellow-brown 'rock debris', (c) green clay, (d) pink cement, (e) white cement, (f) cobbles. Cf. Section 6 level (4) in the South Aisle.
(7) Possible artificial fill to level up below the floors of the Basilica or of the Early Roman building which appears to have preceded it, consisting (from top to bottom) of (a) brown earth, (b) light brown earth, (c) dark brown earth. In studying the section level (7c) was observed as running over the top of the slab which lined the south side of the grave. But this may have been a false impression, since the grave seems likely to have been a later intrusion dating from the same period as the Late Mediaeval (15th–16th century) graves further east.
(8) Sticky reddish brown with occasional sherds.
(9) Brown earth with small stones.
(10) Gritty with small stones.
(11) Brown with stones.

The surviving stump of wall (k) with an inscribed Archaic statue base (l) incorporated in the top of it appears to belong to an older (Early Roman) building used as a base for the Early Christian Basilica. A coin (C1) of the first century BC or AD was found built into the north face of (k), and three more coins, apparently of the same general date, were recovered from beneath the Archaic statue base when it was removed to send to Chios Museum.

The two courses of rough stones (k) together *c.* 0.30–0.40m thick project *c.* 0.05–0.10m beyond the north face of the wall above them and appear to be footings for it. No foundation trench was recognised, however, for (k) through levels (8)–(10) and into (11). Pottery from levels (9) and (10) is said to have been Late Roman. These levels may have accumulated during the life of the Early Roman building. The bottom of level (5) above them seems to mark the surface of the ground at the time of the construction of the Basilica.

FIG. 14. Section 5: trench M (east side) linking South Aisle and Nave

Levels

(1) Surface.
(2) Brown earth.
(3) Brown earth with stones: evidently recent hill-wash.
(4) Brown earth with white specks and stones, apparently washed down ruin debris.
(5) Brown earth with stones, apparently an earlier phase of hill-wash.
(6) Whitish with lumps of cement and many stone chips. Accumulation after the plundering of the ruins of the church complex for stone (cf. level (3) in Section 4, and level (2) in Sections 6 and 8).
(7) Greenish white clay running underneath the block of blue marble (a) which is bedded on small stone slabs: evidently make-up below the floor of the Nave. This seemed to run up against the north face of the South Stylobate (b), which appeared to be set directly on top of the prehistoric level (8).
(8) Dark brown earth with stones, some large but mostly very small: apparently fall from the Bronze Age wall (c).
(9) Dark brown earth with large and small stones: apparently fill behind the Bronze Age wall (c).
(10) Hard light brown.
(11) Dark brown with small stones, continuing below the Bronze Age wall (c). Pottery assignable perhaps to Bronze Age Period II (late Troy I) was recovered from this deposit.
(12) Black with small stones.
(13) Dark brown with small stones, above the soft yellow natural rock. Three obsidian arrowheads were reported from the lowest prehistoric level excavated here: one is described and illustrated in *Prehistoric Emporio* ii 706 fig. 303: 2, where the deposit is assigned to Bronze Age Period I (Troy II), but it was in fact probably of Period II (late Troy I).

Wall (c), revealed in a small deep sounding in the north-east corner of trench M, ran diagonally from south-east to north-west. It may have been an outer defence wall of the settlement towards the end of the Early Bronze Age or in the Middle Bronze Age.

FIG. 15. Section 6: trench X (west side) across east end of South Aisle

Levels
(1) Surface, including trial of 1953 in north part of trench.
(2) Brown speckled with white, with stone chips and larger stones, filling the robber trench (m) of the south wall of the Basilica and that of the Early Roman building used as a base for it (cf. Section 2: Wall E). Accumulation after the plundering of the ruins of the church complex for stone (cf. level (3) in Section 4, level (6) in Section 5, and level (2) in Section 8).
(3) Hard dark brown with white specks and tile, only preserved at south end of trench (south of the robber trench (m)) above a patch of pebble floor (n): evidently ruin debris of the Period I destruction. Pottery of Period I found in the trench may have come from this deposit as well as from (3a) in the South Aisle.
(3a) As (3), but in the South Aisle and only surviving in patches.
(3b) Sandy light brown earth below (3a) at north end of trench. Possibly make-up for mosaic pavement which has disappeared here.
(4) Possible earlier floors forming a base for the make-up for the mosaic pavement of the South Aisle. From top to bottom: (a) thin layer of pink cement (only in places and not in the Section), (b) cobbles, (c) gritty light brown earth with white specks of cement, (d) thin layer of hard sticky light brown clay, (e) thin layer of pink cement, (f) gritty reddish brown with cement, (g) cobbles. Cf. Section 4 level (6) in the North Aisle.
(5) Reddish clay with small stones: apparently rock debris. This may be from a foundation trench dug for the wall of the Early Roman building used as a base for the south wall of the Basilica. Pottery described as Early Roman (including no. 203) evidently came from a patch of yellow sandy soil, which may be the same as (5), at this depth in the north-west corner of the trench. The line of stones (l) at the bottom of (5) appears to belong to some still earlier construction.

FIG. 15. Section 7: trench U (east side) through foundations of the fifth century temple apse

Levels
(1) Surface.
(1a) Trial trench of 1953.
(2) Light brown with lumps of cement.
(2a) As (2), but inside the space bounded by Walls N and O. These walls are later then the church complex and appear to belong to the period of the Late Mediaeval Chapel (15th–16th centuries AD).
(3) Hard red clay with abundant rather worn small sherds. A coin was recovered from this deposit. The fragment of a marble bowl (F 6) found in the south-east corner of trench U also seems to be from here.
(4) Red clay with small stones and stone chips from the plundering of the fifth century temple for stone to build the church complex.
(5) Reddish with some small stones. Early Roman pottery was apparently found in this deposit.
(6) Dark brown with loose stones. Bronze Age pottery was recovered from this level.
(7) Hard black with small stones.

FIG. 16. Section 8: trenches U and R (north side) from west to east across the apse of the Basilica and the fifth century temple foundations

Levels
(1) Surface.
(2) Whitish with stone chips and some larger stones. Accumulation after the plundering of the ruins of the church complex for stone (cf. level (3) in Section 4, level (6) in Section 5, and level (2) in Section 6).
(3) Light brown with lumps of cement, being the same as level (2) in Section 7.
(4) Greenish white clay, apparently make-up for the apse floor.
(5) Soft reddish with large lumps of cement, apparently builder's waste from the construction of the apse. A thin layer of cement (b–b) at the bottom of (4) and (5) and on top of (7) appears to belong with this and date from the time when the apse was built.

(6) Reddish earth with stones, from the plundering of the fifth century temple, as level (4) in Section 7.
(7) Dark brown earth with small fragments of pottery (nos. 5–12) together with bits of lamps (nos 292–6, 309) and five Roman coins (including C3 and C5) of the first to third centuries AD. This may be deposit which accumulated here outside the east wall of the Early Roman building which appears to have served as a base for the Nave and Aisles of the Basilica church. In that case the foundations for the Basilica apse, which was added to it, must have been sunk from the top of level (7), although in studying the section it looked as if the apse foundations were sunk from the top of level (8).
(8) Brown earth with pebbles, apparently hill-wash that had accumulated before the construction of the Early Roman building (cf. level (5) in Section 7 with Early Roman pottery). The foundation trench for the east wall of the Early Roman building which served as a base for the east wall of the Basilica was clearly dug into this, but was not observed cutting through level (7) above. Two coins of the fifteenth/sixteenth centuries AD (C53, C56) assigned to this same deposit, but in trench RR in the northern part of the apse, may have come from Late Mediaeval graves sunk into it. The lower part of the cement face on the west side of the apse wall (a–a) was rough and irregular, as if the cement had been simply poured down the side of a foundation trench when the wall was built.
(9) Light brown earth. This and levels (10)–(12) were of Bronze Age date (cf. levels (6) and (7) in Section 7). Pottery from (9) and (10) included some fragments of wheelmade vases of Troy II type, assignable perhaps to Bronze Age Period I.
(10) Dark brown earth, perhaps the same as (9) above.
(11) Black earth. Pottery assignable perhaps to Bronze Age Period II (late Troy I) was recovered from this.
(12) Dark blackish brown with stones.

FIG. 16. Section 9: trench B (south side) running from west to east from a point *c.* 4m east of the Basilica apse

Levels
(1) Surface.
(2) Light brown with flecks of cement and occasional tile. Pottery from this deposit, which sealed the plundering of the fifth century temple for stone used in building the church complex, included Late Roman fine red ware bowls of *c.* AD 600. The Early Roman lamp fragment (297), and a Late Roman lamp similar to 323 from the Period I destruction level in trench T (Section 2 level (5c)), also came from this deposit, along with a bronze spindle hook like F 63.
(2a) Late Mediaeval (?) graves, dug into level (2), exposed in the north side of the trench. A pair of bronze earrings (?) (F 136) came from the eastern grave.
(3) Red with stones and stone chips, from the plundering of the fifth century temple, as level (4) in Section 7 and level (6) in Section 8.
(4) Reddish brown with small stones. Presumably the equivalent of level (5) in Section 7 and level (8) in Section 8.
(5) Hard dark brown sandy with water-worn chips of stone. Bronze Age pottery was recovered from this deposit.

FIG. 17. Section 10: trench N (north side) from west to east across north end of Narthex

Levels
(1) Surface.
(2) Soft whitish with stones and tile: evidently debris accumulating after the final ruin of this part of the church complex.
(3) Cobbles laid as a base for the mosaic pavement, which was only preserved at the west side of the Narthex.
(4) Light brown clay speckled with white: evidently make-up for the cobbles (3). A coin (C4) of early fifth century date was recovered from this deposit.
(5) Red clay speckled with white, with many small sherds, occasional bits of tile, and scraps of charcoal: apparently fill deposited to level up below the floor of the Narthex. This overlapped the footings on the west side of the wall of the Early Roman building which served as a base for the west wall (a) of the Basilica church. The Early Roman lamp 307 came from this deposit.
(6) Hard gritty light brown with stone chips, continuing into the foundation trench for the footings on the west side of the wall of the Early Roman building, and being in effect an earlier stage of (5).
(7) Brown with stones. Bronze Age pottery assignable to the period of Troy III–V or later appears to come from this level. The footings for the wall of the Early Roman building were laid in a foundation trench cut into this.

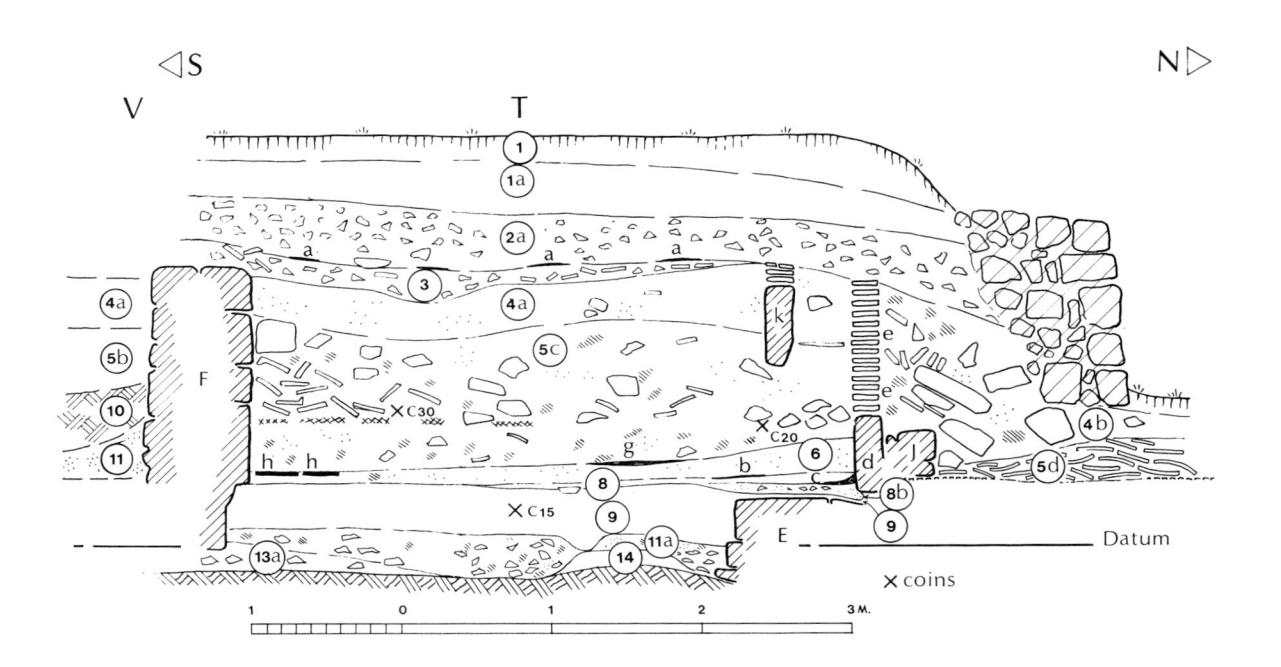

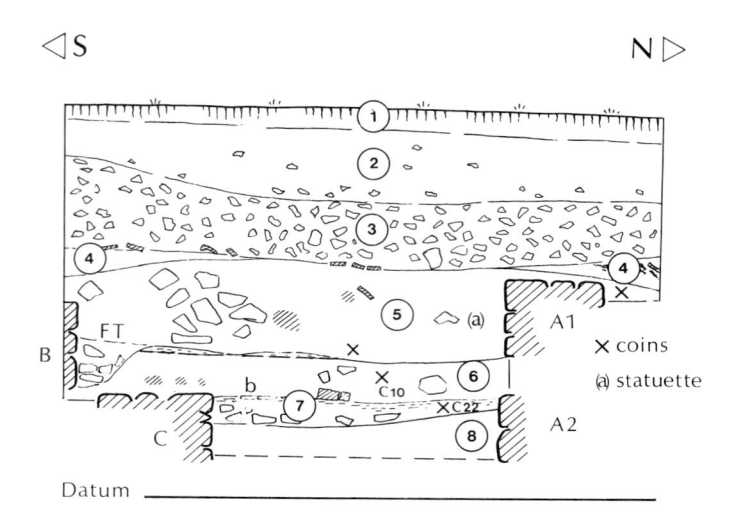

FIG. 13. Basilica Sections 2 and 3.

1. THE EARLY CHRISTIAN BASILICA CHURCH COMPLEX

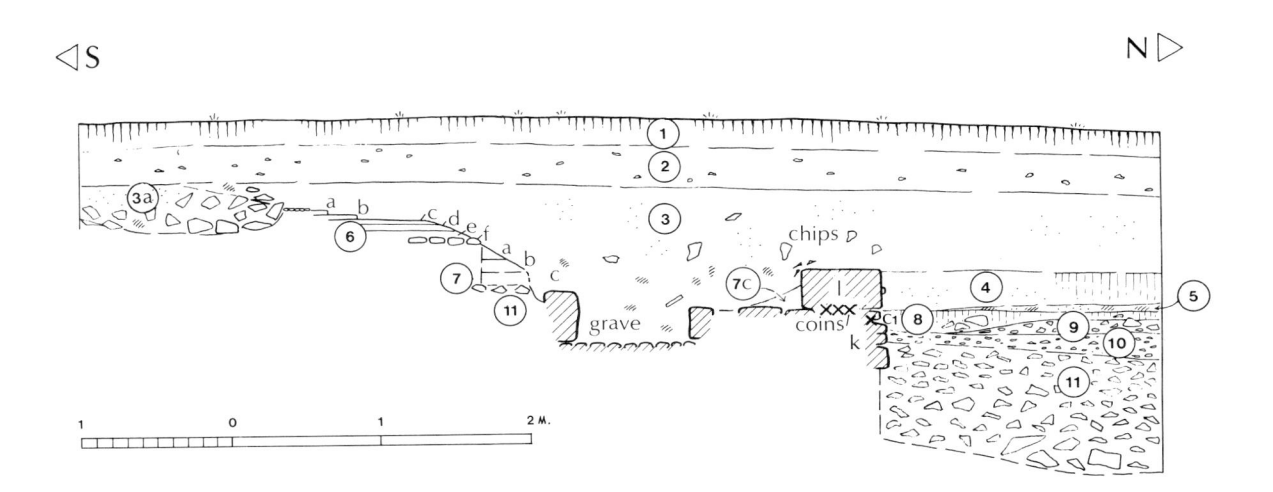

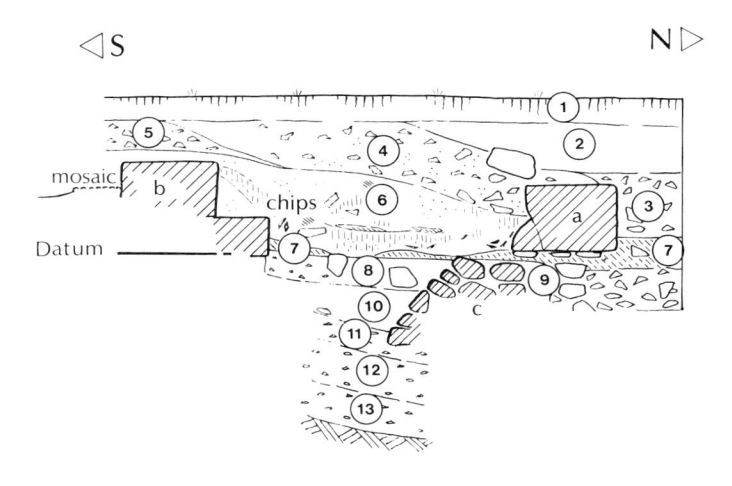

FIG. 14. Basilica Section 4 (north end of E–F) and Section 5.

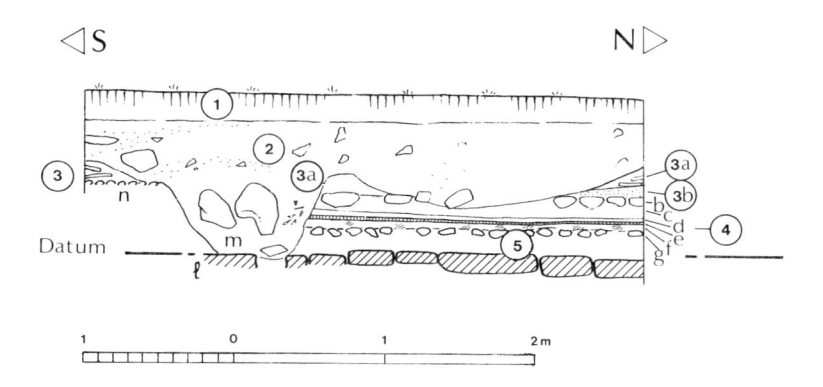

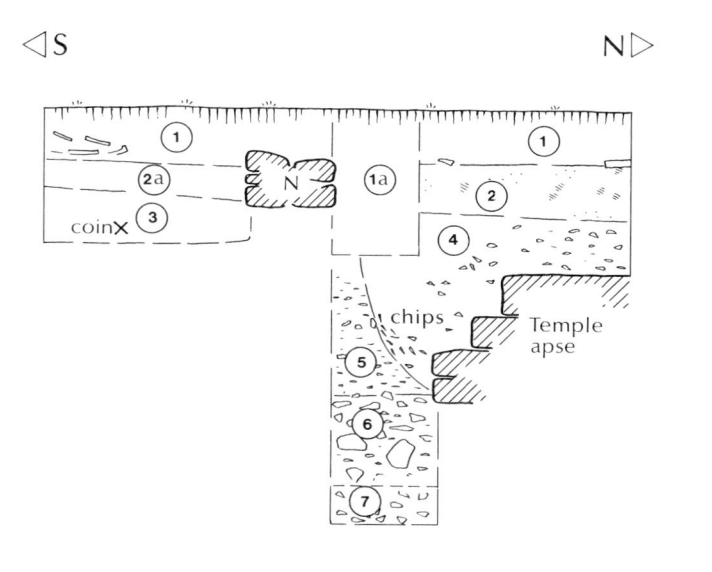

FIG. 15. Basilica Sections 6 and 7.

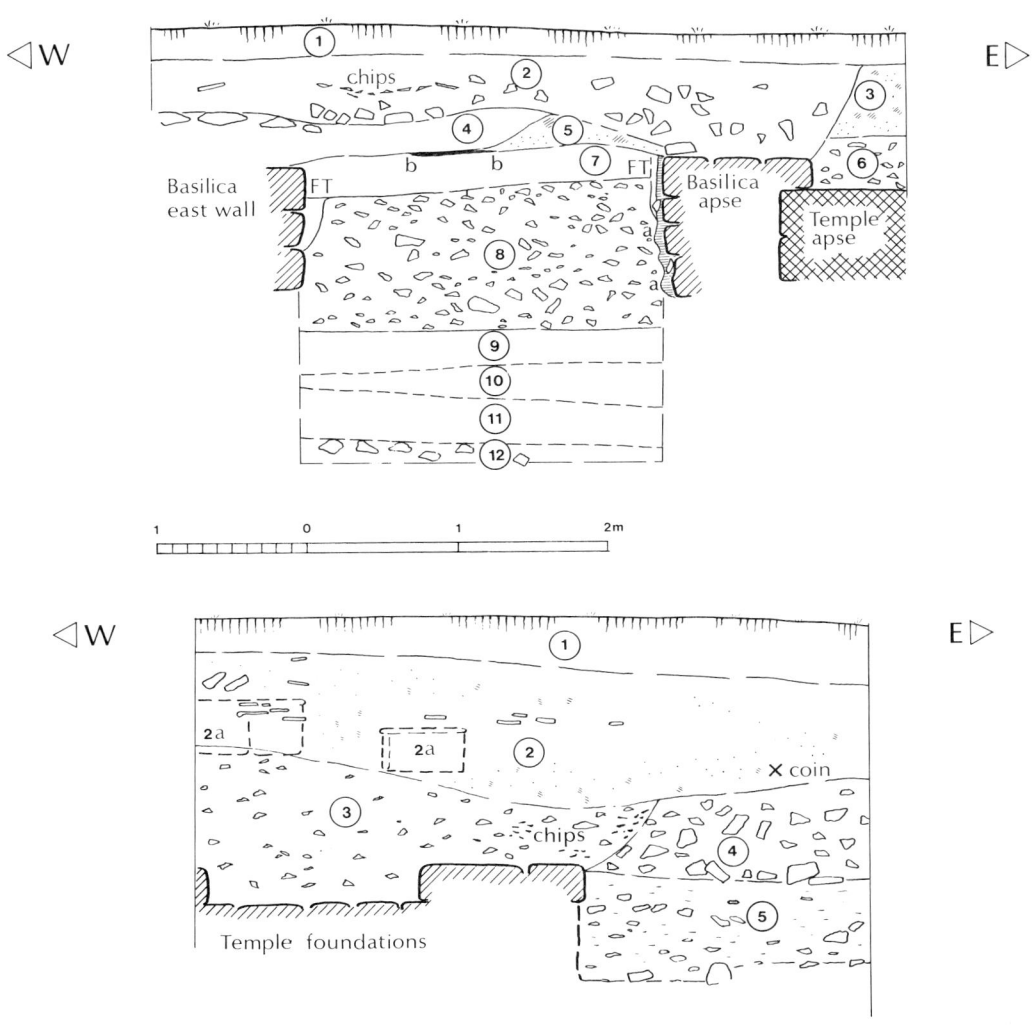

FIG. 16. Basilica Sections 8 and 9.

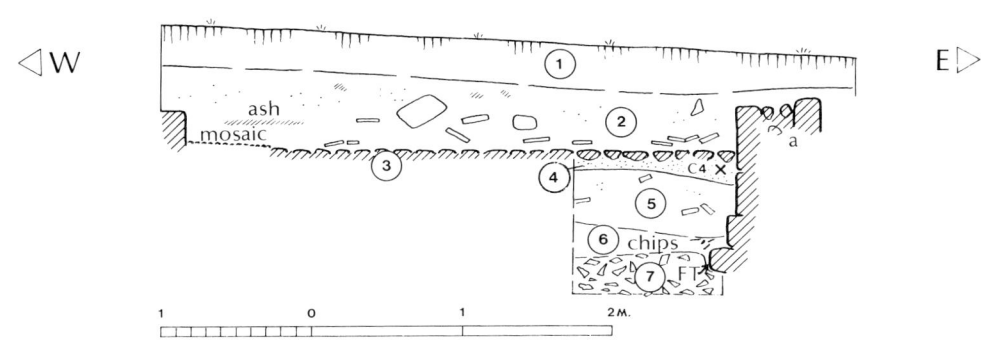

FIG. 17. Basilica Section 10.

5. Index to Finds from the Basilica Church Complex Area

Pottery:

    Pit east of Basilica: H Ext.
        Early Roman: 1–4.

    Fill of apse: U and RR (FIG. 16 Section 8 level (7)).
        Early Roman: 5–12.

    Beneath Basilica floors.
        Early Roman: 13, 20.
        Late Roman: Phocaean Red Slip Ware: 25, 37, 55.

    Basilica Complex area.
        Early Roman: 13–5, 18–9.
        Late Roman:
            Phocaean Red Slip Ware: 21–37, 39–44, 48–50, 52, 54–5, 57, 59, 61, 63, 65, 68, 71–3, 75, 77–94, 96–102, 109–11, 113, 115, 117, 121–3, 126.
            African Red Slip Ware: 132–3, 135–43.
            Cypriot Red Slip Ware: 153, 155–7.
            Other Fabrics: 169, 177.
            The Other Vases: 203, 237, 261.

    Reoccupation Period Vases: 285, 287.

    Graffiti: xiv, xxii.

    Lamps:
        Early Roman: 292–307.
        Intermediary: 308–13.
        Late Roman: 314, 319–20, 322–3, 325–6, 328, 333, 337–41, 343, 345.

Other Materials:

    Marble bowl F6.
    Glass F11–3, F23.
    Bronze: dish F26, hinge fragments F40, chains F52, spindle hook F63, hook F105, pins F132–3, tweezers F138, misc. F146–7, F149–50.
    Iron: ring F54 (c), disc F57, misc. F153.
    Bone: F155–7.
    Mediaeval: bronze earrings (?) F136, lead statuette F137.

Coins:

    C1, C3–5, C8–11, C13–16, C18–20, C22, C26, C30, C34–5, C37, C40, C47–8, C52–60.

Chapter 2
The Settlement and Fortress

1. The Sea Shore Trials (C(hios) E(mporio) S(hore))
Sinclair Hood
(PLATE 10 (*d*))

In 1954 five small trials were made on the edge of the beach on the north side of the bay and in the flat ground behind it to the north-west. The aim of these was to establish whether there had been intensive occupation here in the centuries between the abandonment of the early Greek city on the slopes of Profetes Ilias and the building of the fortress on the Acropolis hill by the harbour. The results of these trials were not conclusive, and the existence of a substantial settlement in the region of Emporio during the later Greek and succeeding Early Roman period remains an open question.

The earliest pottery identified from these trials was Late Roman assignable to the 5th or early 6th century AD (see index at end of this section under Phocaean Red Slip Ware). Coins as well as pottery suggest that settlement continued in this area by the shore into the main Period I of the fortress on the Acropolis. It seems clear therefore that even after the fortress was built occupation in the region of Emporio was not confined to it.

Occupation in the area of the Sea Shore Trials does not appear to have come to an end before the time of the destruction of the fortress. The latest coin of the period of the Arab invasions in the seventh century AD found at Emporio (C49 of Constantine IV (668–85)) was from sounding C of the Sea Shore Trials. It was suggested above (p. 8) that this coin might help to establish a fairly precise date for the Arab destruction of the settlement here and of the fortress. But it could have been lost after the time of the Period I destruction in this area during a phase of reoccupation for which there was evidence, and which, as Boardman notes, may date from an earlier period than the reoccupation of the fortress in Period IIA which came to an end in the first decades of the 9th century.

The first two soundings (A and B), each 3.50m long and 1.50m wide, separated by a metre baulk, were opened where the stumps of two walls were visible in a bank that formed the edge of the beach here. The walls, one in each trench and running across the trenches at right angles to their long sides, were parallel with a space of 2.50m between them. The bottoms of the walls were exposed in excavation, but no floors or surfaces that might have gone with them were identified, and there was no clear evidence for the existence of earlier buildings or occupation levels below them. The trenches were carried down in places to a maximum depth of a metre. A broken and very worn coin of Tiberius II (578–82) (C21) was recovered at a depth of *c*. 0.75m in trench A. The pottery was mostly of the main period (I) of the Fortress with some earlier sherds.

A third sounding (C) 3m long by 1.50m wide *c.* 25m to the west of A was carried down to the rock at a depth of 1.70m at the southern and 1.40m at the northern end. Above the rock was a layer of sand *c.* 0.25m thick, with a deposit some 0.25–0.30m thick above this consisting of small water-worn lumps of pumice, the debris of some ancient eruption (perhaps that of Bronze Age Thera *c.* 1500 BC) which had been washed into the bay and deposited on the shore. Above this again were layers of sand and water-worn sherds. These deposits suggested that the area of the trial (C) had been part of the beach at the time they were formed. The deposit from the surface to a depth of *c.* 0.90m below it consisted of occupation debris with fragments of pottery and a couple of bronze coins (found at depths of *c.* 0.20m and *c.* 0.75m); no walls or traces of floors were recognised, and the area of the trial may have been open ground at the time of the occupation here. The pottery from the lower part of the occupation debris was of the main period (I) of the Fortress. The coin (C49) from depth of *c.* 0.75m associated with it was of Constantine IV (668–85). Pottery from the surface level was mostly nondescript Roman.

A fourth sounding (E), also 3 × 1.50 m, opened *c.* 15m to the north-west of A and B was more productive in terms of traces of occupation. A wall *c.* 0.55m wide with its top some 0.50m below the surface was found running across the north end of the trench (FIG. 18. PLATE 10 (*d*)). It was built of large roughly squared stones with tiles in the joints between them, and was standing to a height of about a metre with four or five courses. This wall belonged with a floor or occupation surface at a depth of *c.* 1.25m from the surface and 0.15m above its bottom (FIG. 18). A scatter of flat slabs of stone at this level may have been the remains of a pavement. Above it was debris consisting of abundant tile and what appeared to be decayed mud-brick walling (level 5). Below this floor or pavement was a layer of hard light brown earth (6) which may have been make-up for it. A deposit of pebbles and sand (7) below this was excavated to a depth of *c.* 0.50m (some 2.15m from the surface). Three late coins were found: two of them in

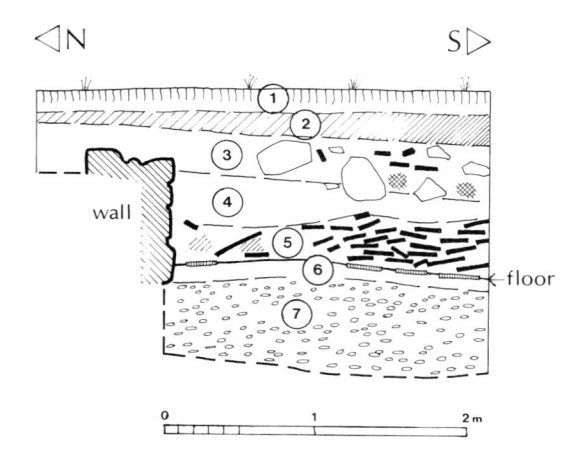

FIG. 18. Sea Shore Trials: trench E (East Section)

(1) Surface
(2) Blackish earth (more marked at S. end of section)
(3) Dark brown with occasional large stones and tile
(4) Hard gritty light reddish brown
(5) Tile and crumbly reddish earth (decayed mud-brick)
(6) Hard light brown
(7) Pebbles and sand

level 6 and one (C17) in 7. One of the coins from 6, recovered from beneath a slab of the possible pavement, appears to be C45 of Constans II dated 642/3 like C46 from the destruction level of Period I in the fortress. This would give a *terminus post quem* for the floor or pavement and for the wall associated with it. Boardman notes that the character of the pottery from above the floor or pavement suggests that it and the wall must belong to a phase of reoccupation dating from after the time of the fortress destruction. This is in harmony with the observation of Ballance that the floors with stone slabs incorporated in them in the area of the fortress on the Acropolis hill were all of Period II. The coin from level 7 was C17 of Justin II (565–78) struck in 575/6. Pottery from the surface level 2 included four or five fragments of Mycenaean and one of earlier matt painted ware.

The fifth sounding (D) was opened *c.* 80m inland to the north-west of E. It was also 3 × 1.50m in area, and it was carried down to a depth of *c.* 1.30m from the surface. Over a metre of earth, alluvium or hill-wash, covered the top of occupation debris which dated from the Early Byzantine period, presumably from the main period (I) of the Fortress. Part of a roughly built wall of rubble *c.* 1.20m wide was found running across the middle of the trench more or less from north to south. Some fragments of glass were recovered from the occupation debris and from the washed-down earth above it.

Index to Finds from the Sea Shore Trials

Pottery:
  Late Roman:
    Phocaean Red Slip Ware: 21, 32–6, 39–42, 45–7, 49, 51, 54–5, 58–73, 80, 83, 86, 90, 92–3, 95, 110–2, 124.
    African Red Slip Ware: 134–6, 139.
    Cypriot Red Slip Ware: 156–8.
    Other Fabrics: 162–6, 168, 171, 173–4.

Other materials:
  Stone: stopper F29, plaque F140.

Coins:
  C17, C21, C45, C49.

2. The Byzantine Fortress

Michael Ballance

(DRAWINGS IV–X. PLATES 12–19)

The steep and rocky promontory to the south of the harbour seems to have been only lightly and intermittently inhabited from the end of the Mycenaean period to the early seventh century AD. No remains of Greek or Roman buildings were found there in the quite extensive excavations carried out between 1953 and 1955; there are only two coins from between the first century BC and the sixth AD (C2,6), and only from the later fifth century AD on does the volume of pottery perhaps suggest some desultory occupation. The only sign of purposeful human activity was a largely destroyed wall (*Prehistoric Emporio* i 164, wall 41, 161 fig. 89, pl. 28 (d)) underlying the main excavated street of the Byzantine settlement; it presumably supported a cultivation terrace similar to those still in use all over the island.

The first of the two main Byzantine settlements on the site (Period I) was presumably laid out about the middle of the seventh century. There was little in either the internal arrangements or the small finds to suggest that it was specifically of a military character; though under the theme system the division between civil and military had become blurred, and the inhabitants of this strongly fortified position commanding the entrance to a good natural harbour must have had their military responsibilities. Not much later, probably in the early 670's the buildings were destroyed by fire, together with most of the household goods of the inhabitants, and abandoned (for the likely chronology see pp. 80–1).

The seventh-century fortifications appear to have survived without very serious damage, and even the bases of some of the house walls could still be used as footings when the site was reoccupied in the eighth or early ninth century (Period II). This reoccupation did not terminate in a fire, and the material lying on the floors is correspondingly less varied and interesting than that in the Period I destruction level. The only sign of occupation after this second abandonment is around the small chapel (perhaps itself part of the Period II layout) near the western summit of the hill (but see pp. 78–80).

PERIOD I

The Period I Acropolis

The Acropolis hill has no attractions as a place of settlement apart from its defensibility and the fact that, while commanding the narrow entrance to the harbour, it is still comparatively accessible from the landward side. Of irregular shape, it measures about 200m from east to west by about 150m from north to south, and rises to two rocky summits, one at about 46m near the eastern end, the other at about 40m near the west. The seventh-century walls enclose a net area of about 4,500m^2 and run at an altitude that varies from about 25m at the main gate to about 38m. at some points on the south side. Outside the walls the ground slopes down at an average gradient of about 1 in 2, except at the east end and along part of the south side, where it falls away in cliffs.

Seen from a distance in its present state, the hill-top appears to be comparatively flat around the edges; but before the building of the fortifications, which support this terrace, this tendency must have been much less apparent.

The only street excavated to any extent was a narrow alley running eastwards from the main gate; but the alignment of the paving found in 1953 just inside the gate suggests that a second and probably more important street may have run south-eastwards in the direction of the saddle between the two summits; a second east-west street parallel to the first may have branched off below the saddle.

The principal excavated area, lying along the north and north-west edges of the site, proved to be thickly built up; trial trenches at various points in the saddle and along the inner face of the wall near the south-east and south-west corners all produced traces of habitation, and it seems that every possible building site, amounting to perhaps half of the total area enclosed by the walls, was utilised, at any rate in Period I. Though less evidence was found of occupation in Period II, this may be partly due to subsequent erosion.

Access to the Acropolis was presumably by a path roughly on the same line as the modern one that approaches the main gate from the north-west; but, as the condition of the threshold of the gate shows, it was not intended for wheeled traffic.

Three vaulted concrete cisterns provide the only evidence of the water supply of the Acropolis. The largest, in C of 1954, could have held about 40m^3. It is likely that others existed, and between them they were probably sufficient for general use in winter and spring and for emergencies during the drier months, particularly if cattle were normally watered at wells in the plain below.

Fortifications of Period I   (DRAWING IV)

The fortifications of the seventh-century Acropolis are reasonably elaborate for a site of such natural strength. The main wall boasts three towers grouped around the north-west corner, as well as a single gate, also on the north-west, and a postern on the south side next to the later chapel. In addition there is an outer wall or *proteichisma* extending from the south-west corner around the whole of the west and north sides.

The main wall varies in thickness from about 1.75 to 2.50m and is of decidedly heterogeneous construction. In most of the visible stretches of the north side, the outer face is constructed of heavy reused blocks of white sandstone up to 0.80m square; the joints are plugged where necessary with small stones, little mortar being used (PLATE 13 (*a*), (*b*)). The foundations, uncovered in L in 1953, are of smaller and rougher stones set in mortar, while the inner face, in B, D and F of 1954, is of rubble either with or without mortar. There is reason to believe that these differences of construction are not all due to differences in date. In F of 1954, the Period I destruction level runs undisturbed up to an unmortared inner face; yet only a few metres away, in B of 1954, a Period I floor runs up to a mortared face (PLATE 16 (*f*)), while the North-west Tower, which is incontrovertibly of Period I, is fully mortared throughout (PLATE 14 (*b*)).

The rest of the circuit is built mainly of rough stones of varying size, including a few re-used blocks. As a rule only the outer face is mortared, while the core and inner face are of rubble laid in earth.

The three towers, which are not bonded to the wall, are all constructed of rubble laid in good mortar and faced on the exterior with roughly dressed blocks arranged in approximate courses. In the North and South-west Towers, the foundations are of larger blocks and project some distance beyond the front wall, presumably in order to spread the weight over a greater area of ground as the soil here can never have been very firm (PLATE 12 (*e*)). In the North-west Tower, which was founded directly on rock, no such projection occurs.

Though generally similar in construction, the three towers are markedly different in plan. The South-west Tower is solid to its whole preserved height of about three metres (PLATE 13 (*c*)). The outer walls have no well defined inner face and the core is of rubble and earth. The North Tower has a small square room in its lower storey, inaccessible except from above and paved with cobbles and small stones (PLATE 12 (*f*)). In the North-west Tower, a rather larger room, also cobbled, was approached down two steps from a passage behind (PLATE 13 (*f*)). The outer end of this tower is unusual in being curved on the exterior and buttressed at the corners, and this was certainly an original feature, as the whole structure is of one build. A drain 0.60m high and 0.30m wide at the inner end runs through the north wall near the east end (PLATE 14 (*a*)).

The gate was of the simplest possible type: a gap in the wall with jambs formed of rather larger stones than were used elsewhere (PLATE 12 (b)). The width (2.25m) suggests that it was arched, though no remains of voussoirs were found. The inner threshold has sockets for a pair of doors, which closed against a slightly raised outer threshold.

The Postern on the south side, immediately below the Chapel, is a steep and partly rock-cut passage 1.60m wide through the main wall (PLATE 13 (e)). A low mortared wall across the outer end must have supported a threshold, and a rectangular posthole behind it presumably served some purpose connected with securing the doors (p. 56).

On the more accessible north and west sides of the circuit a second wall runs at a distance of about two to six metres outside the main one. It is a modest affair varying from 0.75 to 1.25m in thickness and is built of rubble with a variable amount of mortar. At the south-west corner of the circuit it joins, but is probably not bonded into, the main wall (PLATE 13 (d)). At the north-east it seems to have run only as far as the projecting bastion of rock north of the East Cistern. This wall presumably dates from Period I as does the layer of black cobbles (presumably collected on the beach just below the Acropolis on the south) that in many places covers the berm between the two walls (PLATES 13 (c); 15 (b)). Its thinness suggests that it was no more than a crenellated breastwork high enough to cover a man standing on the berm. At one point, however, in the loop that it makes immediately below the North-west Tower, it may have risen into a sort of semi-elliptical tower (PLATE 15 (b)).

It is uncertain what happened to the outer wall at the point where it passed the Main Gate. It does not appear to have returned to join the line of the main wall, but such excavation as was possible here without disturbing a large modern terrace wall failed to reveal any sign of an outer gate.

(1) The Main Defence Wall

The Main Gate (DRAWINGS IV, VI)

Excavation outside the gate involved cutting through two modern terrace walls, each about 1.50m high, down to a sloping layer of large stones and brown loam, the top of which corresponded roughly with the probable Period II ground-level inside the gate. There was no sign of paving, though four parallel lines of small stones suggested that the area had been levelled into a series of rough steps. Below this a further accumulation of stones, interspersed with mortar fragments, may have been the result of the decay and partial destruction of the wall in the interval of time between Periods I and II. The Period I road-level was defined by a number of large worn stones about 0.20m below the level of the outer threshold (PLATE 12 (b)). This rough paving had a well defined edge; so far as could be seen in the very narrow trench, separate paved paths led off to the north-west, along the line of the presumed main access path, and to the north-east, in the direction of the North Tower. The space between the two paths was covered with a thin strew of cobbles.

The outer threshold of the gate was formed of two well-squared stones showing little sign of wear and no wheel-marks. At some period the two stones had been joined together by a pair of metal cramps, the sinkings for which remained. But the presence of an additional sinking at the east end of the east stone, where it could have had no functional purpose, suggests that both the cramps and a series of three square holes near the outer edge of the east stone date from an earlier stage in the history of the stones. The inner threshold (PLATE 12 (c)), 0.14m below the outer one, consisted of two stones with two pivot-holes 0.10m in diameter and 0.05m deep set about 0.25m from the ends, so that the effective opening of the gate would have been rather less than 1.35m. There was no trace of sinkings for wooden jambs to block the spaces between the door-pivots and the stonework, though a band 0.35m wide passing across the west pivot-hole had been slightly smoothed down. A semi-circular cutting in the outer edge of the west stone allowed rainwater to drain into a small stone channel under the outer threshold.

Further clearance of topsoil and stones inside the outer wall to north and north-west of the gate revealed more cobbles further down the slope but no trace of the main access path.

The North Tower (DRAWING VI and FIG. 19)
The interior of the North Tower was partly cleared in 1953 (Y), and in 1954 a trench (G) was cut into the accumulation of rubble immediately outside it on the west.

The room inside the tower (PLATE 12 (*f*)) was floored, at a height of about 1.00m above the berm, with cobbles and small stones, covered by tiles of the Period I destruction level. The filling above the tile-layer consisted of loose stones and earth.

The cutting outside the tower revealed the outer face of the tower wall, in roughly faced small blocks with a few larger squared stones. The usual black cobbles appeared on the surface of the berm, though erosion had removed those at the north end of the trench. In the angle between the tower and the main wall was a shallow cemented trough. The pottery in the last few centimetres above the cobbles included none of Period II, confirming that here as elsewhere they belong to Period I. No definite Period II ground-level could be established in the rubble higher up.

The foundations of the north wall of the tower take the form of a solid concrete raft projecting some 1.50m beyond the wall itself and supporting a stepped footing faced with large blocks. The builders no doubt distrusted the stability of the ground, which here probably consisted of Bronze Age occupation levels.

The main wall at this point is built of very large blocks, without mortar; the inner face, visible in D and F of 1954, is of smaller stones but also unmortared. There are some signs at the north-west corner of D that in Period II a trench was cut into the Period I destruction level and the wall repaired down to just above the Period I floor; the stones above this point, though laid in earth, bear traces of mortar and were presumably salvaged from some damaged part of the Period I defences. At the north-west corner of B (1954) also, the wall shows signs of hasty repair.

In L of 1953 the wall was founded upon Bronze Age occupation deposits (as also in S and K of 1953, F, D, B of 1954) and was preserved to a total height of 2.80m. The lowest 0.80m of the outer face was of smallish stones well set in mortar. Above this point it was of reused blocks of white sandstone up to 0.80m wide, laid in rather irregular courses, sparingly mortared and liberally wedged with small pieces of sandstone and basalt (PLATE 13 (*b*)).

From here to the projecting rock that forms the north-east corner of the circuit the general line of the wall is clear because of the terrace that it supports, though actual remains, of mortared rubble, can be seen at only two points (6 & 7 on the plan, DRAWING IV). Traces of mortar on the rock itself (8 on plan) were insufficient to show whether, as might have been expected, there was a tower at this commanding point.

Just beyond the rock (at 9) a short section of the outer face, in large rubble and good mortar, was cleared at the base of a modern terrace wall. Further on (at 10) a considerable stretch of very decayed wall was visible, with a mortared outer face of boulders and large rubble and a core of rubble and earth.

To the south of the rock outcrop at the eastern end of the circuit, the wall reappears (at 11), this time without visible mortar. Parallel to it on the inside is a short stretch of what seems to have been a house wall.

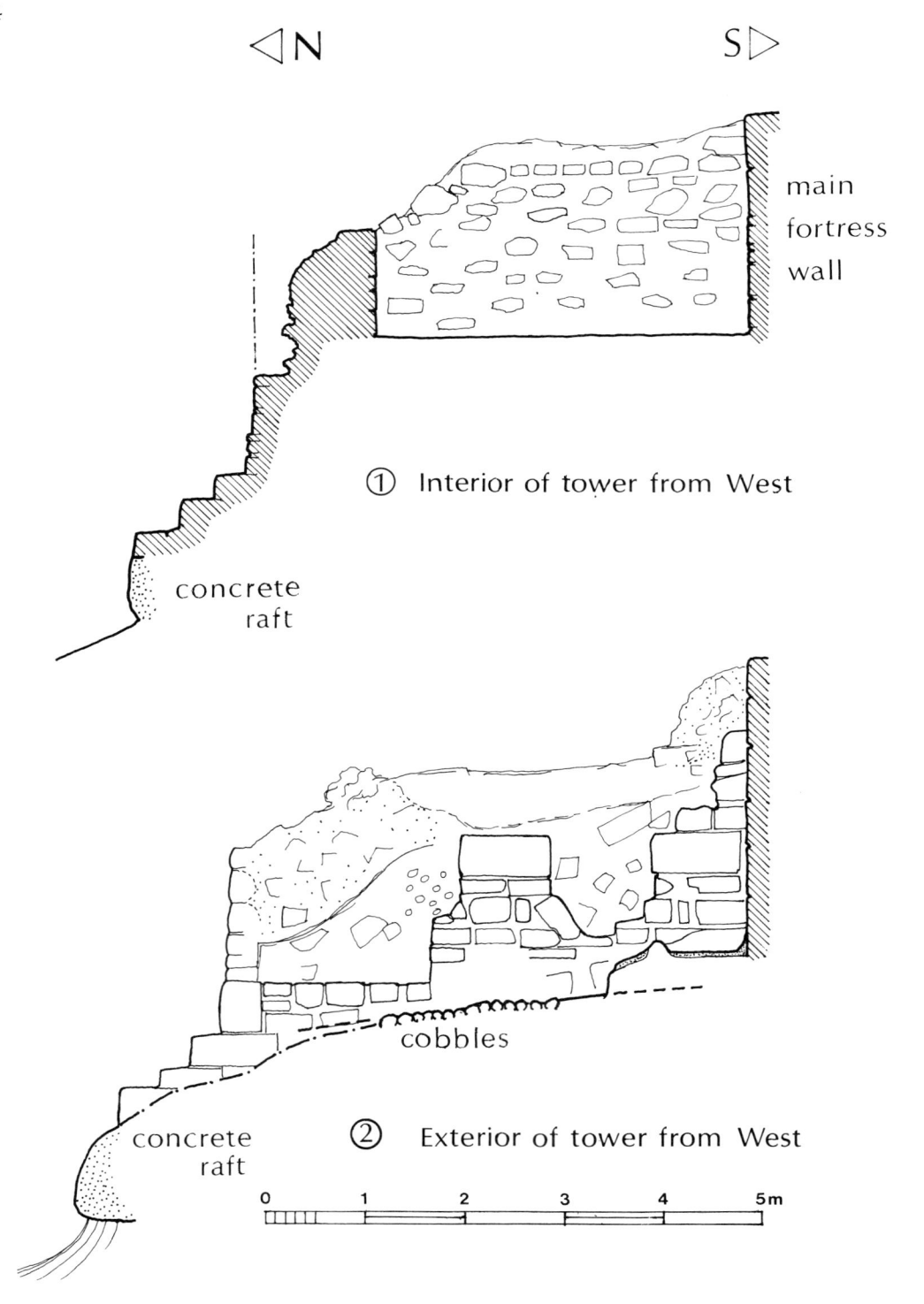

FIG. 19. The North Tower: elevations of (1) interior and (2) west side.

South and south-east of the main summit of the hill, traces of the wall are visible intermittently westwards from 12 over a stretch of about 25m. The outer face, standing to a height of about four courses, is mortared, but the core is of rubble and earth. About 0.50 or 0.60m behind the inner face of the main wall, which is here about 2.00m thick, runs what appears to have been a continuous smaller wall (12 & 13; cf. 11).

A small trench (O of 1955) cut across the two walls showed that the inner one was of normal domestic type, about 0.60m thick and built without mortar (Plan, FIG. 20). It was joined roughly at right angles by another similar wall, on both sides of which, but especially on the east, lay a deposit of brown earth, pottery and tile fragments. A whitish level below this in the northeast corner of the trench appeared to have been a house floor. The narrow space, 0.45 to 0.60m wide, between the fortification wall and the house wall alongside it, was covered with a layer of cobbles that ran up against both walls. In view of its narrowness, this passage was presumably intended for drainage rather than access.

The fortification wall reappears some 35m further on, in the saddle between the two summits of the hill; but the inner face (at 14 and 15) is dubious and even the outer face seems to contain little mortar.

From the saddle as far as the Postern by the Chapel nothing remains of the wall except two little scraps of mortared rubble; one (16) immediately west of the western summit of the hill, the other only 3m east of the postern.

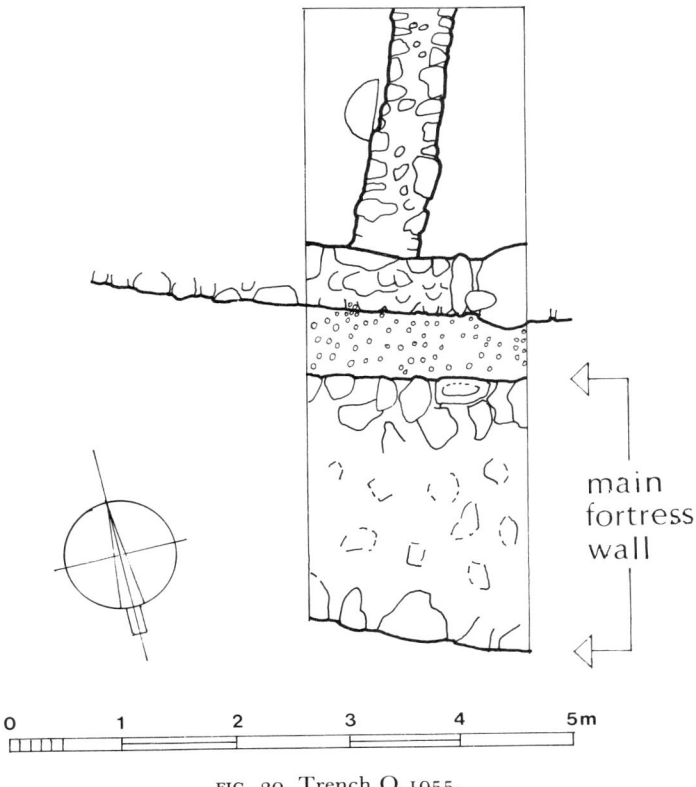

FIG. 20. Trench O 1955.

The Postern Gate (FIG. 25)
The Postern was excavated in 1953 as an extension to the excavation of the Chapel (A) and further work was done on it in 1955 (N). The path descending to the Postern was largely rock-cut, but the inequalities of the surface were filled in with the usual cobbles (PLATE 13 (*e*)). At the outer end it was crossed by a mortared sleeper wall, 0.65m wide and at least 0.25m high, which had presumably supported the threshold. Immediately behind the centre of this was a hole about 0.50 by 0.25m; the sides were lined with stones set in mortar, while the back (north side) was formed by a projection of the rock. It went down to a depth of about 0.40m (0.50m below the probable level of the cobble pavement), and the bottom was covered by a large stone and some cobbles. The filling of the hole consisted of softish earth with many sherds.

The purpose of this hole is uncertain. There seem to have been no indications that it was a drain, and at the time of excavation in 1955 it was presumed to have held a gate post. But a gate post in the centre of the passage requires explanation, and the only logical one seems to be that at some time, not necessarily long after the original building of the walls, the width of the Postern was reduced from about 1.80 to 0.80m. The mortar bedding for a rectangular object (presumably a stone) was noticed just to the east of the hole and it is thus possible that the sleeper wall was built up and thickened on this side. But the evidence is at best uncertain.

Just sufficient evidence was found to establish the position and thickness (2.20m) of the fortification wall on the east side of the Postern. On the west, where the rock was higher, only the rear corner was preserved, underpinned by a small separate mortared wall. The fortification wall was well mortared on both sides of the postern.

The steeply sloping alley inside the Postern was defined by two unmortared walls belonging to the original scheme. Although neither was bonded into the fortification wall, that on the north-east had been cut back at the time of the building of the Chapel, and was partly cut into and partly overlaid by the lining of Tomb II (see below). The cobble paving of the passage ran right up to its base. The south-eastern wall, which stood on the rock at a level higher than the cobbles, had tiles of the Period I destruction level piled against it.

The paving of the passage was covered by a layer containing much tile and pottery typical of Period I, with no sign of later pottery. No evidence was recovered of any measures taken to repair or block the Postern in Period II.

Immediately west of the Postern, the walls bent out to the south to include a rocky spur. As it ran southwards (18) both faces were visible to a height of one or two courses. Mortar was confined to the outer face, here built of very large but rough stones. Just before the southernmost point, the outer wall branched off (at 19) (PLATE 13 (*d*)).

The outer face of the main wall, still of boulders and large rubble set in mortar, was visible all the way from here to the South-west Tower, though there was no certain trace of the inner face.

The South-west Tower
The South-west Tower (20) was of roughly squared smallish blocks (PLATE 13 (*c*)). The well mortared walls were about 1.20m thick and had no defined inner face, simply merging with the core of rubble and earth. This tower, like the North Tower, was not bonded to the main wall and had a projecting stepped footing at the downhill end.

Just to the north of the tower, a small area (W) was cleared in 1953, showing a well preserved strew of cobbles on the berm.

The main wall behind the tower, excavated in Trench L (1955), proved to be of unusual construction; the outer skin, with an average thickness of 0.70m, consisted of mortared masonry and had a distinct inner face. A similar skin, but rather thinner and mortared only on its exposed face, formed the back of the wall. The space between the two skins was packed with rubble and earth. This gave the wall a total thickness of 2.50 to 2.70m at this point as against the normal maximum of 2.20m. This form of construction was not specially noticed in any other stretch of the wall, but may have been used elsewhere; apart from a short length of the south wall in O of 1955 the only other stretches of wall fully excavated and cleaned were near the north-west corner of the circuit.

Three roughly parallel walls of the usual domestic type butted against the inner face of the fortification wall immediately behind the tower. The central one was at a considerably lower level than the others, and a thick strew of sherds and tiles that ran up to its southern face seems to have been a Period I destruction level.

The southern wall lay on top of the tile strew and should thus be of Period II; the same probably applies to the northern one, which was preserved almost up to the modern ground level. A thick layer of brown earth overlying the central wall may have been the makeup for a Period II floor, and the layer above that, containing mortar fragments and rubble, should thus represent the final decay both of the Period II domestic walls and of the fortification wall.

The wall north of the South-west Tower was of the same type as that to the south of it. The outer face was visible for some distance to a height of up to two metres, but the inner face could only be seen at 21 where excavated (M of 1955, where a house wall was butted against it).

The North-west Tower (DRAWING V and FIGS. 21, 22)

The interior of the North-west Tower (22), together with the area immediately behind it, was excavated in 1953 (F of 1953). The stony reddish-brown earth under the floor of the tower contained prehistoric and probably Mycenaean pottery, but no other sign of occupation; the presence of stone-chips near the bottom suggested that it was a fill contemporary with the building of the tower, which was founded on rock throughout. An unusual feature of the upper part of this fill was that it included, especially near the centre, a large quantity of beach pebbles of the type used for the cobble-strew on the berm outside.

Apart from a few of these pebbles and a faint trace of mortar perhaps dropped from above by the builders, the Period I floor was defined only by the destruction level that overlay it; at the south-east corner a knob of rock, blackened by fire, rose to a height of about 0.80m above it (PLATE 13 (*f*)). Immediately inside the door, a thin layer of mortar and amphora-fragments, presumably the bedding for a gutter, led round to a drain-hole through the north wall of the tower (PLATE 14 (*a*)). Unfortunately this area was confused by the presence of a stone-robber's or treasure-hunter's pit, though this did not extend as far as the drain-hole itself. A very shallow depression 0.20m wide in the floor just to the south of the doorway seemed to have been the seating for a wooden partition running westwards, perhaps to support a pile of earth used as bedding for some amphorae in the south-east corner of the room.

The destruction-level contained a number of complete but crushed pots (Plan, DRAWING V. PLATE 14 (*b*)). An amphora and four pithoi, two of them with lids (one inscribed, 274) had stood against the west half of the south wall; further to the east were four large amphorae, which had apparently been standing well away from the wall, accompanied by three smaller amphorae and a small cooking-pot (PLATE 14 (*c*)). Other objects included table ware, an iron pruning-hook (F86), an iron ring (F54a) and some bones, all under the pithos in the south-west corner, and two bronze sockets (F142–3) and a bronze handle ?(F151) lying against the wall by its immediate neighbour. A rotary quern (F98) was propped against the east wall. A coin of Constans II (dated 645/6) was found by the wall, halfway along the north side, while the Period I floor was being cleaned (C41).

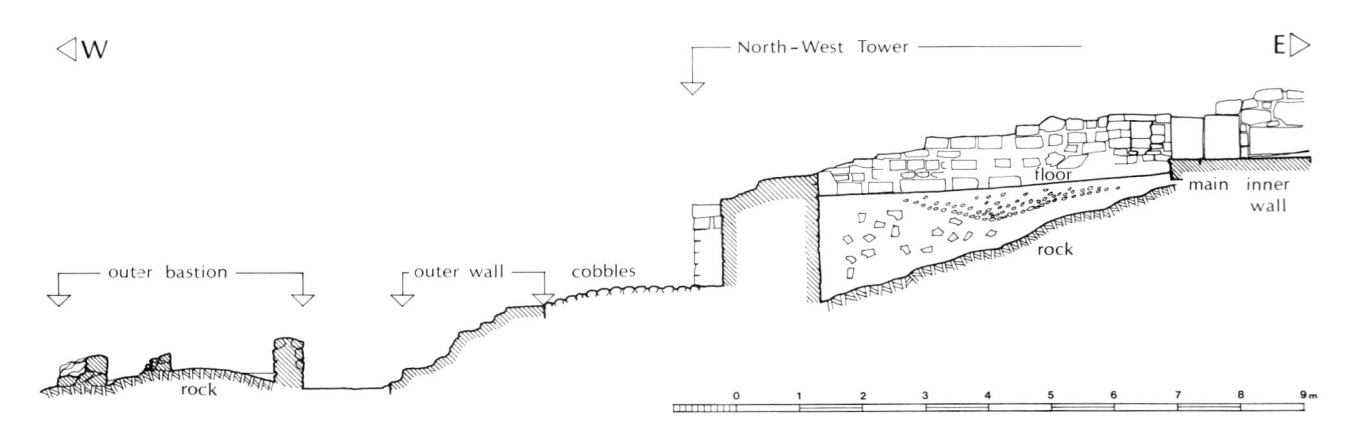

FIG. 21. North west Tower Section 1 (DRAWING V) through tower and outer bastion.

Immediately overlying the floor and its associated objects was a layer of burnt earth, pebbles, ash and charcoal; in this and especially in the upper part of it were numerous large fragments of white stone slabs, 0.02 to 0.05m thick, showing traces of mortar on one face, and sizable fragments of white mortar incorporating large pebbles on one face and in some cases showing signs that slabs had been attached to the other face; the total thickness of pebbles and mortar varied from about 0.10 to 0.15m. Most of the tiles found were flat ones, though some roof-tiles also occurred. These tiles, slabs and lumps of mortar suggest two possible reconstructions of the flat roof, or upper floor, of the tower. The slabs, perhaps mixed with tiles, either constituted the paving over a vault (modern parallels exist in this part of Chios), or alternatively were laid on closely-spaced wooden beams to support a floor of pebbles set in mortar.

Above this burnt debris was a thin (0.10 to 0.20m) layer of brown earth and small stones, and above this, almost reaching modern ground-level except at the west end where it had been completely eroded away, a "white level" containing stones, stone chips and fragments of decayed mortar presumably derived from the natural decay or intentional destruction of the upper parts of the tower walls. In this were found a virtually complete Period I amphora (231), perhaps fallen from above, and a fragment of marble column.

No certain Period II floor was found, though in retrospect it seems possible that the thin brown layer below the "white level" was the makeup for a floor.

Access to the ground floor of the tower was through an opening 1.50m wide, presumably arched though no voussoirs were noted (PLATE 14 (a)). At the west end of this opening was a fine stone threshold with a moulded edge, on which part of the southern jamb of the door was found in position; the northern jamb had presumably been removed by the diggers of the pit already mentioned, but traces of mortar showed where it had stood. The passage was paved with slabs and with flat tiles 0.30 m square and sloped up at the east end towards a roughly-laid step about 0.25m high running along the line of the inner face of the fortification wall.

Immediately to the south of the passage, a Period I house-wall (DRAWING V wall 1) ran at right angles to the fortification wall and formed the southern border of an alley leading eastwards from the tower door (PLATE 13 (f)). The ground surface in the alley consisted of gritty brown earth and small stone-chips, lying on, and sometimes failing to cover, the bedrock. On the north side of the alley, at the west end, another rough step at a higher level gave access to an area that was never excavated.

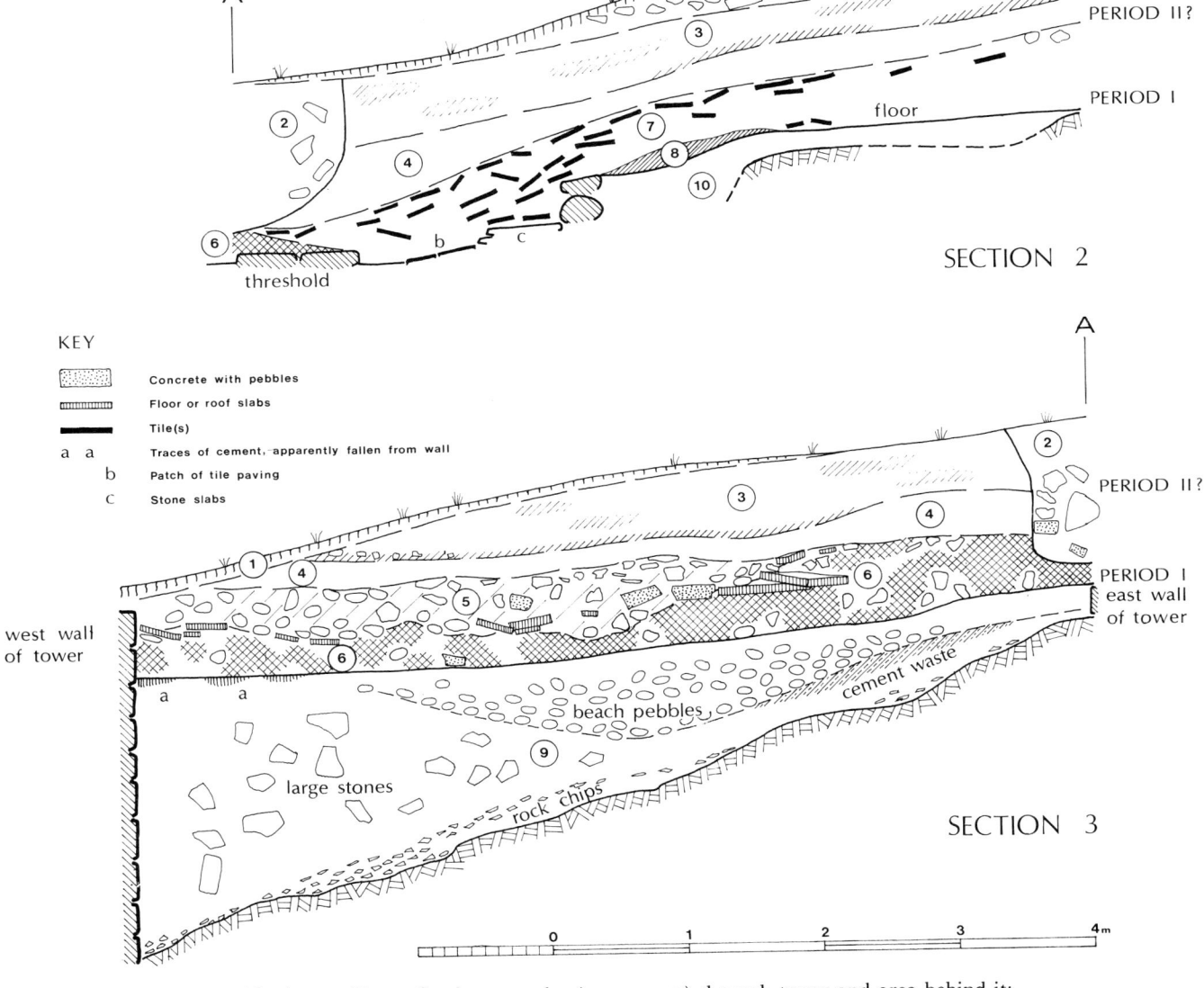

FIG. 22. North-west Tower Sections 2 and 3 (DRAWING V) through tower and area behind it:

(1) Surface
(2) Pit with earth and stones filling robber trench for east wall of tower
(3) Hard whitish earth, above surface of Period II (?)
(4) Hard brown earth with small stones
(5) Ruin debris of Period I destruction of tower, with grey ash and stones (Section 3)
(6) Ruin debris of Period I destruction of tower, with black ash and stone slabs from upper floor or roof (Section 3)
(7) Earth and tile of Period I destruction (Section 2)
(8) Ash above floor of Period I (Section 2)
(9) Fill of earth, rock waste, stones and large beach pebbles, dating from time of construction of tower (Section 3)
(10) Gritty brown earth with small chips of rock (Section 2)

The only other Period I wall (DRAWING V wall 2) that was found ran northwards from the alley and presumably represented the end of a curved wall (4) excavated in the next trench (V).

The wall to the south of the alley proved to belong to a house, the floor of which lay about 0.80m above the lowest ground-level in the alley. On it was a cooking-pot, some other small pots, jar-lids (262) and some fragments of glass, covered by the thick tile-layer characteristic of the Period I destruction-level.

The destruction-level in the alley also consisted of from 0.30 to 0.50m of tiles and brown earth, suggesting that this area also had been roofed; as in the tower, there was no certain Period II ground-level, though two Period II walls were found, one (35) running north-south across the house-floor, the other (36) east-west above the north side of the alley.

Five metres beyond the tower the fortification wall made a rather sharp bend (DRAWING IV (23). PLATE 14 (d)). A reduction in width from 2.20 to 1.80m seemed to be due to inaccurate setting-out rather than to any difference in date. Both faces were of roughly coursed rubble and large lumps of rock; the core was of rubble laid in earth, and mortar was confined to the faces. Three metres beyond the bend, a hole or drain ran through the wall from the inside almost to the outer face before turning eastwards within the thickness of the masonry.

The immediate area of the bend was excavated in 1953 (V) together with part of a house inside the wall and part of an oven built up against the outer face. The rest of this oven and the whole of a second in the angle of the tower were cleared in 1954.

Both ovens were roughly circular and about 1.50m in inner diameter (PLATE 14 (e)). They were built of small rubble laid in earth; the northern one still had part of its domed roof which consisted largely of tile fragments; there was no sign of the doors, which had presumably faced west. Both ovens were floored with gritty earth containing small beach pebbles. The pottery from below the floors was very mixed, but the presence of Period II sherds just above bedrock in the southern one, 0.25m below the likely floor-level, provides a *terminus post quem* for both; the northern one is structurally secondary, being built up against the other. The bones of a small animal were found in one of the ovens. A blackened level excavated in 1953 just outside the bend of the fortification wall may have been the ash-heap for the ovens, though only Period I pottery was recorded from it.

(2) The Outer Defence Wall

At the point (DRAWING IV (19)) where it branches off from the main wall at the south-west corner of the circuit, both faces were visible and the wall was 1.20m thick and mortared right through.

The outer face was traceable almost all the way to the South-west Tower; at one point (24) the thickness could be measured as 1.20 m

The wall appears (at 25) to have passed very close to the South-west Tower but the exact line was uncertain. Two more short stretches were visible (26 and 27) between here and the North-west Tower.

Below the North-west Tower it ran out into a loop (28) to include a projecting spur of rock (DRAWING V. PLATE 15 (a), (b)). The thickness decreased to 0.75m, and there were signs of a presumably original mortared cross-wall cutting off the extremity of the loop. The surviving upper structure of the cross-wall, however, was not mortared, nor was a low revetment, excavated in 1953, immediately inside the loop. In 1954 further clearance showed that this revetment continued outside the cross-wall to the south-east. It consisted only of a single face of small stones, up to about 0.40m high, and presumably supported the inner edge of a bank of earth resting against the wall. As the cobble strew, which seems to be a feature of the original Period I layout, ran on behind it, it was presumably secondary.

On the south side of the loop, just outside the area enclosed by the cross-wall, a large flat stone forming part of the inner face of the outer wall may have been the threshold of a small postern or sally-port.

The reconstruction of the loop in either its original Period I or its later form is somewhat problematical. In particular the purpose of the cross-wall is obscure unless the loop was carried up to form a sort of semi-elliptical tower, parallels for which could be found. But the lack of a doorway in the cross-wall, which in its rebuilt form was preserved to a height of over 0.50m above the Period I cobbles, is hard to explain on this assumption; possibly the ground-level inside the loop was much higher in Period II, but this involves the attribution of the revetment (which rests directly on the rock) to Period I or at least to an earlier date than the rebuilding of the cross-wall. Beyond the loop, the outer wall disappeared under modern terrace walls, reappearing 10 or 12m further on at 29 on DRAWING IV and running more or less straight almost as far as the Main Gate.

Clearance in front of the Main Gate in H 1954 revealed nothing but a scatter of mortared stones at the point where the path to the Gate might have been expected to pass through the outer wall. A further short stretch of the outer wall (DRAWING IV (30)) was visible between the Gate and the North Tower. A longer stretch began 6m beyond the tower and ran for some 18m. At one point (31) the wall had cracked and the part to the west of the crack had bulged out. Though the bulge itself did not seem to have been repaired, an extra skin of very sparingly mortared masonry had been added to the east of the crack in order to make the outer face appear unbroken.

Two more short stretches (32 and 33) give the general line of the outer wall as far as the projecting rock outcrop at the north-east corner of the circuit (8). At this point it probably returned to join the inner wall; no trace of it could be seen along the north-east side which, though slightly less steep in its higher reaches than the north side, was protected by cliffs lower down.

Period I Occupation Levels

After the building of the Acropolis wall, to the permanence of which we owe the fact that anything more than the footings of the seventh-century settlement have survived, the site had to be levelled into a series of rough terraces before building could start. In the main excavated area east of the gate, an earlier terrace wall existed, but was in such a ruinous state that the builders seem to have disregarded it, though they made some effort to raise the level of the area between it and the fortification before laying a road over the top of it. Even so, the earliest floors in Rooms VIII to XVII were some way below the level of the street, which must have caused the inhabitants some inconvenience in wet weather. Up the slope to the south, the terracing was achieved mainly by cutting into the gritty yellow clay of the hill side, which, though not entirely natural (it seems to have contained some Bronze Age sherds), was sufficiently compact to form a firm foundation for floors and even walls. Floors were surfaced with the same clay, or perhaps in some cases with a grittier equivalent from elsewhere on the site; only rarely was it possible to distinguish a floor surface as such except where it was overlaid by the destruction level. In the street, a general strew of small stones with some distinctive black beach pebbles and a few large slabs, most of them just inside the Main Gate, seems to mark the original Period I surface. The destruction debris lies on a rather higher level that probably represents a gradual accumulation during the period of settlement rather than a systematic attempt at resurfacing. Though great efforts were made during the excavation to distinguish two or more successive Period I street surfaces, the variety of materials found at different points was such that no firm conclusions could be reached.

Except in the more open spaces around the cistern in C (1954) and to the west of it in E (1954), as well as in some parts of the street, the most distinctive level over the whole excavated area was the destruction level that marked the end of the Period I settlement. This layer of tiles, charcoal and pottery was often 0.20m and in places up to 0.40m deep. Some stones occurred in it, but in most cases the walls do not seem to have collapsed until after the fire, and some were probably standing to a fair height at the time of the Period II rebuilding.

The Period I Settlement (PLAN, DRAWING VI)

(1) General Characteristics of the Period I Buildings

Where the builders were not constrained by rock outcrops or fortifications, they were able to adopt more or less rectangular plans; some idea of what may have been the typical plan can be got from the line of buildings backing onto the fortification wall eastwards from the main gate. The street wall was 0.55 to 0.60m thick and consisted of small rubble laid in mud mortar, with occasional larger stones used either as quoins or at random; it seems to have been built more or less all at once, with a doorway every 4 or 5m. The space thus enclosed, about 3.5m wide, was divided up by cross walls, which were not bonded to the street wall and in one case (wall 15) by no means perpendicular to it. The cross walls were also of variable construction; nos. 10 and 17 were virtually identical to the street wall, but no. 8 was thinner and contained many tile fragments; no. 12 was of mud brick on a stone footing, while nos. 13 and 15, of which only footings survived, seem to have been of lighter than normal construction. Roofs were of timber, though the remains of burnt beams were never complete enough to show the exact construction, and the tiles used for covering them were re-used ones of very varying types.

If these buildings are typical of the Period I settlement, they are surprisingly small units, all under 20m^2 and all but one consisting of only a single room. Of the buildings on the south side of the street, Rooms XIX–XX, XXII and XXIV may also originally have been separate single-room units, though the subdivision is uncertain. None of the Period I buildings excavated elsewhere on the Acropolis was complete enough to throw any light on the question.

Since there is no positive evidence of an upper storey in any of them, we are left with the conclusion that the seventh-century inhabitants of Emporio lived in single-room hovels with an average area of 15m^2. The quantity and variety of the equipment found in the destruction level seems to rule out the possibility that these were regular barrack-rooms; at the other end of the scale one can almost see them as shops — *pantopoleia* in the most literal sense of the word — but the problem of where the shopkeepers lived then becomes more acute still.

(2) Period I Buildings and levels by the Main Defence Wall

The part of the settlement most intensively examined in 1953 and 1954 lay along the western half of the north side. The reason for this choice was simply that the greater depth of earth here gave a better chance of finding well-stratified deposits. These, as it turned out, comprised occupation levels of the Early Bronze Age, the Mycenaean Period and both Byzantine settlements.

Trench V (1953) (DRAWING V)
Trench V, excavated in 1953, covered the bend in the fortification wall to north-east of the North-west Tower (PLATES 14 (*d*); 15 (*c*)). Within the wall, the trench included a single room (III) bounded by the fortification wall and walls 3 and 4; there was also a buttress or stub wall (5) built against the fortification wall, probably as part of the latter, though it was unmortared and not bonded in. Wall 3 appeared to be a double one, though the cramped conditions in the corner of the trench made it difficult to examine in detail.

The floor sloped rather steeply downwards towards the north. Distributed about it were a number of objects, mainly of iron, including a pick-head, bill-hook blade, and saw (F54b, 75, 80, 82–3, 89, 92–3, 154); several weights (F115–7, 119), probably two steelyards (F110, cf. 102), fishing gear (F70–1, 73) and also a large thin marble slab. A stone mortar (F7) was found against the south-east side of the trench at a high level behind wall 4, presumably on the floor of the next room. The whole floor was thickly covered with tiles, which had been little, if at all, disturbed at a later date, and with some pottery (PLATE 15 (*d*)).

Trench T (1953) (DRAWING VI)
In Trench T, excavated in 1953, the only Period I wall apart from the fortification wall was wall 6, which contained some unusually large stones at its north end. At the south end, a door led from the street (Room V) into a large space (Room IV) the south and west limits of which lay outside the trench. The ill-defined floor of Room IV lay immediately on top of Bronze Age levels; a hearth, about 0.60m in diameter, occupied the centre of the room, and six pithoi seemed to have been sunk into the floor, one near the hearth, the others distributed along the sides. Several fragments of lead, glass and iron were found on or a little above the floor, including a hollow iron point near the centre of the room. (See F19, 39, 58, 59, 62, 71.) Above the floor lay the usual layer of roof-tiles, together with pebbles, apparently disturbed in Period II since many Bronze Age sherds, presumably from below the Period I floor, were mixed with it and a Period II wall was founded immediately on top of it.

The roadway from the Main Gate (Room V) was a ramp paved with irregular slabs leading up from the threshold already described (PLATE 14 (*f*)). Few interesting objects were found except an iron knife (F81), a glass handle and a Mycenaean figurine (*Prehistoric Emporio* ii 629, no. 16) just inside the gate and an iron knife (F79) at the south-east corner of the trench.

Trench S (1953) (DRAWING VI)
In Trench S, also dug in 1953, only two Period I walls were found (PLATE 15 (*e*)); one, wall 8, was a thin one containing an unusually large proportion of tile fragments; wall 7, by contrast, was unusually thick at about 0.80m, and was at first thought to be a ramp or causeway rather than a wall, though the fact that it joined wall 8 and was not overlaid by the tiles of the destruction-level seems to disprove this.

The space enclosed by these two walls (Room VI) appears from the thick deposit of tiles in it to have been roofed, but there were no objects of any significance on the floor.

The destruction level in Room VIII was rather more productive, yielding a pithos (250, cf. 252), several iron nails, a bronze link (F51), a weight (F114), a piece of mother-of-pearl; and near the north end of wall 8, a coin of Phocas (C23, dated 606/7), though this may have belonged to the makeup for the Period II floor rather than to the destruction level proper. The floor was overlaid by a thin layer of charcoal and by the usual tile-level. A good many tiles were also found in the street (Room VII).

Trench F (1954) (DRAWINGS VI, IX)
Trench F of 1954 was the north-westernmost of a group of six trenches (originally planned as five-metre squares) dug to amplify the picture of the settlement already provided by the 1953 trenches.

The western room (VIII), most of which had been excavated in S the previous year, produced nothing more of interest.

Room IX, on the other hand, produced an exceptionally rich destruction-level with about ninety complete pots and other recognisable objects (Plan, DRAWING IX). The owner's name, Theodotos, is inscribed on 199. The fire had in places been fierce enough to fuse glass and calcine marble; a quantity of lead, perhaps derived from net-weights, had solidified on cooling to form sheets up to 5 mm thick on the floor. For other marine gear see F67, 69, 71–2. The furniture had included cupboards or chests, the hinges (and perhaps locks) of which were found not far out from the centre of the east wall (F31, 34, 37, 42–3). A large saw (F91) and a small brazier (279) lay near the north-west corner, and fish-hooks were scattered about the floor. Various nails and iron spikes had presumably fallen from the roof. There were three weights (F111, 120–1; cf. F101, 103–4, 108–9), four lamps and a very full range of domestic pottery including table ware, eight amphorae and water-pots, four pithoi, ten jugs (one unbroken) (PLATE 16 (*a*)), seven cooking pots, a vessel very like a tea pot (209), and some glass (F18, 20). One cooking-pot contained carbonised beans. There were even one or two objects of earlier date: an intaglio of Asklepios (F123), a fragmentary cameo (F124) and one handle of a bronze kylix (*Greek Emporio* pl. 93, 394), presumably chance finds or derived from grave-robbing. The general impression was of a prosperous farmhouse kitchen, or even a general store, though two large marble trays or table-tops (F2,3) (PLATE 16 (*b*)) leaning against the north wall suggested something rather higher up the social scale. A spearhead (F74) was the only sign of military preoccupations.

As usual on the Acropolis, there was a complete absence of objects in precious metals; the contents of the destruction-level were scattered in a way that could be accounted for by cursory looting, or by hurried abandonment, or even by the collapse during the fire of wooden furniture and fittings of which no trace was recovered. A few objects were found on top of, rather than under, the tiles: a jug, a pithos-lid, an unidentified piece of bronze sheet (F27). This may have been due to their positions in the room; e.g., on top of furniture or shelves that collapsed only during or shortly after the fall of the roof. But there had also been some disturbance, especially at the north-east corner, at or before the establishment of the Period II settlement.

The actual floor was of a very sandy soil containing some small black beach-pebbles, and the final level at the time of the destruction was only a few centimetres above the top of a Mycenaean wall (*Prehistoric Emporio* i 161 fig. 89, wall 34), so that there was no possibility of there having been any making-up of the floor to correspond to the rise in the level of the street outside (PLATE 15 (*f*)). Just outside the doorway of Room IX the original Period I ground-level was probably marked by a large flat slab, which lay just above another earlier wall (*Prehistoric Emporio* i fig. 89, wall 30) and on top of a layer containing almost pure Bronze Age pottery. Against wall 9, a little to the west of the doorway of Room IX, lay a coin of Heraclius (C25, dated 610–613) at a level very slightly above that of the slab. But the road was soon raised by a 10–15cm layer of light sandy soil containing Bronze Age sherds and topped with a few cobbles and small stones. As a result of the raising of the road-level the inhabitants of Room IX set up a large slab (their original threshold?) on edge outside the door to keep the street out of the room. It was on this road-surface that the tiles and pottery of the Period I destruction-level lay, thinly at the east end of E and F, much more thickly at the west.

Trench D (1954) (DRAWINGS VI, VIII section 5, IX)
Room XI–XII, immediately to the east of IX, was separated from it by a mud-brick wall (12) on stone foundations, the only one certainly identified on the Acropolis. A good-sized door led into the street, and the room was divided into two unequal parts by a narrow north-south wall (13) (PLATE 16 (*c*)); there was presumably a doorway in the southern end of this wall, but evidence of this had been destroyed by the building of the Period II wall (50) that overlay it. The narrowness of the foundation suggests that like its neighbour to the west it originally had a mud-brick superstructure. The south wall (11, 14) separating the two rooms from the street, was preserved to a height of about 0.30m from floor-level and was overlaid by Period II walls (49 and 51) that were not exactly aligned on it. The street door, like that of Room IX above, had a large rough slab turned up on edge on a line with the outer face of the wall to prevent the street collapsing into the building (PLATE 16 (*d*)).

The floors of Rooms XI and XII lay on top of a series of layers representing the accumulation of soil at the foot of the pre-Roman terrace wall (*Prehistoric Emporio* i 164, wall 41) further south and some intentional filling, which contained scraps of Period I pottery, at the back of the fortress wall during or soon after its construction. At the extreme north-east corner of Room XII the foundations of the Period II wall 52, resting only partly on the foundations of its Period I predecessor 15, went a little below the Period I floor. In both rooms the floors as such were of yellowish gritty clay and would hardly have been recognisable if they had not immediately underlain the conspicuous destruction level.

The destruction level in Room XI included eleven complete pots of various kinds, among them six jugs: four of the jugs lay together in a group near the north-east corner, with two fish-hooks, several net-weights (F69, 71) and a polished stone axe (*Prehistoric Emporio* ii 651, no. 25); there was a large pithos half way along the west side, and a further group of an amphora, a jug and a cooking-pot in the centre of the southern half of the room. A first-century B.C. coin of Elaea (C2) lay somewhat above the floor near the north-east corner.

In Room XII most of the twelve complete but mainly broken pots lay in the south-eastern quarter of the room; they included two pithoi, a smaller jar, two lids, two cooking-pots, four or five amphorae, a lamp and part of a plate; there were also a well-preserved fragment of a steelyard (F100, cf. 110), five fish-hooks and a number of net-weights (F69, 71). A coin of Heraclius (C36, dated 630–1) lay among the tiles near the centre of the room. A sample of carbonized wood was collected.

In the street to the south (XIII), the original Period I surface lay from 30 to 40cm higher than the floors of the rooms, with only a thin layer of mixed fill separating it from the top of the pre-Roman terrace-wall. In places, particularly outside the door of Rooms XI and XII, it was marked by a fairly well defined strew of cobbles and small rubble. But there was no trace of burnt debris at this level, and the road surface at the time of the destruction, marked in many places by a line of ash, was an irregular one, with no attempt at proper paving, from 10 to 20cm above the earlier one and immediately below the thick cobble strew of the earlier Period II road. It contained a coin of Heraclius (C28, dated 613/4?, found in Baulk BD).

Trench B (1954) (DRAWINGS VI, VIII section 2)
The only walls of Period I were Walls 14 and 16 (PLATE 16) along the north side of the street, which were broken by a door about half way across the trench, and a very thin Wall 15, which perhaps, as it did not penetrate below the floor, was only the stone footing of a lightly constructed partition that separated Room XII from Room XIV–XV. The floor was normal in that it consisted only of the top of a fill of yellowish-brown sandy clay put down to level off the previous sloping ground-surface, which appeared to have been a natural accumulation between a jumble of stones derived from the pre-Roman terrace wall (PLATE 16 (*f*)). What was remarkable was the lack, above the floor, of the heavy tile and pottery strew characteristic of the Period I destruction level. The only significant small finds from the room were two lead weights for a steelyard (F118, 122), a small fragment of a silver dish (F25) and a very simple bronze ring (F135). In fact the only point at which the tile-level, 20 to 30cm deep, did occur was in the doorway to the street; here it was overlaid by the Period II rebuilding of the wall, which, exceptionally, was on exactly the same line as that of Period I. So it would seem that the room was cleared to floor-level by the rebuilders; one reason for this may have been that they wanted access to the rear face of the fortress wall, which had collapsed at a point corresponding to the north-west corner of the trench; but the very careless nature of the repairs done to it contrasts strangely with the thoroughness of the clearance work. An actual reoccupation of the room at the original floor level, soon after the Period I destruction and long before the main rebuilding of the settlement, seems unlikely, if only because there is no sign of a door at the appropriate level. One possibility is that during the repairs to the fortress wall something worth recovering was found in the destruction level; the silver object found in 1954 may be a clue; if this had been the workshop of the local silversmith there might have been a sufficient incentive for the removal of the destruction debris.

The Period I street-level outside was marked by a fairly generous strew of tiles and burnt material lying on an irregular surface of yellowish clay at an average height of about 0.60m above the floor of the room. In this case there was no convincing evidence of an earlier surface corresponding to that in Trench D.

Trenches K and J (1953) (DRAWING VI)
K was a small trench, only two-and-a-half metres square. Apart from the fortress wall it produced only one Period I wall (17), which had formed the east wall of Room XIV–XV; the back of this wall, hidden in Baulk BK, was never excavated, so that there is no indication of its thickness, nor was there any evidence in the section that its upper parts had been of mud brick. The Period I floor had a similar makeup to that of Room XIV–XV, and, like it, was not covered by a conspicuous burnt destruction level.

The south wall of this room (16, 18), with a Period I doorway, was excavated in Trench J (1953), and proved, like its continuation in B, to have had its upper parts rebuilt in Period II on the original line but with a new doorway to the street 0.90m above the original one and offset 0.20m to the east (PLATE 17 (*a*)). The street, after being constricted by a projecting buttress on the south side, continued eastwards at about the same width as in B; its final Period I level was again marked by a tile strew, and there was a possible earlier Period I surface of small stones about 0.20m below it.

(3) Period I Buildings and Levels South of the Street
Whereas the Period I deposits between the street and the fortress wall were all buried at a

considerable depth and overlaid by a coherent Period II layout, the rise in the ancient ground levels to the south of the street meant that, except at the east end of the main excavated area, recognisable Period II remains were rare and the Period I ground level along the southern edge was only just below the limit of recent disturbance. In addition, much of Trenches C and E (1954) was taken up by a Period I vaulted cistern lying in what seems to have been an open courtyard; the limits of this could not be determined, as the Byzantine ground level on the south had been removed by subsequent erosion and ploughing, while the area to the west was covered by our main dump.

The continuity of this description can best be maintained by returning boustrophedon from east to west along the south side of the street, beginning with trenches J (1953) and A (1954) in which the two periods of intensive settlement with intervening destruction follow much the same lines as in the area north of the street, and concluding with the less heavily built-up areas in C and E (1954).

Trenches J (1953) and A (1954) (DRAWINGS VI, VIII section 2, X)

The part of J corresponding to the Period I street has already been described. The remainder of the trench consisted in Period I of a single large space (Room XIX–XX), the west end of which ran through into A while the east end lay in unexcavated ground (PLATE 17 (c)). There were two doorways onto the street; the eastern one, in J, had two lines of stones across it, perhaps intended to carry a stone threshold (a large flattish block lay in the street outside; PLATE 17 (b)), while the western one, in A, had a fragmentary stone slab apparently in situ. In both doorways there were large deposits of charcoal perhaps derived from the doors themselves or from thick wooden lintels. A gap was also found in the west wall (22), but this may have been the result of stone-robbing in Period II, when the wall was rebuilt on more or less the same line, rather than a doorway.

With two doors to the street and a length of nearly 7m, this space might be expected to have been divided into two; an alignment of stones running south from a point between the two doors might possibly have been footings for a light partition analogous to wall 15 in B, though a pithos sunk in the floor further south blocked its line of advance. The unexcavated baulk between the two trenches was only about 0.40m thick and can hardly have concealed any sort of wall.

The floor of this room was as usual of yellowish gritty clay and lay partly on an accumulation of pre-Byzantine deposits; but in the southern half of the area the natural clay had been cut into to form a terrace. The south wall (23) rested on a separate shelf cut in the clay about 0.40m above floor-level.

The Period I destruction level excavated in J included complete roof-tiles, remains of fallen pithoi (in addition to the one sunk in the floor); a basalt mortar (F8, cf. 9) upside-down on the floor just west of the alignment of stones; an iron and bronze object that may have been a lock (F44); a number of iron blade fragments including small knives (F78, 87) a bronze needle (F68) and numerous iron nails and staples. Even the five square metres of the floor excavated in A yielded two pithoi, part of an amphora, three jugs of various sizes (PLATE 17 (d)), a small handled beaker, a cooking-pot and a clay lamp (330). One vase names its owner, John the Boatswain (Graffito ii).

Room XXII, to the west of this, was rather less than 4m square and was bounded on the west by a wall (25) resting on the east end of the cistern in C (1954). The gap in this wall shown on the plan is due to its destruction where it passed over the crown of the cistern vault, and as the top of the vault lay 0.60m above the Period I floor-level in A, it is most unlikely that there was a door here. The south wall (23), resting directly on the natural clay, was well enough preserved to show that it was not broken by a doorway (PLATE 16 (*e*)). The north wall facing the street (21) was only one course high as excavated, and the ashes of the destruction ran over it at the west end, showing that it was never any higher at this point. Moreover the large flat stones that formed the outer face of it suggested that it was never more than a stylobate and that the room was open to the street or, more probably, divided from it only by wooden shutters that left no permanent trace.

The floor, of the usual yellowish gritty clay, lay directly on the natural clay subsoil in the southern third of the room, and elsewhere on a stone fill behind the pre-Roman terrace wall. Two coins of Heraclius (C24, 31; dated 610/1 and 616/7) were found not far apart near the south wall (23), both a few cm below the apparently undisturbed Period I floor-level. These should logically provide a terminus post quem for the laying of the floor.

The destruction level covered the whole floor except an area about a metre square in the north-east corner (PLATE 17 (*e*)). Marks on the floor showed the positions of burnt roof timbers and suggested that most of the roof had fallen in one piece. A group of three complete tiles leaning against the south wall (23) demonstrated that the rafters ran north-south, and this orientation was confirmed by other substantially complete tiles. Bronze hinge (F33, 35) and latch fragments (F45) from near the north-west corner of the room may indicate the presence of a chest or cupboard. Pottery included two pithoi, three amphorae and a cooking-pot; there were also some fragments of glass and a few nails. A coin of Constans II (C44; dated 642/8) was found at floor-level under the group of complete tiles against the south wall. Two more coins (C33, Heraclius, 624/5; and C42, Constans II, 642–8) turned up in the northern part of the room, but just above the tile strew in circumstances that suggested they reached their final positions during the fall of the walls. Two iron blades (F84, 88) were also found among the fallen stones above the tiles and should probably be assigned to Period I.

If Room XXI, which lay further to the south, was indeed a room rather than an open space, it must have had its floor at least a metre above the Period I floors elsewhere in A. In fact erosion or cultivation had removed virtually everything above the hard clay subsoil. Wall 24, which bounded it on the west, survived only as a single course of footings.

Trenches C and K (1954) (DRAWINGS VI, VIII section 5)
The dominant feature of Trench C, extending also into the adjacent E (1954), was the cistern (FIG. 23. PLATE 17 (*f*)). Strongly built of rubble laid in good lime mortar, it was about 5.30m long and 2.80m wide internally and was laid out somewhat on the skew. The vertical walls were about 1.70m high and the total internal height to the crown of the stilted semicircular vault was about 3.50m. A ledge 10–15cm wide at the top of the vertical wall must have supported the centering for the vault. The average thickness of the walls was about 1.00m on the long sides and 0.60m on the ends. The *opus signinum* lining of the floor was originally covered with flat tiles about 45cm square, though most of these had later been removed, leaving impressions on the lining.

At the centre was a rectangular basin 1.20m by 0.90m and about 0.50m deep, the bottom of which sloped down on all sides to a central depression 0.40m in diameter. This would have facilitated the drawing of water when the cistern was nearly empty.

The rectangular hole in the roof over this basin was originally about 0.80 by 0.70m across, but the breaking away of the crown of the vault on the west side had more than doubled the size of the opening. There was no indication of any raised coping round the hole or of any catchment system by which the cistern might have been filled.

2. THE SETTLEMENT AND FORTRESS 69

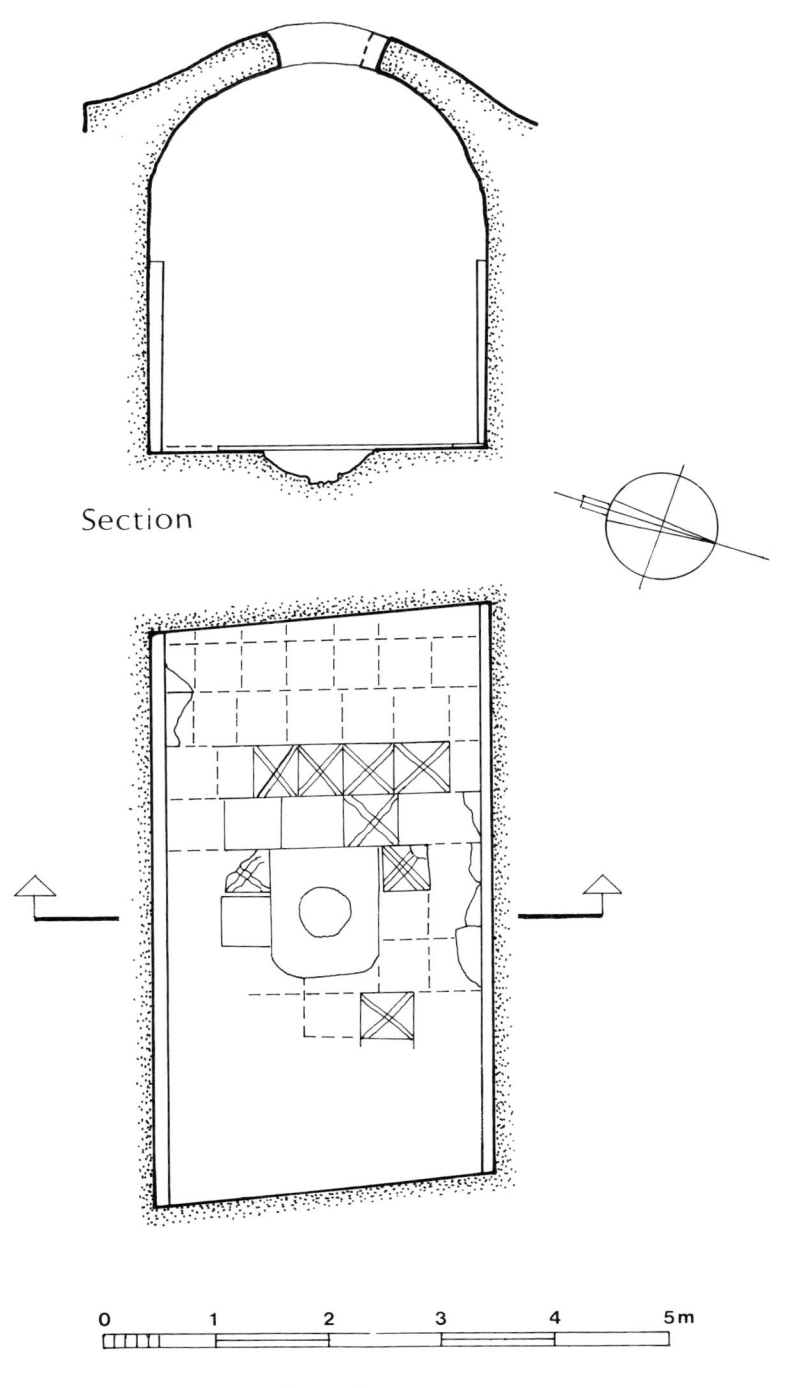

FIG. 23. Cistern in C 1954.

The deposit within the cistern varied from almost pure silt at the bottom to a mixture of soil and stones higher up; the top of the deposit was merely a conical pile of material tipped, apparently quite recently, through the hole. A line of darker soil 0.40 to 0.60m from the bottom suggested plant growth after the abandonment of the site. The pottery in the bottom 30cm of the silt consisted almost exclusively of Period II water-jars, many of them substantially complete. There were also a bronze hook (F106) and one or two small objects of bronze sheet.

The cistern almost certainly dates from Period I. The original floor surface to the north of it, at the level of the external shoulder of the vault, is marked by a layer of cobbles that corresponds to the earlier of the two Period I street levels; a later arrangement of slabs in the eastern one of the two doorways to the street overlaps the shoulder of the cistern vault (PLATE 18 (*a*)), corresponds to the later Period I street level, and is overlaid by a burnt layer that can only be that of the Period I destruction. Wall 26, which is built directly on top of the south shoulder of the cistern vault, forms the north boundary of a room (XXIV) higher up the slope with an apparently intact Period I floor. The east end of the cistern, surmounted by wall 25, forms the west boundary of Room XXII, which again has an intact Period I floor. Lastly, in both C and A, no certain Period II pottery was found at a level lower than about 0.15m below the outside crown of the cistern vault. Indeed the only evidence that might suggest a Period II date for the cistern is that almost all the abundant pottery found in the 30–40cm of mud lying directly on the bottom of it and representing the accumulation of silt while it was still in use consisted of Period II water-jars. This is easily explained if the people who reoccupied the site after a century of abandonment took the trouble to clean out their cistern before using it; this cleaning would account for the lack of Period I deposit and also for the removal of much of the original tile paving.

Wall 26, standing on the south edge of the cistern, proved to be the north wall of a Period I room that was bounded on the west by wall 27 (of one build with 26) and on the east by wall 24. Further clearance (Trench K 1954) revealed the south wall and a door in the south-west corner. Wall 29, the westward continuation of 26, had only one course of footings preserved. It was not of one build with 26, and stood at a much higher level, on top of a clay fill overlying the edge of the cistern. The evidence for dating it was scanty and it may have been either an afterthought of the Period I builders or a Period II addition.

Wall 25 standing on the east end of the cistern, must, as explained above, have been of Period I, and the same must be true of the three short lengths of wall 30 (PLATE 16 (*d*)), 31, 32 (PLATE 15 (*f*)) that divided the cistern area from the street, as the Period I levels run through the two doorways that they form and none of the three is preserved above the earliest credible ground surface of Period II.

As very few tile fragments were found in the area of the cistern it can probably be assumed that it was an open yard. In that case the only function of the wall between it and the street was to act as a barrier, though it is not clear why there should then have been three openings in it (the two in C and a larger one in E).

On the south side of the cistern the only possible Period I ground level was on top of a fill of largely sterile yellow clay lying on the shoulder of the vault and reaching up 0.70m to a point about 0.20m below the outside of the crown. Here there was a strew of cobbles on a level with the bottom of wall 29. The fact that there was Period II pottery in the level immediately above this cobble strew — Period II pottery very rarely occurs below the earliest Period II ground surface — coupled with the fact that the lowest and only surviving course of wall 29 lay 0.60m above the bottom of wall 26 might well suggest that both the cobbles and the wall were of Period II. In that case we are left with no Period I surface at this point. Fortunately this is not of any importance, as nothing of much interest was found either in the clay fill or above the cobbles.

In Room XXV, the area south of wall 29, no floor was found above the apparently natural clay. The 20cm of brown loam surviving below the limit of modern cultivation contained only scraps of Period I pottery and could have been the makeup for a Period II floor.

In Room XXIV, south of wall 26, and immediately below the limit of cultivation, the lower part of a typical Period I destruction level was found, with tile fragments, charcoal and burnt soil. The floor below consisted of 10cm of the usual gritty clay on top of the clay subsoil. On the floor lay large Period I sherds, a clay lamp, and an iron axe-adze so similar to those the workmen were using that they refused to believe it was ancient (F94); tucked against the face of wall 26, perhaps a little below the final surface of the floor, was a coin of Constans II (C46; dated 641–3). Extension of the trench further to the south (as K 1954) revealed no more of the destruction level, which had been ploughed out, but located the footings of the walls that defined it. A well-preserved bronze hinge was found (F38).

Trench E (1954) (DRAWING VI)
Trench E was the least rewarding of all the main 1954 group on the Acropolis. Apart from the west end of the cistern and the wall 32 (PLATE 15 (*f*)) to the north of it (discussed above), the only structures were a small group of stones over the south-west corner of the cistern (which in retrospect seem to have formed the end of the footings of wall 29) and the ends of two Period I walls (33, 34) just projecting into the trench on the west. The southern one (34) had been robbed out, probably by the Period II builders, almost to the level of the Period I floor.

The Period I destruction level was fairly well marked, especially in the northern half of the trench, as a strew of tile, charcoal and sherds lying on a partly cobbled surface. There were no small finds of any importance. Below the cobbles, yellowish loam, with a little pottery, most of it prehistoric, overlay the natural yellow clay in most parts of the trench.

The function of this area of the site was not entirely clear; it seems to have been simply an open yard connected to the east-west street; most of the tile in the destruction level was near the north-west corner and could have fallen from the building of which walls 33 and 34 formed part; further excavation to the west, to determine its relationship with other buildings or with the main street that ran south from the gate, was prevented by the presence of a very large dump.

(4) Outlying Trenches

Trenches M, N and O (1953) (DRAWING IV)
Three small trial trenches were dug in 1953 to test for further buildings up the slope south of J (1953). Footings of walls were found in all three, but only in the lowest (M) was there sufficient soil cover for a floor to be preserved.

Trench O, the highest of the three, produced two more or less parallel east-west walls, of which only one course of footings survived, and an intermediate one traceable only as a slight cutting in the bedrock.

The east-west wall in N also survived only as a single course of footings. In M, again, only one course of an east-west wall survived, but the floor immediately downhill to the north of it had escaped ploughing, as it lay a little lower than the shelf cut for the wall in the natural clay. On it lay several square metres of a typical Period I destruction level, with two lamps (316), a pithos containing carbonised beans (248), a pithos-lid with a small jug (193) under it, a large nail and some fragments of an iron blade.

It can probably be assumed from the fact that all the walls found in these trenches were laid directly on the subsoil that they were all of Period I.

A cistern in the angle between N and O is of the same general type as the Period I cistern in E and the probably Period I example in J (1954).

The East Cistern: Trench J (1954) (FIG. 24)

This cistern, lying on a comparatively gentle slope to the north of the eastern summit of the hill, was partly exposed at the downhill end, while the crown of the vault at the uphill end was only about 0.20m below ground level (PLATE 18 (*b*)). Excavation was confined to the clearance of the buried part of the top of the vault, which revealed a north-south wall lying on the south-east corner and two short stretches of east-west wall running across just to the north of the opening in the vault. The inaccurate alignment of these east-west stretches and the unusually large stones used in them suggested that they were intended to form two separate piers rather than a continuous wall; if so, they may perhaps have served to support a pulley or some other

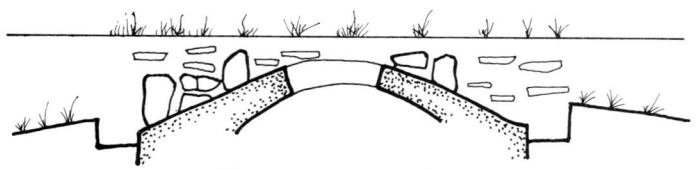

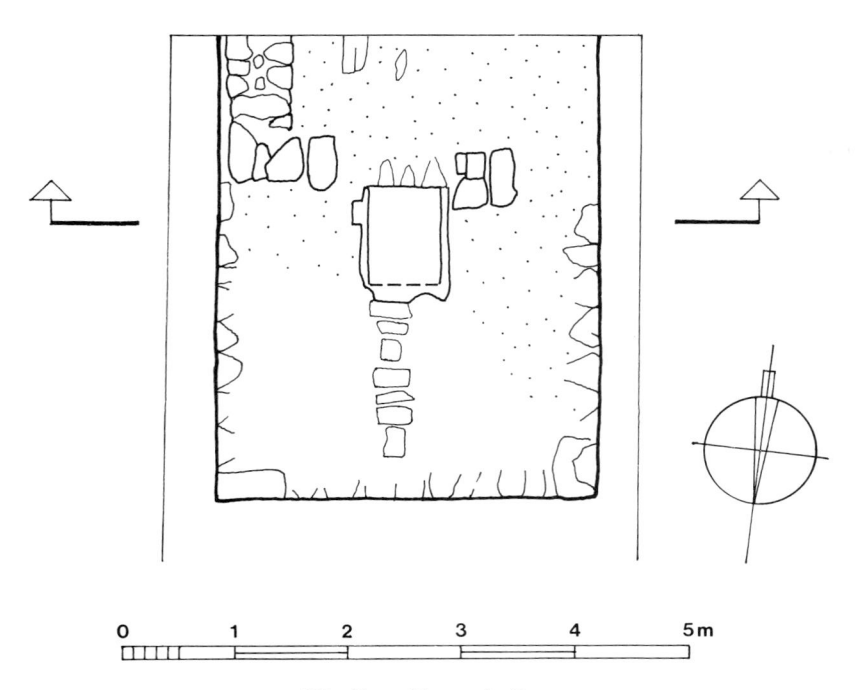

FIG. 24. The East Cistern in J 1954.

simple device for drawing water. As in the cistern in C there was no sign of a coping round the opening or of any inlet from a catchment area, which in this case might have been the now bare rock of the eastern summit. A heavy strew of tile over the upper parts of the vault suggested a Period I destruction level. No attempt was made to excavate the deep deposit inside the cistern.

The cistern itself, 3.40m wide and at least 4.30m long on the exterior, was built of stones of all sizes, the largest along the edges and in a line along the crown of the vault, set in good lime mortar; much of the rendering of the exterior had survived. The opening, which had originally measured 0.60 by 0.90m, was well preserved except at the north end.

PERIOD II

The Period II Settlement (PLAN, DRAWING VII)

The Period II rebuilders of this area of the site probably found a good many of the Period I walls standing in good condition to a reasonable height above the Period I ground level. In Trenches A and B of 1954 and J of 1953 they rebuilt the wall along the north side of the east-west street using the surviving parts of the original one as a footing. In D of 1954 the rebuilding was more complete; most of the Period I remains were robbed out and the new wall, in two sections divided by a doorway, was not built on the same line. Of the north-south partition walls only one (10) was reused. The one in K 1953 (17) was probably robbed out to what was then ground level, while the others, not being of stone above the footings, were simply levelled off, if indeed they were still recognisable as walls.

On the south side of the street the only coherent Period II building was a single room (XX), apparently freestanding, that used parts of several earlier walls as footings. Further west, the cistern was cleared out for reuse; walls 23 and 26 were probably rebuilt on the same footings and wall 29, unless it already existed (p. 70), was built as an extension on the same line. There may have been further buildings to the south of this point at too high a level to survive subsequent erosion and cultivation. In E and the northern half of C, there is no sign of any Period II walls and the whole area was probably an open space opening directly off the street.

In general quality the Period II walls were not markedly different from those of Period I; no doubt the same stones were reused and the mud mortar, containing scraps of Period I pottery, was made from earth collected on the site. Floors were normally of gritty whitish or yellowish earth; occasionally slabs were used, at any rate at points where there was likely to be much wear; patches of lime occur on some floors, but as none of them covers a whole room, they should perhaps be regarded only as evidence for the mixing of mortar, presumably for repairs to the upper parts of the fortress wall. On exterior ground surfaces such as the street, considerable quantities of large beach pebbles were strewn about, though no attempt seems to have been made to set them into a regular cobble pavement.

(1) Period II Buildings and Levels by the Main Defence Wall

Trench F (1953) (DRAWING V)
The relatively slight remains of Period II in this trench have been discussed on p. 64.

Trench V (1953) (DRAWING V)
In V two roughly parallel stretches of Period II wall (37 and 38) were found; both overlay the

tile level of the Period I destruction. The Period I wall 4 is unlikely to have survived into Period II as tiles were found on top of it. But in the "white level", containing numerous fragments of mortar, that overlay the tiles and presumably represented the debris from the destruction and rebuilding of the Fortress wall, there was no clear trace of a floor to go with the walls.

For the ovens outside the Fortress wall, which are fairly certainly of Period II, see above, p. 60.

Trench T (1953) (DRAWING VII)
In Trench T, three Period II walls were found. Wall 41, at the east end, was largely hidden in Baulk ST (PLATE 14 (*f*)). It stood directly on the paving slabs of the Period I roadway leading south from the gate, and presumably formed the west wall of the range of rooms described below in S, though it extended further to the south, at least as far as the south edge of T. The Period I wall 6 was apparently not rebuilt but replaced by a roughly parallel wall 40 further to the west. A short length of east-west wall 39 in the south-west corner of the trench may have formed a room with 40, the Fortress wall and another wall presumably hidden in Baulk TV; but the details are uncertain. The floor-level within was probably marked by the rather uneven top of a layer of light earth and small stones with fragments of white mortar, about 0.25m thick, that overlay the tile-level of the Period I destruction.

The Period II road through the gateway may have been the top of a level of rough stones mixed with tile-fragments and pebbles, about 0.30m above the Period I threshold. But there was no sign of a separate Period II threshold at the higher level, and it remains a possibility that the roadway was cleared down to the Period I level and the original threshold reused in situ. The alternative assumption that there was no threshold, and thus no gates, seems very unlikely in view of the evidence that the defences as a whole were repaired in Period II.

Trench S (1953) (DRAWING VII)
In Trench S none of the Period I walls was reused except the Fortress wall, but two new north-south walls (43, 45) were built parallel to the reused Period I wall 10 in Trench F (1954) and the Period II wall 41 in T (1953) to form three rooms, apparently unconnected with one another (PLATE 18 (*c*)). The corresponding Period II south wall (42, 44) was well enough preserved to show the street doors of the western and central rooms (VI, VIa) clearly, but further to the east the only trace of a possible Period II street wall was a corner (46) projecting from the south face of the trench at 45°. The relationship of this corner to the street wall in F (1954) was never examined. The footings of all these walls lay in or on top of the Period I destruction level, and in places at least there was a layer of light hard earth that presumably represented the makeup for the Period II floors.

The destruction or abandonment level above the floors varied in composition: in Room VIII at the east end there were few stones but some small tile-fragments; in Room VI, large stones and a considerable quantity of broken tile; in Room VIa, large stones as well as unbroken tiles, a complete globular vase near the south-east corner and fragments of water-jar near the centre of the room. A coin of Heraclius (C32, dated 618/9) was found in the topsoil.

Trench F (1954) (DRAWING VII)
Two walls, 9 and 10, seem to have survived the Period I destruction sufficiently well to be reused; a new north-south wall 48 with footings about 0.50m above the Period I floor level was built along the east side of the trench. The Period I street door seems to have been reused, somewhat narrowed by the end of the new wall 48 and with the threshold raised to suit the

higher street level. Inside the room thus formed (IX), the top of the destruction level, still some 0.50m deep, was apparently levelled off and a quantity of gravel containing scraps of Period I pottery was used to raise it to what seems to have been a very uneven floor, or even a series of successive floors. Subsequently the level was again raised with a fill of fairly clean yellowish sandy loam. At this point the part of wall 9 just east of the junction with 10 seems to have been demolished and a new wall 47 built just behind it, with a doorway at the west end replacing the earlier one at the east; only two courses of this new wall were found, and the narrow gap at the east end corresponding to the earlier doorway seems to be due to the accident of survival rather than to the intentions of the builders.

The only floor that ran up to this new wall was marked by the equivalent of a destruction level, or rather an abandonment level as there was no sign of burning and no strew of tiles. A group of stones at floor level against the west end of the north face of wall 47 seems to have been a rough hearth. Scattered about the floor were a wine glass, an inverted cooking-pot, four other substantially complete pots of which at least one was an amphora (280), and a coin of Leo V (C51, 813–820) which should provide a terminus post quem for the abandonment. The level immediately above the floor was of yellow clay, presumably rainwash after the abandonment (unless it was a yet later floor as suggested on p. 81).

In the street outside (X), the original Period II surface seems to have been a fairly generous strew of cobbles about 0.25m above the earlier of the floors inside the building, and there was a rather indeterminate later ground level that might have corresponded to the later house floor. It was at this level that a lead sealing (F139) was found in 1955 in Baulk DF.

Along the west edge of the trench, a strip about 0.60m wide behind wall 10 belonged to room VIII, most of which had been excavated in 1953 in Trench S. Here there was a well marked floor at about 0.70m below modern ground level, covered first with broken tiles (mainly of gently curved rather than rectangular section, with a slight lip at the top end of the concave surface) and above that with a strew of large stones. The amount of tile seemed to imply at least a partial collapse of the roof rather than dismantling.

At the east side, wall 48 came so near to the edge of the trench that no floor could be identified between them, though the section confirmed the floor level found in Trench D, Room XI.

Trench D (1954) (DRAWINGS VII, VIII section 5)
None of the Period I walls in D was reused in Period II, and two new L-shaped walls (49, 50 and 51, 52) were brought out from the Fortress wall to form two new rooms. Both overlay Period I walls for part of their length, without keeping strictly to the same line; indeed they were very carelessly laid out even by Period II standards. In each case the doorway was simply the gap between the toe of the L and the next wall that happened to be there. The room on the east (XII) had a threshold of slabs with a little rough wall along the outside forming a step up into the street (PLATE 18 (*d*)); the western room (XI) had a cobbled threshold.

The earliest Period II floor level inside these rooms was never satisfactorily established, except that it presumably corresponded more or less with the inner thresholds. In Room XII it seems also to have been marked by a hearth against the south wall (51), cut into the top of what remained of the Period I south wall (14) (PLATE 16 (*d*)), and by the crushed but substantially complete remains of an amphora lying on what must at the time have been a floor, though careful cleaning round it failed to establish the exact surface and there was no apparent change in the whitish loam above and below. In Room XI it was clear that the lowest Period II floor could not have been below the top of the Period I mud-brick wall 12 about 1.00m below modern ground level.

The top of this whitish level, about 0.30m above the presumed earlier floors, could be thought of as a possible floor, though no clear signs of habitation were found on it. Above it was a heavy strew of stones representing the collapse of the walls, which, like the stumps of the walls themselves, extended up to the limit of modern cultivation. Patches of yellow sandy soil and blackish loam between the stones presumably represented subsequent rainwash and plant growth.

In the street to the south (XIII), the earliest Period II road surface was about 0.80m below modern ground level; in the west part of the trench it was clearly defined by a thick strew of cobbles; further east the cobbles faded out over a heavy fall of stones probably due to the collapse of a Period I wall. A less clearly marked surface of cobbles and stones immediately below the limit of modern (not necessarily recent) cultivation and about 0.40m below the present ground level seems to have been the latest Period II road surface corresponding to the presumed later floors in Rooms XI and XII. It produced a coin of Constans II (C43, 642–8), but must have been of 9th century date; other 7th century coins were found in the upper levels (C27, 613; C39, 635/6).

Trench B (1954) (DRAWINGS VII, VIII section 2)
The Period I street frontage (walls 14 and 16) was, as already described (p. 66), rebuilt on its original lower courses; the rebuilt wall was carried on across the Period I doorway and a new and narrower doorway formed above the western half of it at a level about 0.90m above the Period I floor (PLATE 18 (*e*)). A north-south wall (53), joining the rebuilt street wall (16) just to the east of the new door, was structurally secondary to it and stood on a fill of whitish soil containing fragments of lime mortar and even a mass of stones still mortared together that had presumably fallen from the Fortress wall (PLATE 18 (*f*)). In the north-west corner of the trench the Fortress wall had been carelessly repaired down to below Period I floor level.

The oldest Period II surface rested on this whitish layer in the western room (XIV) and on an intermediate fill of alternate thin layers of fine and coarse sand in the eastern one (XV). The actual surface consisted of a thin but conspicuous lime strew covering the southern two thirds of each room. This may have been only a mortar-mixing floor for repairs to the Fortress wall (compare the layer of lime in A, p. 77); in this case it may be structurally earlier than wall 53, which only just penetrates below it. The only object of any significance found directly on it was a large pithos with a pointed or rounded bottom terminating in a knob (282), which had been broken while lying on its side in the southern part of XV, and near the east edge of the trench some of the fragments were above the lime level and were supported by the whitish loam of the next layer up (visible in section, level (5)). No convincing later floor was found at the top of the whitish loam, under the thick strew of stones from the final collapse of the walls.

In Room XIV nothing was found on the lime floor, but there were indications of settlement near the top of the whitish level immediately below the stones. Two paving slabs were in situ just inside the door to the street, but about 0.40m below the threshold (PLATE 18 (*e*)), and a further slab at the north end of the room, at a slightly lower level, probably belonged to the same floor. A large broken amphora (281) beside the first pair of slabs appeared to have been lying on a floor at the level of the slabs, but the actual surface could not be distinguished. Two iron spikes found among the fallen stones above may have come from the roof.

In the street (XVI) there were 50–60cm of stones immediately on top of the tiles and ash of the Period I destruction. The most probable Period II road surface was a thin layer of grit and small pebbles 40–50cm. below modern ground level, only just below the tops of the Period II walls where best preserved. The door into Room XIV was protected by a thick slab set on edge outside and above the threshold (PLATE 19 (*a*)). There may have been an earlier Period II street level below it, but the evidence was not conclusive.

The final stone-strew over Rooms XIV and XV extended up to the tops of the Period II walls as preserved, the whole having been levelled off by later cultivation at a depth of 50–60cm below present ground level.

Trenches K and J (1953) (DRAWING VII)
In K, the continuation of Room XV (XVII in Period I) was excavated without any conclusive signs of a floor. The east wall (54) of the room was visible in the side of the trench, and seems to have been entirely of Period II, joining up with the street wall in J (18), which, as in B, was a rebuild of the Period I wall, with a narrower door offset slightly to the east (PLATE 17 (*a*)). The rebuilt wall came to a neatly finished end 1.70m east of the door (PLATE 17 (*b*)); this seems to have been the beginning of another door, the other side of which was probably a north-south wall (54a), with only one or two courses preserved, that projected like a buttress for about 0.40m into the street. The end of another Period II wall (54b), resting partly on the Period I south wall of the street (19), appeared on the east side of the trench.

(2) Period II Buildings South of the Street

Trenches J (1953) and A (1954) (DRAWINGS VII, VIII section 2)
In Period II it seems that the only roofed building south of the street was a single-roomed affair, half in J and half in A (PLATE 19 (*b*)). Except for a short stretch just south of the door, the walls were built partly over (rather than on) the remains of Period I walls and partly on or over the Period I destruction level, which had been little if at all disturbed and had in places been covered with a fill or natural accumulation of brown loam. A straight joint just west of the south-east corner suggests that the building was put up in two phases, the south wall (58) before the east wall (56), but there was no evidence of a long interval between the phases. The Period I wall 23 seems to have remained in use, since the new wall 58 was butted up against it; but no sign of a Period II (or even a Period I) floor was found to south of it; in Period II it may well have been kept simply as a retaining wall to exclude rainwash from the hill above.

Within the building an intermittent slab floor comparable to that in B Room XIV was found 0.65m below modern ground level, only just above the bottom of the walls (PLATE 19 (*c*)). Two broken but more or less complete pots lay either on or immediately beside slabs; a coin of Nikephoros I (C50; 803–811) lay just below one of these pots at a level almost certainly that of the earth floor between the slabs. Like most of the Period II floors, this was not traceable as a distinct change of level. A possible level for a later floor was 0.30m above the slabs and immediately below the stone strew resulting from the final collapse of the walls; but here there were no complete pots or tiles or other certain indication of an ancient surface.

The space to the east of the building (Room XIX) was covered over with the same closely packed pebbles and grit as the Period II street; stones from the Period I destruction level below projected in places, and further fallen stones and tiles lay on top of it, especially at the south side of Trench J.

In A (1954), to the west of this building, the Period I destruction level was overlaid by a thick fall of stones probably from wall 23. In Period II this seems to have been levelled off with a fill of brown clay containing mortar fragments to form the ground surface of a yard about 0.60m above the Period I floor.

A layer of lime up to 5cm thick covered much of the southern part of this area; but stones from below protruded up through it and it seems likely to have been not so much a floor as the remains of a pile of lime intended for repairs to the Fortress wall or perhaps to the cistern in C.

The space to the north of the lime patch was open to the street, and the thin grit and pebble strew of the street appears to have extended over it. The soil above this level seems subsequently to have been cultivated, and there was no trace of the post-abandonment stone-strew found on other parts of the site.

A coin of Maximianus (C6, 292–5) was found in the topsoil of J.

Trench C (1954) (DRAWINGS VII, VIII section 5)
The cistern (FIG. 23) that had formed the principal feature of the Period I layout was cleaned out and reused in Period II (p. 68); there was no obvious sign that it had also to be repaired. Wall 26, to the south of it, probably survived into Period II, if only as a retaining wall, and its extension 29 may even have been built at this time. Any Period II occupation levels that may have existed further south were eroded long ago. The south end of wall 25, resting on the southeast corner of the cistern, may have survived as a buttress to wall 26. No wall seems to have survived north of the cistern, and the line of the thick strew of cobbles put down in the street in the earlier phase of Period II seemed to be continued southwards by a rather vaguely marked ground level of stones and yellowish clay that reached a point just below the top of the cistern vault. An apparently Period I cobbled surface at the same level as the south shoulder of the cistern vault may have remained in use in Period II (p. 70).

A more distinct strew of cobbles about 20–30cm above this, just covering the crown of the cistern vault and only a little below the limit of subsequent cultivation, ran right across the street as well, and seems to have been the final Period II surface.

Trench E (1954) (DRAWING VII)
None of the Period I walls seems to have survived in Period II and the whole area (apart from the south end of the trench where even the Period I levels had been removed by erosion and cultivation) was simply covered with a series of rough strews of cobbles and small stones, the highest of which corresponded to the later Period II surface in the street and came only just below the limit of modern cultivation.

The Chapel: Trench A (1953) (FIG. 25)

Between the two highest outcrops of the western summit of the headland and just inside the Postern stood what seems to have been the latest building on the Acropolis, a chapel 6m long and just under 4m wide externally. It consisted of a single room with a door in the centre of the west side and a roughly semicircular apse at the east (PLATE 19 (*d*)). The walls varied in thickness between 60 and 70cm and were built of rough stones of varying size laid more or less horizontally as two mortared faces with a mortared core of small stones and tile fragments. The massive south jamb of the door had a vertical groove cut in its north face.

The internal arrangements were confused by a large stone-robbers' or treasure-hunters' pit sunk in the middle, but a number of very irregular stone floor-slabs remained in situ at the foot of the north wall. In the apse the floor was presumably at a higher level as there was an outcrop of rock about 0.50m high; traces of mortar along the chord of the apse may have marked the change of level.

Deeper excavation outside the west end produced a 20cm layer of mortar rubble, presumably fallen from the walls, at about the same level as the floor inside; below this was

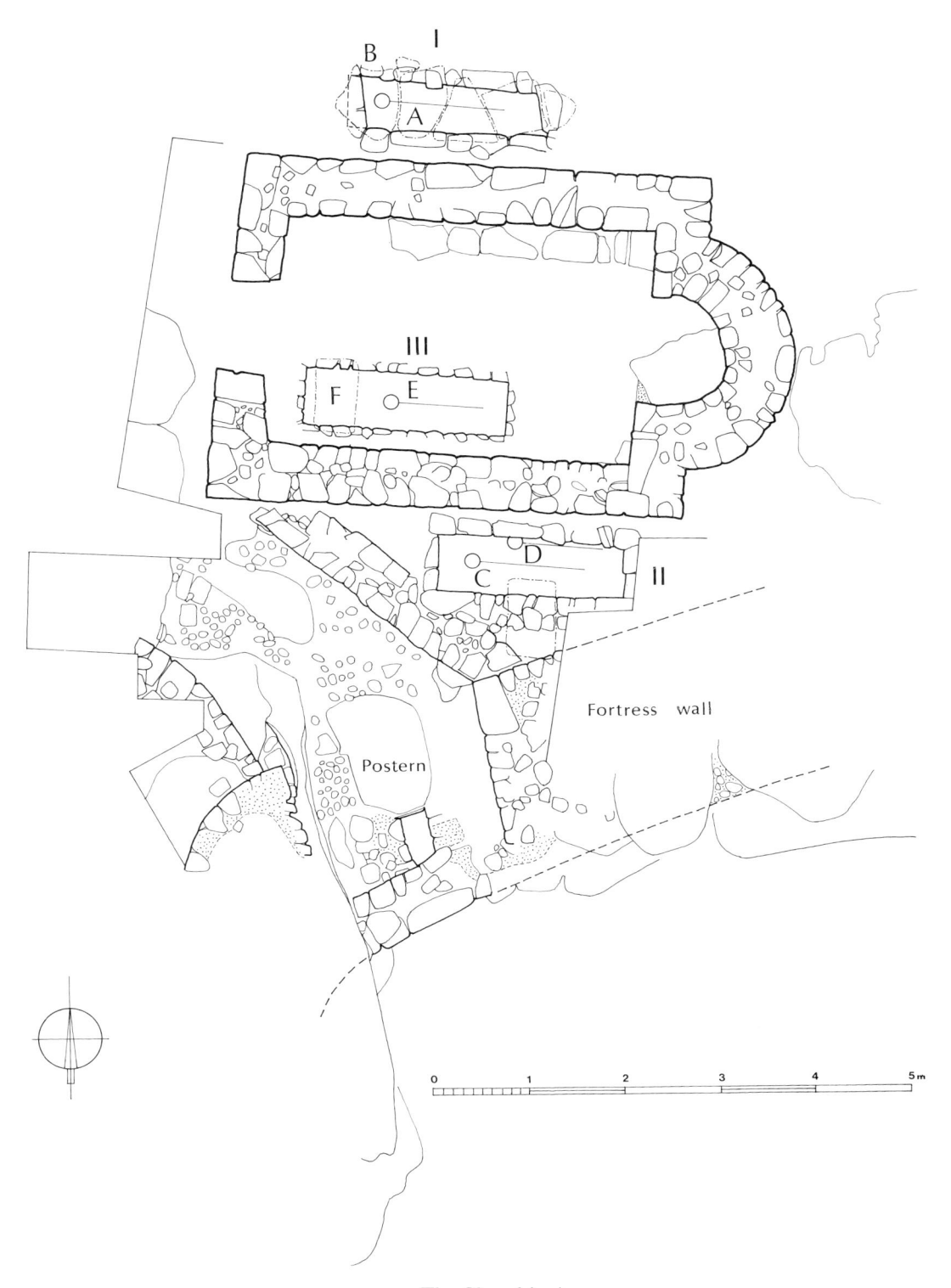

FIG. 25. The Chapel in A 1953.

0.40m of clean brown earth in which was found a coin of Heraclius (C38, after 629/30); below this again lay 40cm of tiles and other debris characteristic of the Period I destruction.

Associated with the Chapel were three shallow stone-lined graves originally covered over with slabs. Tomb I, just outside the north wall, still had its cover consisting of four rough stone slabs and a large flat tile no less than 7.5cm thick (PLATE 19 (*e*)). The grave was 0.70m deep, lined with unmortared stone, and contained a well preserved skeleton (A) about 1.50m tall, lying on its back with head to the west, upper arms at its sides and forearms apparently raised so that the hands rested on the shoulders (PLATE 19 (*f*)). A pendant in the form of a cross in a circle (F131) lay high up on the chest and a bronze plaque beside the chest. A second skeleton (B), presumably an earlier occupant of the grave, was piled in disorder at the west end.

Tomb II, lying outside the south wall of the Chapel, was cut into the north-east wall of the Postern passage. It was generally similar in construction to Tomb I, but only one of the cover slabs remained and that had been displaced. It also contained two bodies; one (C) was laid along the south side of the grave with the arms folded over the lower chest; most of the skull was missing. The other (D) lay mostly along the north side, though some of the leg-bones were on the south; the pelvis was missing.

Tomb III, inside the church, was built of smaller stones laid, unlike those in the other graves, in mortar; one of its cover slabs remained in situ near the west end. One fairly well preserved skeleton (E) of a child about 0.70m tall lay in the centre and bones from probably two earlier bodies (F) had been gathered together towards the west end. The fill of the grave included fragments of glass and glazed pottery as well as an almost complete glazed jug with decoration in black and green on a white ground (288–90). This may have belonged to the filling of the robbers' pit rather than to the original contents of the grave.

Date of the Chapel. The only absolute evidence of the date of the Chapel is that its south wall cut through the north-east retaining wall of the probably Period I sunken passage leading down to the Postern, while its west wall lay at a higher level than the Period I destruction debris excavated outside it. The tiles found in the upper levels and presumed to have belonged to the Chapel are also of a later type than those used elsewhere on the Acropolis.

Dating the Period I Fortress

The logic of the coin evidence discussed in the following Section 3 would suggest that the final surfaces of the Period I street and house-floors were laid later than the early part of the reign of Heraclius and probably later than 642/3, early in the reign of Constans II, though the only coin of this Emperor (C46) found in, rather than on, a floor cannot have been more than two or three centimetres below the final surface, and, on the not unreasonable assumption that the more house-proud members of the community occasionally re-surfaced their floors with fresh earth, may not have been there for more than a year or two before the destruction. None of these coins found below the latest Period I floor-level is properly sealed as it would be if a wall or solid pavement had been laid on top of it. Any of them might have resulted from a child burying its pocket-money and forgetting the exact spot, or someone dropping a coin into a pot-hole in the street immediately before filling it in with a donkey-load of beach pebbles.

The only conclusion that can safely be drawn from the coins is that the settlement inside the Fortress was destroyed not earlier than the beginning of the reign of Constans II; the presence in the area of the basilica of two coins of the latter part of his reign (C47, 655/8, C48, 659/60) suggests that even that area, more vulnerable than the Fortress lasted on into the 660's when the Arab fleet was closing in on the Aegean and Propontis.

Historically, one might suggest that the Arabs' attack on Cyprus in 649, their first major naval venture, may have been the stimulus that resulted in the building of the Fortress. Its destruction can hardly have come long after 668, when Mu'awiya made his first foray into the Propontis and plundered Ephesus on his return. The little fort on the headland would have been clearly visible from the main shipping route up the Asiatic coast; with its splendidly sheltered harbour it must have been potentially, if not actually, a useful base for a Byzantine naval squadron, and its elimination must have been an early priority for the Arabs as soon as they developed an interest in maintaining their own freedom of passage into the northern Aegean.

Dating the Period II Reoccupation

The second, ninth-century group, comprises only two coins, of Nikephoros I and Leo V (C50, C51; 803–820) both found on floors in association with more or less complete pots that must represent a destruction or abandonment level. Though two or more separate Period II levels were tentatively detected in several areas of the site, the homogeneity of the soil used in the make-up of the floors was such that certain identification of occupied floors depended entirely on the presence of occasional slabs, complete pots and, for what they were worth, strews of lime.

Both the floors on which the coins were found were covered by further layers of similar soil, which in their turn were overlaid by a heavy strew of stones from the collapse of the walls, implying that the abandonment dated by the coins was followed by a further reoccupation, perhaps contemporary with the latest Period II floor (with slabs and an amphora) in the western room (XIV) of B (1954), though the alternative possibility remains that the floor in XIV is contemporary with the dated floors but was not made up in the final reoccupation suggested above.

The apparently precise dating of one moment in the history of the Period II settlement is of no help in determining its duration. The general impression gained during the excavation was that comparatively little Period II pottery was found on the site as a whole (except in the cistern), but this picture is distorted by the enormous quantity of Period I pottery, originating in the destruction level, that was put back into circulation by the operations of the builders of the Period II settlement. Judged by the depth of the deposit resulting from the successive raising of the floor levels, on the other hand, Period II would seem to have lasted considerably longer than Period I.

Archaeological sections (DRAWING VIII)

The two north-south sections on DRAWING VIII through trenches A–B and C–D are on the lines of ones already published in *Prehistoric Emporio* i as Sections 2 and 5. The same numbers have therefore been retained for them here.

DRAWING VIII. Section 2: trenches A–B (east side) (*Prehistoric Emporio* i 162 fig. 91)

(1) Surface.
(2) Dark brown earth with pebbles and stone chips.
(3) Earth with large stones and some tile above floor of Period IIb.
(4) Dark brown with many large stones.

(5) Light reddish brown with some pebbles, stone chips, stones and tile fragments, above floor of Period II.
(6) Brown with pebbles: make-up for road of Period IIb.
(7) Brown with stones.
(8) Yellowish brown with pebbles and stone chips above floor of Period IIa.
(9) Yellowish brown with pebbles, stone chips and some large stones, overlying foundations of wall 58.
(10) Layers of coarse and fine sand, virtually sterile: evidently make-up for floor of Period II.
(11) Earth with stones and some tile, representing accumulation between Periods I and II.
(12) Large stones with mortar, apparently fallen from fortress wall after the Period I destruction.
(13) Brown with few stones above yellow clay floor of Period I.
(14) Period I burnt destruction level with black ash and tile.
(15) Yellowish brown sandy, apparently make-up for road of Period Ib.
(16) Dark brown with stones (see *Prehistoric Emporio* i 162 fig. 91 (1)).
(17) Thin layer of yellow clay above undisturbed clay subsoil.

DRAWING VIII. Section 5: trenches C–D (west side: section reversed in drawing) (*Prehistoric Emporio* i 164 fig. 94)

(1) Surface.
(2) Dark brown earth with some small pebbles and stone chips.
(3) Dark brown with large stones.
(4) Whitish brown with a few stones.
(5) Yellowish sandy with fragments of mortar.
(6) Yellowish brown.
(7) Brown with small pebbles and stone chips.
(8) Hard yellow with a few stones: probably Period I fill.
(9) Yellowish with stone chips and fragments of tile.
(10) Yellowish sandy with cobbles and fragments of tile and mortar.
(11) Reddish brown sandy with a few stones and tiles.
(12) Yellowish brown sandy with a little stone or tile.
(13) Yellowish with small stone chips.
(14) Brown with pebbles and stone chips.
A. Wall 41 of *Prehistoric Emporio* i 161 fig. 89, 164 fig. 94.

3. Analysis of Coins from Settlement and Fortress

Sinclair Hood

Nineteen identifiable coins were recovered from the Acropolis. All except two of these were datable to the first half of the seventh century AD. The exceptions were C2 of the first century BC, and C6 of Maximian (AD 292–5). The seventh-century coins include one (C23) of Phocas (AD 602–10), eleven of Heraclius (AD 610–41) ranging from the beginning of his reign (C24) to 635/6 (C39), and five of his successor, Constans II (AD 641–68) none of which it seems is datable later than 648.

The coin situation on the Acropolis forms a striking contrast to that in the area of the Early Christian basilica complex, where the range of coins is entirely different, with a heavy concentration (thirteen in all) assignable to the fifth and sixth centuries, but only five of Heraclius and three of Constans II. The clear implication is that intensive occupation of the fortress area on the Acropolis cannot have begun until considerably later than the building of the basilica complex which seems to date from the time of Justin II (AD 565–78) in the third quarter of the sixth century.

Four coins of Heraclius (C24, C25, C28, C31) were recovered from below floors or other surfaces of the main Period I of the fortress. Two of these (C24, C31) came from a deposit just below the Period I floor in Room XXII in trench A (DRAWING VIII Section 2: below the floor at the bottom of level (14)). The other two coins were embedded in the make-up of the Period I street, C 25 in that of the latest phase of it (Period IB) in trench F just outside the door into Room IX. The latest of these four coins is assigned to 616/7. The completion of the fortress can hardly therefore date from before that time.

It seems possible, although not certain, that one or two of the five coins of Constans II recovered on the Acropolis (C41, C46) also came from below floors of Period I. C46 datable to 642/3 appeared to be from a deposit with pottery akin to that of Period I but underneath the floor of the Period I destruction in Room XXIV in the south-east corner of trench C. C41 datable to 645/6 was found in cleaning the irregular earth floor in the main North-West Tower: it might have come from below the floor, or could have been trodden into it later, or lost on it at the time of the Period I destruction.

If no coins later than C31 of Heraclius dated 616/7 came from below the fortress floors it would suggest that the fortress might have been constructed during the period of the Persian and Avar threat to Constantinople, but presumably before the end of the Persian war in 628. In that case the fortress would have enjoyed a life of some forty years or more before it was destroyed by the Arabs around AD 670.

Alternatively the fortress may have been erected in the 650's after the Arab threat by sea had become manifest, and this is likely enough if the two coins of Constans II (C41, C46) did in fact come from below the floors of Period I. In that case the fortress would only have been in existence for a period of some 15–20 years before it was destroyed about AD 670.

A difficulty in the way of such a late date for the contruction of the fortress is that it leaves only three coins of Constans II that might have been lost in it at the time of its final destruction. One of these (C44) dated between 642 and 648 was found on the floor of Room XXII in trench A and was certainly from the Period I destruction level. The other two coins (C42, C43) which were similar in date may also have been lost in the destruction. All three of these coins were badly worn and had no doubt survived in circulation for the twenty years or so between the time when they were struck and the destruction of the fortress around 670.

Two of the coins of Heraclius found on the Acropolis similarly came from deposits of the Period I destruction. These were C33 and C36, datable to 624/5 and 630/1. A third coin (C39, assigned to 635/6) was in a deposit sealed by the Period II floor in Room XI on the west side of trench D. All three of these coins are later than any of the four coins of Heraclius (C24, C25, C28, C31) recovered from below the Period I floors. These three coins may well have survived in circulation until the time of the Period I destruction of the fortress around 670 in the light of the long life of copper coins in provincial areas during this general period (cf. Metcalf 1962, 19 note 25, citing Charanis 1955). Three earlier coins of Heraclius recovered from surface levels (C27, C29, C32) could also have been lost when the fortress was destroyed, but might equally well have been dropped at the time it was built along with C24, C25, C28 and C31, found beneath its floors.

It is worth noting that a coin of Constans II (C45) assigned to the same date (642/3) as C46, which might have come from below a floor of Period I in the fortress, was apparently found beneath a slab thought to be part of a pavement in one of the Sea Shore Trials (FIG. 18 trench

E). The pottery from above the pavement, however, suggested that the building here dated from a reoccupation some time after the Period I destruction of the fortress.

No coins of Constans II later than C41 dated 645/6 or C42–C44 dated 642–8 were recovered from the fortress on the Acropolis. But two of the coins (C47, C48) from the area of the basilica complex were datable to his later years, 655/6–657/8 and 659/60.

More significant perhaps for the date of the Period I destruction of the fortress, and for that of the presumably contemporary destruction of the basilica complex, is the solitary coin (C49) of Constantine IV (668–85) from the Sea Shore Trials (FIG. 2 trench C). This coin cannot be earlier than 668 and may have been struck in 673, the year when the Arabs occupied Rhodes and only a year before the beginning of the five-year siege of Constantinople (674–8). It was found in association with occupation debris apparently assignable to Period I of the fortress, but might have been lost on the occasion of a subsequent reoccupation of the area.

The end of the first phase of reoccupation (Period II) in the fortress is dated by two coins, C50 of Nikephoros I (803–11) from on a Period II floor in trench A, and C51 of Leo V (813–20) from on one in Room IX (trench F).

4. Index to Principal Findspots in the Fortress

John Boardman

[Bracketed numbers indicate that a find is referred to under that item.]

North-west Tower 159, 191, 201, 213, 221, 224–6, 231, 236, 247, 263, 265, 274, 329; graffiti xviii, xxi, xxx; F54a, 55, 86, 98, 142–3, 151; C41.
Room I behind North-west Tower 129, 148, 185, 245–6, (256), 257–9, 262; F4.
Room III 16–7, 94, 116, 120, 147, 264, 278, 286, 319, 331; F1, 7, 51, 54b, 70–1, 73, 75, 80, 82–3, 85, 89, 92–3, 102, 110, 115–7, 119, 144, 154.
Room IV F19, 39, 58, 62, 71, 79, 81, 97.
Room V 291.
Room VIa C22.
Room VIII 230, 250, 252; F51, 114; C23.
Room IX 103, 144–5, 149, 160–1, 184, (185), 187, 189–90, 196, 199, 200, 206–7, 209–10, 216, 218–20, 223, 232, (238), 240–1, (241), 243–4, 266, 271, 279–80, 284, 315, 317–8, 321, 334; graffito xxviii; F2, 3, 18, 20, 27, 31, 34, 37, 42–3, 47–8, 50–2, (53), 54d–e, 56, 59, 67, 69e–q, 71–2, 74, 77, 90–1, 96, 101, 103–4, 108–9, 111, 120–1, 123–4, 139; C25, 51.
Room XI 104, 106, 146, 179–83, (184), 198, 202, 229, 233, (238), 242, 254, 335; graffiti xiii, xvi, xix; F5, 46, 65–6, 69, 71, 76, 113, 125–6; C2, 27.
Room XII 105, 150, 197, 211, 217, 222, 234, 238, 255, 273, 283, 336; F28, 32, 49, 69, 99, 100, 127, 134; C28, 36.
Room XI–XII graffiti xi, xx; F29, 41, 95, 110; C43.
Room XIV (238), 281.
Room XV 282; F25.
Room XIV–XV 267; F52, 118, 122, 135, 152.
Room XVI (238).
Room XIX (246), (250), 251, 253, 272; F8, 9, 44, 63, 68, 78.
Room XX 178, (180), 186, 188, 194, 227–8, 253, 256, 277, 330; C50.

Room XIX–XX 21–5; graffito ii; F(27), 51, 87, 112, 145.
Room XXII 208, 239; F33, 35–6, 45, 84, 88, 148; C24, 29, 31, 33, 42, 44.
Room XXIV F38; C46.
Chapel 288–9; F131; C38.
Cistern in Trench C 192, 212; F30, 51, 64, 94, 106; C49.
Trench DF C39.
Trench E 342; graffito xii; F107; C17.
Trench K 128.
Trench L 107.
Trench M 130, 193, 205, 248–9, 260, 316.
Trench V 291.
West of North Tower F10.
Pindakas 65, 137, 140; F15e, (129); C12.

Chapter 3
The Finds

John Boardman

(PLATES 20–33)

1. Introduction

Some measure of Roman occupation on the site is suggested by the finds for the fifth century AD continuing into the seventh, when the Fortress was built, and there was a subsequent period of reoccupation in the ninth century; it is the pottery, lamps, coins and other finds of these years that form the bulk of the material published here. The beginning is marked only by an increase in the amount of pottery and number of coins found on the site, since there seems to have been continuous occupation on a small scale through the early Roman period, and probably ever since the eighth century BC or earlier. The end of the main period can readily be associated with the coming of the Arabs, probably in the 60's of the seventh century.

The material derives from three main areas of excavation and since the circumstances of excavation largely determine both the character and value of the finds, these sources are briefly discussed.

The Fortress
The most important level was that of the destruction debris on the floors of the main period in the fortress. The excavations uncovered both living rooms and storerooms in which pithoi, amphorae, bowls, jugs and lamps were found, sometimes complete or at least in a readily mendable condition, and all this pottery with the other finds must have been in use in the mid-seventh century. There were also heavy levels of mixed destruction debris which included material from the upper slopes of the acropolis on which the fortress stood: these yielded pottery of the sixth and perhaps latest fifth centuries AD as well as a certain amount of earlier pottery, all in a most fragmentary condition. There was little glass found in the destruction level. The coins are almost all of the seventh century, down to the 640's AD. There were no earlier Roman levels of occupation found on the acropolis hill, but reoccupation, dated by coins to the ninth century, yielded some complete vases.

The Basilica
The building was apparently destroyed at the same time as the fortress but only in one or two of its outbuildings were there any near-complete vases found and the mass of pottery, lamps and

glass is from the accumulation of destruction debris and is very fragmentary. As well as a fair proportion of Greek, and almost all the early Roman pottery published here, the Basilica area yielded both the earliest of the late Roman pottery and the only fifth-century coins found on the site. Most of the fragmentary pottery is of the earlier seventh century and there seems to be less in proportion of the type found in the destruction levels of the fortress. There is a little pottery from the reoccupation period.

The Sea Shore
Excavations on and near the sea shore immediately NW of the harbour were confined to trial pits dug to determine the stratigraphy, if any, and periods of occupation in that area. No complete vases were recovered but the yield of fragmentary pottery, especially of tableware was considerable. The range of date is, at the beginning, as for the fortress, that is to say appreciably later than the earliest pottery from the Basilica area: the latest tableware, however, is of the destruction period and it seems likely that occupation in this exposed area was abandoned no earlier than that within the fortress walls. Since the only floors found seem to belong to a reoccupation in the area, perhaps not as long after the fortress destruction as the ninth-century reoccupation, the late Roman houses may have stood a little further from the shore.

Other sources
A farmhouse, part of which was excavated on a site about one kilometre from the harbour at Emporio, at Pindakas, yielded scraps of pottery and glass of late sixth- or seventh-century date. The site was published in BSA liii/liv (1958/9) 295–309, with its pre-Roman and some later finds, except the pottery. Between here and the harbour a low hill also carries fragments of the same period and may be the site of another farmhouse, but late Roman pottery can be found all over this part of the island: for example, a sixth-century glass cup was found broken at the site of the Archaic Greek temple of Athena on the hill top north of the harbour, no doubt from a picnic party there (*Greek Emporio* 22).

These main sources are abbreviated below as Fort, Bas and SS. 'Fort × 3' means that three examples of the form were found in the fortress.

The organisation of this material, the basic catalogue, drawings and commentary, were completed by about 1960. The organisation therefore depends on the knowledge of the material available then. The commentary and comparanda have, however, been modestly updated, mainly with reference to Hayes' magisterial work on pottery (Hayes, *LRP*) which was written with only partial knowledge of the finds from Emporio. The catalogue is selective, especially of the larger, coarse pottery shapes which were common finds in Fortress rooms, but all types and shapes are represented. Photographs and drawings are mostly by the writer.

2. The Pottery

Early Roman Pottery

There is very little early Roman pottery from Emporio. The best was found in two small groups, one from an earth fill below the apse of the Basilica (5–12, whence also the lamps, 292–6), and the other from the area of the prehistoric settlement (1–4). No structures of the early Roman period were found though coins (C1–6), as well as this pottery, attest occupation and activity here in this period. The lack of any amount of middle Roman pottery suggests that the site may not have been so heavily occupied again until the fifth century. The two groups seem consistent in date both in themselves and with each other. 'Çandarli' ware (*LRP* 316–22) or imitations of it, is well in evidence (1–11), as well as fragments in a rather different pink fabric which may be local but which keeps to the profiles typical of the period. 9 and 10 have poorer surfaces and appear later though they may be local products. The date for most of the material in both groups (1–4; 5–12) should be the second to third centuries AD. 15 is somewhat earlier. 16 may well be later than the rest of this pottery since its stamped decoration is reminiscent of later Roman styles (cf. *LRP* 218–9 Style A of African red slip ware, fourth/fifth century). 17, with low relief pattern, is from a late Roman level and placed here for lack of dated parallels for its decoration. There was no early Roman pottery from the fortress site, and very few lamps of this period.

1. FIG. 26. Complete open bowl. H. 8.0. Pinkish-ochre clay with good red wash. Cf. S. Loeschke, *AM* xxxvii (1912) Type 19. Pit east of Bas.
2. FIG. 26. Rim of bowl. Diam. 24.0. Clay as 1. Cf. Waage no. 473n. Pit east of Bas.
3. FIG. 26. Wall of bowl. 'Thorn' decoration below a groove. Closest probably the barbotine ware described by Jones in *Tarsus* I 188f. Pink clay with dull red wash. Pit east of Bas.
4. Other fragments from the same pit are as Waage nos. 450k and 473p. Pink clay with a poor red wash.

Samian

5. FIG. 26. Rim of open bowl. Pink clay with orange-red wash. On the lip graffito (FIG. 44, i). Bas apse fill. Two other fragments from the same level have the slightly flattened top to the rim; cf. *LRP* 321 Form 3. Second/third century.
6. FIG. 26. Upper half of open bowl. Diam. 12.0. Pink clay with little mica, good red wash. Cf. Waage, no. 470. Basilica apse fill.
7. FIG. 26. Complete open bowl. H. 6.0. Pink clay with red wash, carelessly applied near the foot. Fragments of a similar bowl from the same level. Cf. *LRP* 321 Form 4. Third century. Basilica apse fill.
8. Straight wall of bowl, as Waage, no. 465. Pinkish brown clay with little mica, good red wash. Basilica apse fill.
9. FIG. 26. Foot of open bowl or dish. Diam. 14.0. Pink clay with good red wash. Cf. Waage, no. 417. Basilica apse fill.
10. FIG. 26. Rim of open bowl. Diam. 12.0. Pink clay with red-brown wash. Basilica apse fill.
11. FIG. 26. Rim of bowl. Diam. 14.0. Pink clay with red-brown wash, carelessly applied. Basilica apse fill.
12. FIG. 26; PLATE 20. Corner palmette from a model altar. The upright leaves lean out slightly and at the corner a flame-palmette is modelled. The section suggests how the floor was fitted to the walls. The inside is finger-smoothed and stained by fire or oil. Cf. Kaufmann, *Graeco-Agyptische Koroplastik* pl. 38. 302–5. Pink clay fired grey in core. Basilica apse fill.
13. Two bowl fragments as Waage, no. 460h. Light rouletting at top of rim, pink clay with good red wash. One fr. from beneath Basilica floor, one from Bas area.
14. Fragment from bowl as Waage, no. 470. Pink clay with good red wash. Bas.
15. FIG. 26. Bowl with upright lip, part of base missing. H. 3.5. Samian A, mid-first to mid-second century. Bas.

3. THE FINDS

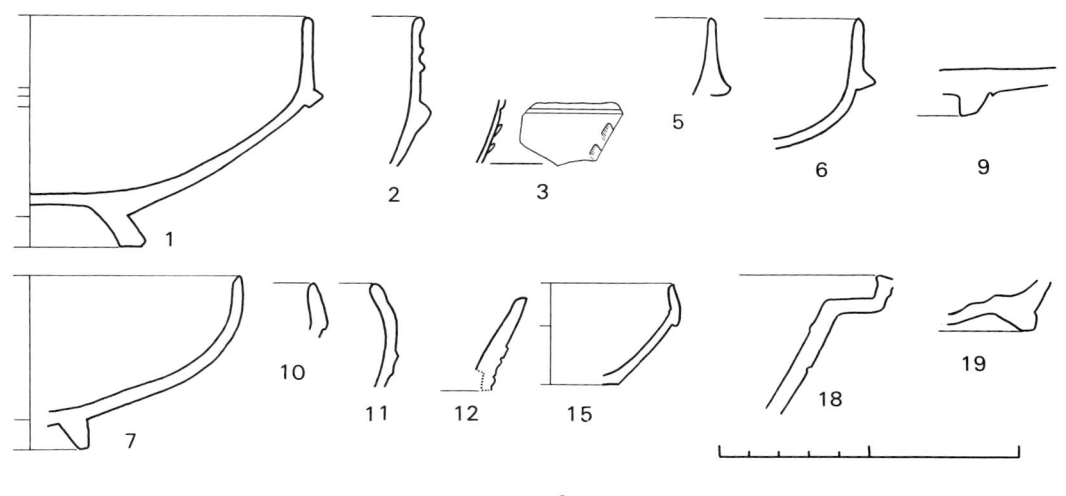

FIG. 26.

16. PLATE 20. Wall of open bowl. L. 4.5. Within, impressed decoration of leaves, dots, and rosettes. Pink clay, no paint preserved. Fortress debris, Room III.
17. PLATE 20. Fragment from heavy wall of moulded bowl (?). Tendrils in low relief, apparently moulded. Pink clay, no paint. Fortress debris, Room III.
18. FIG. 26; PLATE 20. Rim of bowl. Diam. ca. 30.0. Recurrent stamp on flat of rim, an X and toes in *planta pedis*. Pink clay with some mica, apparently a pale cream wash outside. Bas.
19. FIG. 26. Base of closed vase. 'Roman Pergamene' fabric: buff body with red wash (covering whole base ring). Bas.
20. Fragment from bowl as Waage, no. 670. The only certain middle Roman fragment. Pink clay with poor red wash. Beneath Basilica floor.

Late Roman Pottery

Table Ware Bowls

The value and limitations of the material published here may be mentioned since the ware is susceptible to fairly close stylistic and chronological study. The quantity found permits a fairly detailed stylistic arrangement of shapes for the major class of imported table ware ('Late Roman C' or Phocaean) through to the abrupt end of occupation on the site; and the terminus which can be closely dated (in the 660's AD) from coins and general historical considerations gives the destruction material considerable chronological importance. This is a rare dating point for the seventh century and seems to bring us almost to the end of the history of late Roman red table ware. For the earlier pottery, however, there are no dating points at Emporio. The fortress may have been built in the seventh century (its coins are all of that date) but the earliest late Roman pottery from it seems to be of the fifth century and there must have been considerable occupation before the site was fortified, although in the only places on the steep slopes where a sufficient depth of earth remained no intermediate levels between the Mycenaean and the levels of the fortress construction were observed, nor were earlier Roman levels found elsewhere on the site.

For the earlier pottery, therefore, we rely on the evidence of other sites. Most of the pottery is Phocaean ('Late Roman C') and 21–111 present a series of what appear to be significant stylistic changes in the development of the rim profiles. There are small quantities of African red slip ware (131–51) and some other fabrics were detected (152–77) although where the shapes are as for Phocaean they are illustrated and discussed with that ware and the results summarised. Base fragments are included with the appropriate rim fragments, judging from the evidence of complete shapes elsewhere.

The shapes are almost all open bowls, some with quite steep sides, which seem to have served as plates, soup plates, broth bowls and even cups: at least, few other clay, metal or glass vessels were found which might have served this purpose, and this in a wine-growing area. The latest type of profile could hardly then have promoted the best in table manners. The ancient names seem to have been *patane, patella, patellion*, terms applicable to open bowls and cups (Pollux, *Onom.* VI 85, 90, X 107–8; Koukoulis, *Vie et civilisation byzantines* v 156). (Diameters of complete bowls are given as maximum diameters; of fragments, at the top of the rim and approximate.)

Phocaean Red Slip Ware

This has been generally designated 'Late Roman C', following Waage, but for its identification as Phocaean see *LRP* 525. For a description of the fabric see Waage, 51f., *LRP* 323–4. In *Hesperia* xi (1942) 299f. Waage notes the grey or black outside to the rim on some fragments, which he suggests is due to uneven firing of this part, a phenomenon discussed also in *LRP* 324. This feature is apparent in varying degrees on examples from all groups, most common on the latest. From many examples it seems that the effect was sometimes deliberately sought (cf. PLATE 20 (*a*), (*c*)) whatever the accident that originally suggested the decoration — probably the stacking of bowls within the kiln. As well as the grey or black rim produced in this way some bear a broad pale cream band on the outside of the rim (PLATE 20 (*b*)) presumably again due to the uneven firing of a wash that overlapped this part of the vase. That this was simply a pale wash intended to fire in this way is rendered rather doubtful by the examples from Emporio which show alternate patches of cream and grey on the discoloured rim (see 103, PLATE 21). The development of rim shapes during the two centuries represented by the fragments numbered 21–111 is clear and simple. A high thin moulding becomes squatter and broader, and eventually lengthens laterally to become little more than slight grooves and ridges or an extension of the wall of the bowl itself. No two rims are quite alike so I have grouped together those that seem to mark approximately the same stage in the general development of the shape.

21–34. The upright rim is thin and concave outside. These correspond to Waage nos. 940–943, and the sequence 21–73 is *LRP* 329–38 Form 3. Such development as there is appears in the flattening and lengthening of the bottom overhang of the rim, which starts curved and ends straight; this is probable in the light of the future of the shape in which this feature lengthens while the height of the rim diminishes. There are varieties. On most the rim is rouletted in different fashions except for 25, 28, 30. The fabric is consistent (variations in 22, 28) and on many the orange-red wash is notably better than that on later examples. Waage assigns these to the fifth century, as does Hayes (*LRP* Form 3, Types B–D).

21. FIG. 27; PLATE 20. Rim. Diam. 38.0. Bas × 2; SS; all rouletted.
22. FIG. 27. Rim. Diam. 40.0. Bas × 2; rouletted; pink clay.
23. FIG. 27; PLATE 20. Rim. Diam. 40.0. Fort; Bas × 2. All rouletted.
24. FIG. 27; PLATE 20. Rim. Diam. 30.0. Bas × 2; rouletted.
25. FIG. 27. Rim. Diam. 36.0. Bas × 11, one example below Basilica floor.
26. FIG. 27; PLATE 20. Rim. Diam. 40.0. Bas; rouletted.

3. THE FINDS

27. FIG. 27. Rim. Diam. 22.0. Fort; Bas × 2; rouletted.
28. FIG. 27. Rim. Diam. 30.0. Fort; Bas; buff, micaceous clay.
29. FIG. 27; PLATE 20. Rim. Diam. 24.0. Bas × 2; rouletted; one in buff micaceous clay.
30. FIG. 27. Rim. Bas.
31. FIG. 27. Base. Diam. 18.0. Bas.
32. FIG. 27. Base. Diam. 18.0. Fort × 5; Bas × 9; SS × 2; one with stamped device on floor, see 118.
33. FIG. 27. Base. Diam. 12.0. Fort × 2; Bas × 11 with two from below the Basilica floor; SS × 3; one in pink clay.
34. FIG. 27. Base. Diam. 16.0. Fort × 5 including one with light rouletting above the foot; Bas × 3; SS × 5; one in pink micaceous clay.

35-49. The rim height diminishes without much lengthening horizontally but some thickening. Endless varieties but probably no great range in date. On most the back of the lip meets the inner wall at an angle, unlike the following group. Rouletting is less common and the pale pink clay recurs in 35, 40, 43. A dark brown micaceous clay appears in 42, 46. 38 has fired red with a grey core and the rim is black. These are Waage nos. 944-5, perhaps still fifth-century; *LRP* Form 3, Type E.

35. FIG. 27. Rim. Diam. 26.0. Fort, in pink clay; Bas; SS.
36. FIG. 27. Rim. Diam. 24.0. Bas; SS.
37. FIG. 27; PLATE 20. Rim. Diam. 26.0 Fort × 2; Bas × 3, one rouletted; one each from below the Basilica and Fortress floors.
38. FIG. 27. Rim. Fort.
39. FIG. 27. Rim. Diam. 34.0. Fort × 3; Bas × 4; SS × 4; rouletted.
40. FIG. 27. Rim. Diam. 30.0. Bas × 6; SS; one rouletted, one in pink clay.
41. FIG. 27; PLATE 20. Rim. Diam. 28.0. Fort × 2; Bas × 2; SS × 2; two rouletted.
42. FIG. 27. Rim. Diam. 32.0. Bas × 3; SS in brown micaceous clay.
43. FIG. 27. Rim. Diam. 30.0. Bas × 5, three in pink clay with one rouletted.
44. FIG. 27. Rim. Diam. 18.0. Fort × 3; Bas; one rouletted.
45. FIG. 27. Rim. Diam. 30.0. SS.
46. FIG. 27. Rim. Diam. 32.0. Fort; SS × 4; one in brown micaceous clay.
47. FIG. 27. Rim. Diam. 32.0. SS.
48. FIG. 27; PLATE 20. Rim. Diam. 30.0. Bas × 2; rouletted.
49. FIG. 27. Base. Diam. 12.0. Fort × 2; Bas × 6; SS × 2.

50-57. The rim lengthens horizontally and its back mainly passes smoothly into the inner wall. The pink clay recurs in 51 and a red micaceous in 50. There is little rouletting (54, 55). These are Waage nos. 946-7, near the end of the fifth century into the sixth; *LRP* Form 3, Type F.

50. FIG. 27. Rim. Diam. 28.0. Fort × 3; Bas × 5; one in red micaceous clay.
51. FIG. 27. Rim. Diam. 16.0. SS; pink clay.
52. FIG. 27. Rim. Diam. 26.0. Bas × 2; one in buff micaceous clay.
53. FIG. 27. Rim. Diam. 26.0. Fort.
54. FIG. 27. Rim. Diam. 22.0. Fort; Bas × 3; SS × 2; two rouletted.
55. FIG. 27. Rim. Diam. 28.0. Fort × 4; Bas × 9; SS × 4; two rouletted, two from below the Basilica floor.
56. FIG. 27. Rim. Diam. 20.0. Fort.
57. FIG. 27. Rim. Diam. 30.0. Bas.

58-64. The outside of the rim is here straight or slightly convex, otherwise close to the last groups but rather later since there is no rouletting. These are the latest types associated with the Antioch earthquake of AD 526 (Waage no. 947a-f); early sixth-century.

58. FIG. 27. Rim. Diam. 30.0. Fort; SS × 2.
59. FIG. 27. Rim. Diam. 30.0. Bas; SS × 2.
60. FIG. 27. Rim. SS.
61. FIG. 27. Rim. Diam. 30.0. Fort; Bas; SS × 4.

62. FIG. 27. Rim. Diam. 34.0. SS.
63. FIG. 27. Rim. Diam. 30.0. Bas; SS.
64. FIG. 27. Rim. Diam. 28.0. Fort × 2; SS × 2.

65–73. As the last but the indentation behind the rim is barely perceptible. As Waage no. 947k–n. The bases 71–3 may belong here or with the last group. Perhaps second quarter of sixth century.

65. FIG. 28. Rim. Diam. 26.0. Bas × 2; SS × 3; Pindakas.
66. FIG. 28. Rim. Diam. 26.0. SS.
67. FIG. 28. Rim. Diam. 40.0. Fort; SS.
68. FIG. 28. Rim. Diam. 30.0. Fort × 2; Bas; SS × 4.
69. FIG. 28. Rim. Diam. 32.0. SS.
70. Rim. Diam. 38.0. SS.
71. FIG. 28. Base. Diam. 14.0. Bas × 6; SS × 3.
72. FIG. 28. Base. Diam. 10.0. Fort × 3; Bas × 11; SS × 3.
73. FIG. 28. Base. Diam. 10.0. Fort × 2; Bas.

74–79. The convex outside to the rim is now the rule and with the diminished height the development is now horizontally. These are Waage no. 949a, dated to the mid sixth century. Waage leaves a no. 949 for the missing link between 947n and 949a but there is here enough variety to demonstrate the immediate transition. Three examples of 75 are in pink clay. A complete example (79) is from the Basilica. These, and the successive examples of the ware listed here, are *LRP* 343–6, Form 10.

74. FIG. 28. Rim. Diam. 30.0. Fort × 2.
75. FIG. 28. Rim. Diam. 26.0. Fort × 3; Bas × 3; three in pink clay.
76. FIG. 28. Rim. Diam. 28.0. Fort.
77. FIG. 28. Rim. Diam. 30.0. Fort; Bas × 2.
78. FIG. 28. Rim. Diam. 28.0. Bas × 3.
79. FIG. 28. Complete bowl. Diam. 31.6. Bas.

80–87. The flat top to the rim grows to equal the depth of the flat underhang; also a noticeable slimming. As Waage no. 949f–n, to the end of the sixth century.

80. FIG. 28. Rim. Diam. 30.0. Fort × 3; Bas; SS.
81. FIG. 28. Rim. Diam. 26.0. Fort; Bas × 3.
82. FIG. 28. Rim. Diam. 26.0. Bas × 2.
83. FIG. 28. Rim. Fort × 3; Bas × 6; SS × 2.
84. FIG. 28. Rim. Diam. 30.0. Fort; Bas × 12.
85. FIG. 28. Rim. Diam. 26.0. Bas × 2.
86. FIG. 28. Rim. Diam. 28.0. Fort × 6; Bas × 6; SS.
87. FIG. 28. Rim. Diam. 28.0. Bas × 2.

88–95. The rim is slimmer and longer; Waage no. 949y, where he saw the death of Late Roman C in the middle of the first half of the seventh century (coin associations down to Heraclius). The pink clay recurs in 89, 93. The concavity of the upper part of the rim in 92, 93 leads to the exceptionally thin profiles of the next and last group. The complete 94 was on a Fortress floor and about half the rims of this group are from a level immediately overlying the plunder pit dug to rob stones from the Archaic Greek temple for the church building. The bases 95 should be of this or the preceding group.

88. FIG. 28. Rim. Diam. 28.0. Fort × 5; Bas × 5.
89. FIG. 28. Rim. Diam. 28.0. Fort; Bas × 15; one in pink clay.
90. FIG. 28. Rim. Diam. 28.0. Fort × 4; Bas × 7; SS × 2; two lightly grooved below the rim.
91. FIG. 28. Rim. Diam. 28.0. Bas × 7.

3. THE FINDS

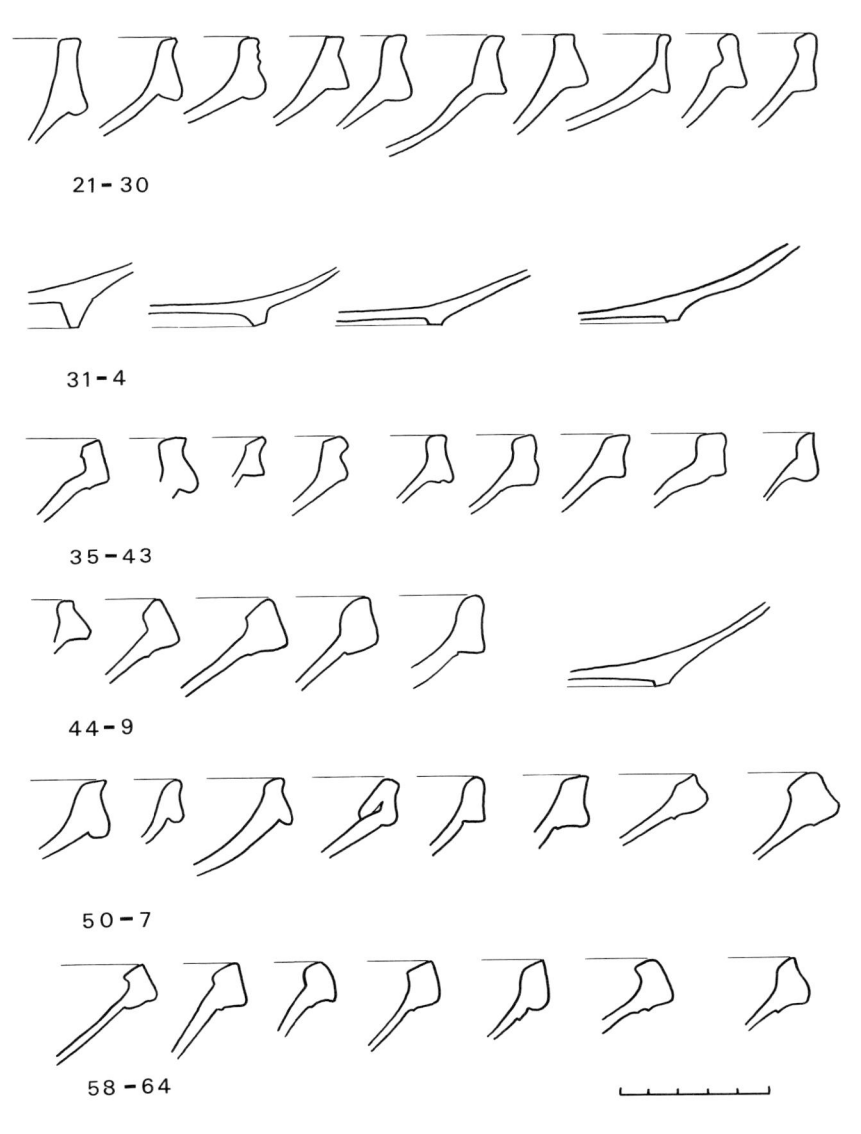

21-30

31-4

35-43

44-9

50-7

58-64

FIG. 27.

92. FIG. 28. Rim. Diam. 26.0. Fort × 2; Bas × 5; SS.
93. FIG. 28. Rim. Diam. 26.0. Fort × 9; Bas × 18; SS; two in pink clay.
94. FIG. 28. Complete bowl. Diam. 27.6. *LRP* Form 10, 11, fig. 71.Fortress floor, Room III.
95. FIG. 28. Base. Diam. 10.4. Fort × 5; Bas × 8; SS.

96–111. These are the latest of the table ware and may be dated into the 660's when the fortress was destroyed. The complete examples are from the Fortress floor. The excessive thinness and occasional concavity of rim does not occur at Antioch where this variety must have ceased to arrive earlier in the century. This may be the true 'death' of Roman red. The

FIG. 28.

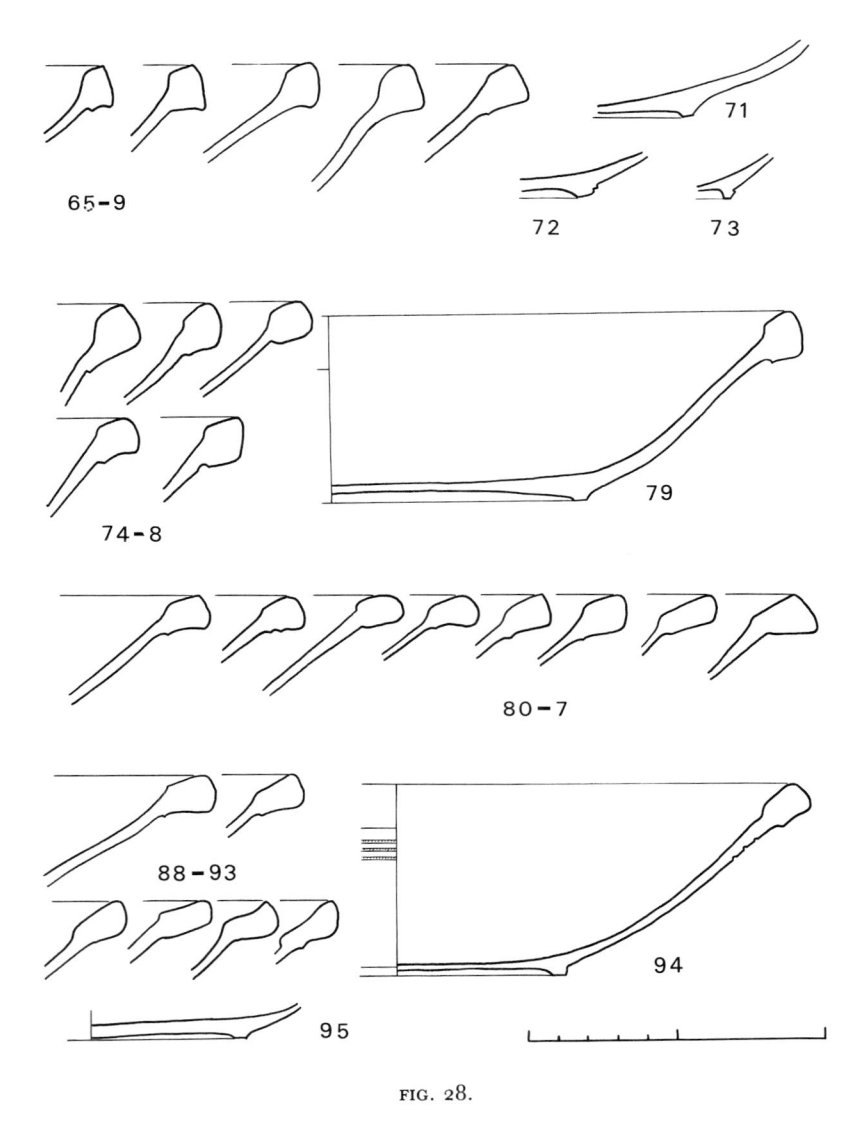

pink clay occurs often here (97, 101). A fragment of 102 in a dark grey gritty clay is like a complete example in the Athenian Agora (P 23106) which has a twisted hollow handle, like a frying pan. 108 is a similar handle in the same clay, but perhaps earlier (cf. *Agora* V G 113, pl. 72).

96. FIG. 29. Rim. Diam. 28.0. Fort × 3; Bas × 4.
97. FIG. 29. Rim. Diam. 28.0. Fort × 17; Bas × 21; SS; ten in pink clay.
98. FIG. 29. Rim. Diam. 24.0. Fort; Bas × 8.
99. FIG. 29. Rim. Diam. 26.0. Fort × 2; Bas × 2.
100. FIG. 29. Rim. Diam. 24.0. Fort × 7; Bas × 11.
101. FIG. 29. Rim. Diam. 24.0. Fort × 8; Bas × 11; four in pink clay.
102. FIG. 29. Rim. Diam. 22.0. Fort × 12; Bas × 4; one in gritty grey clay.

3. THE FINDS

103. FIG. 29; PLATE 21. Complete bowl. Diam. 26.2. Fortress floor, Room IX.
104. FIG. 29. Complete bowl. Diam. 25.0. Fortress floor, Room XI.
105. FIG. 29. Complete bowl. Diam. 25.8. *LRP* Form 10, 14, fig. 71. Fortress floor, Room XII.
106. FIG. 29. Complete bowl. Diam. 26.0. Fortress floor, Room XI.
107. FIG. 29. Complete bowl. Diam. ca. 28.0. Fortress floor, Trench L.
108. PLATE 21. Handle. Gritty grey clay. Fort.
109. FIG. 29. Base. Diam. 11.6. Fort × 4; Bas × 2.
110. FIG. 29. Base. Diam. 12.0. Fort × 7; Bas × 9; SS × 3.
111. FIG. 29. Base. Diam. 10.0. Fort × 3; Bas; SS × 2.

112–123. Fragments of Phocaean bases with stamped decoration of crosses, once a bird and once a hare. *LRP* 346–68 for the types. Ours are mainly sixth-century.

112. Simple outlined cross. *LRP* Motif 73. SS.
113. PLATE 21. Double outlined cross. *LRP* Motif 71. Bas.
114. Triple stroke arm of a cross on a base as 95. Fort.
115. Part of a Maltese cross. Bas.
116. PLATE 21. Part of double outlined Maltese cross. *LRP* Motif 72. Fortress debris, Room III.
117. PLATE 21. Cross monogram. *LRP* Motif 61. Bas. Trench LL 3.
118. PLATE 21. Cross monogram on base as 32. *LRP* Motif 67. Fort.
119. PLATE 21. Cross monogram. Fort.

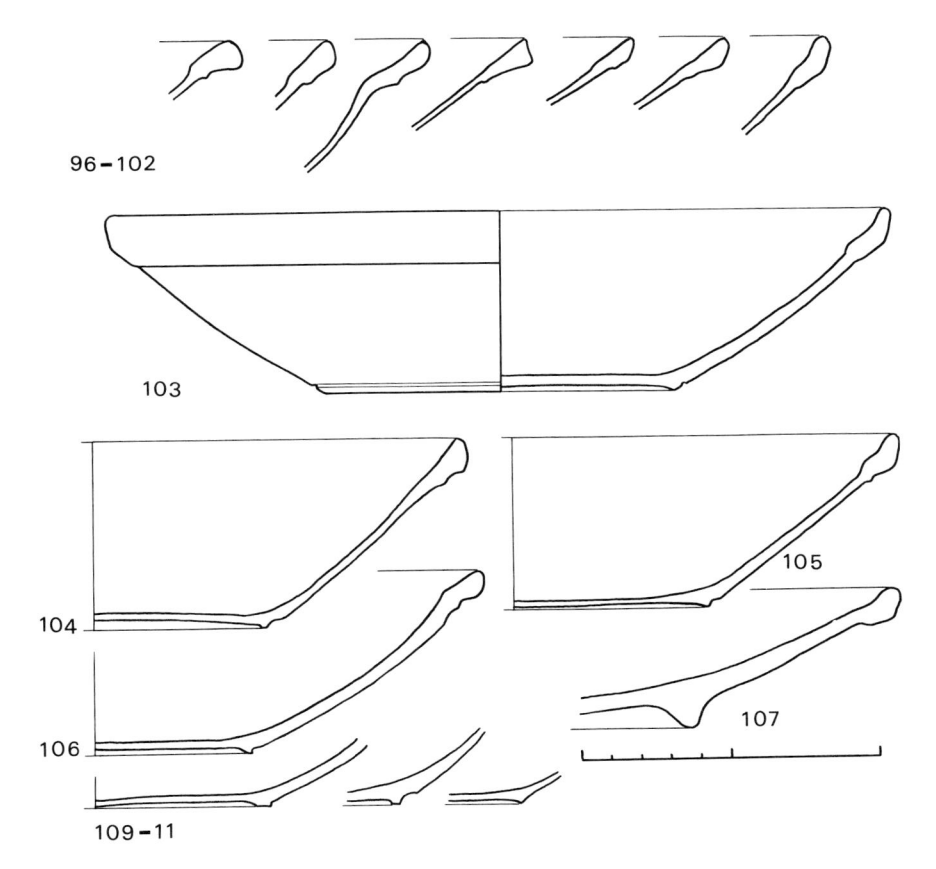

FIG. 29.

120. PLATE 21. Part of a jewelled cross. *LRP* Motif 77. Fortress debris, Room III.
121. PLATE 21. Cross and diamond. *LRP* Motif 34. Bas.
122. PLATE 21. Tail and legs of a bird (cock). Cf. Waage fig. 33. Bas.
123. PLATE 21. Hare. *LRP* Motif 35t. Bas. V, section 1 level (5b) DRAWING III (b).

124–130. The fabric is as Phocaean but the profiles seem unusual.

124. PLATE 21. Wall with bands of rouletting (usually confined to the lip in this fabric). SS.
125. FIG. 30. Rim. Cf. Waage nos. 930–2? Fort.
126. FIG. 30. Rim. Rather grey clay. Bas. B, section 9 level (2) FIG. 16.
127. FIG. 30. Rim. The outside discoloured. Cf. Waage no. 930a. Fort.
128. FIG. 30. Rim. Flat top with parallel incised wavy lines. Cf. Waage no. 924. Fortress floor. Trench K (1953).
129. FIG. 30. Rim. Early profile but fabric is Late Roman C. Fortress floor, Room I behind NW Tower.
130. FIG. 30. Rim of dish or lid; heavy profile. Fortress floor, Trench M.

African Red Slip Ware

For the fabric see Waage, 44f., *LRP* 13–14. The second commonest fabric for bowls at Emporio. Comparatively early examples are 131–3. The main series, 134–51, corresponds to Waage nos. 801–5, *LRP* 160–71, Forms 104–6, Suppl. 507–9. The seven complete examples (144–150) and many fragments from the destruction level of the fortress show that they belong to the latest years, the mid seventh century. They are uniformly shallow with heavy walls and rounded lips; their diameters are appreciably greater than the contemporary Phocaean bowls. The 'spiral burnishing' within, noted by Waage, 44, 51, appears on most examples and is marked on 145.

131. FIG. 30. Rim. Cf. Waage no. 873; Hesperia 11 (1942) pl. 9. 158. Early fifth century. Fort.
132. Rim. Cf. Waage nos. 881–3. Bas.
133. FIG. 30; PLATE 21. Base with stamped decoration of a man's head; cf. Waage, fig. 32. 5, the foot like no. 878. Bas.
134. FIG. 30. Rim. Diam. 38.0. Fort × 3; SS.
135. FIG. 30. Rim. Diam. 36.0. Fort × 7; Bas × 3; SS.
136. FIG. 30. Rim. Diam. 36.0. Fort × 2; Bas; SS.
137. FIG. 30. Rim. Diam. 36.0. Fort × 6; Bas; Pindakas.
138. FIG. 30. Rim. Diam. 26.0. Fort × 4; Bas.
139. FIG. 30. Rim. Diam. 40.0. Fort × 4; Bas; SS.
140. FIG. 30. Base. Diam. 14.0. Bas; Pindakas.
141. FIG. 30. Base. Bas × 2.
142. FIG. 30. Base. Diam. 16.0. Fort × 2; Bas.
143. FIG. 30. Base. Diam. 4.0. Bas; a very narrow ring base with steep walls; not an ordinary bowl, then.
144. FIG. 30. Complete bowl. Diam. 28.7. Fortress floor, Room IX.
145. FIG. 30. Complete bowl. Diam. 37.8. *LRP* Form 105, 16, fig. 32. Fortress floor, Room IX.
146. FIG. 30. Complete bowl. Diam. 38.6. Fortress floor, Room XI.
147. FIG. 30. Complete bowl. Diam. 33.8. Fortress floor, Room III.
148. FIG. 30. Complete bowl. Diam. 38.0. Fortress floor, Room I behind NW Tower.
149. FIG. 30. Complete bowl. Diam. 35.6. Fortress floor.
150. FIG. 30. Complete bowl. Diam. 40.6. LRP Form 105, 15, fig. 32. Fortress floor, Room IX.
151. FIG. 31. Rim with flat grooved top. Fort × 2.

Cypriot Red Slip Ware

The fabric is similar to that of the African red slip ware but the surface often somewhat greyer. Shape and the occasional double grooves on the rim are like Waage no. 970; *LRP* 379, Form 9, Suppl. 529. 153 and 157 are like Late Roman C fabric and on the analogy of the upright rims of 21–64 should be earlier sixth-century. Rouletting on the bodies of some (154, 158–161) seems

3. THE FINDS

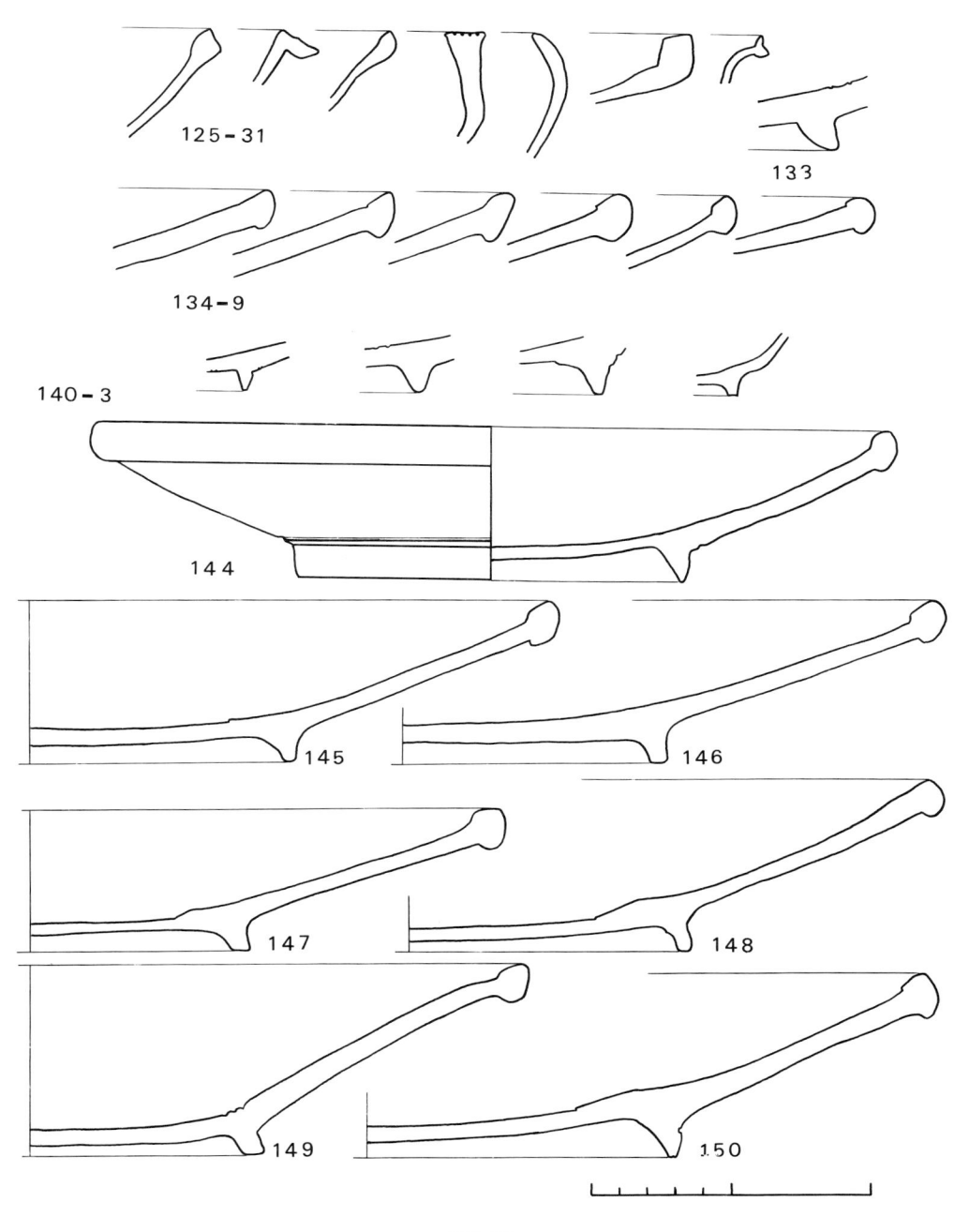

125-31

133

134-9

140-3

144

145

146

147

148

149

150

FIG. 30.

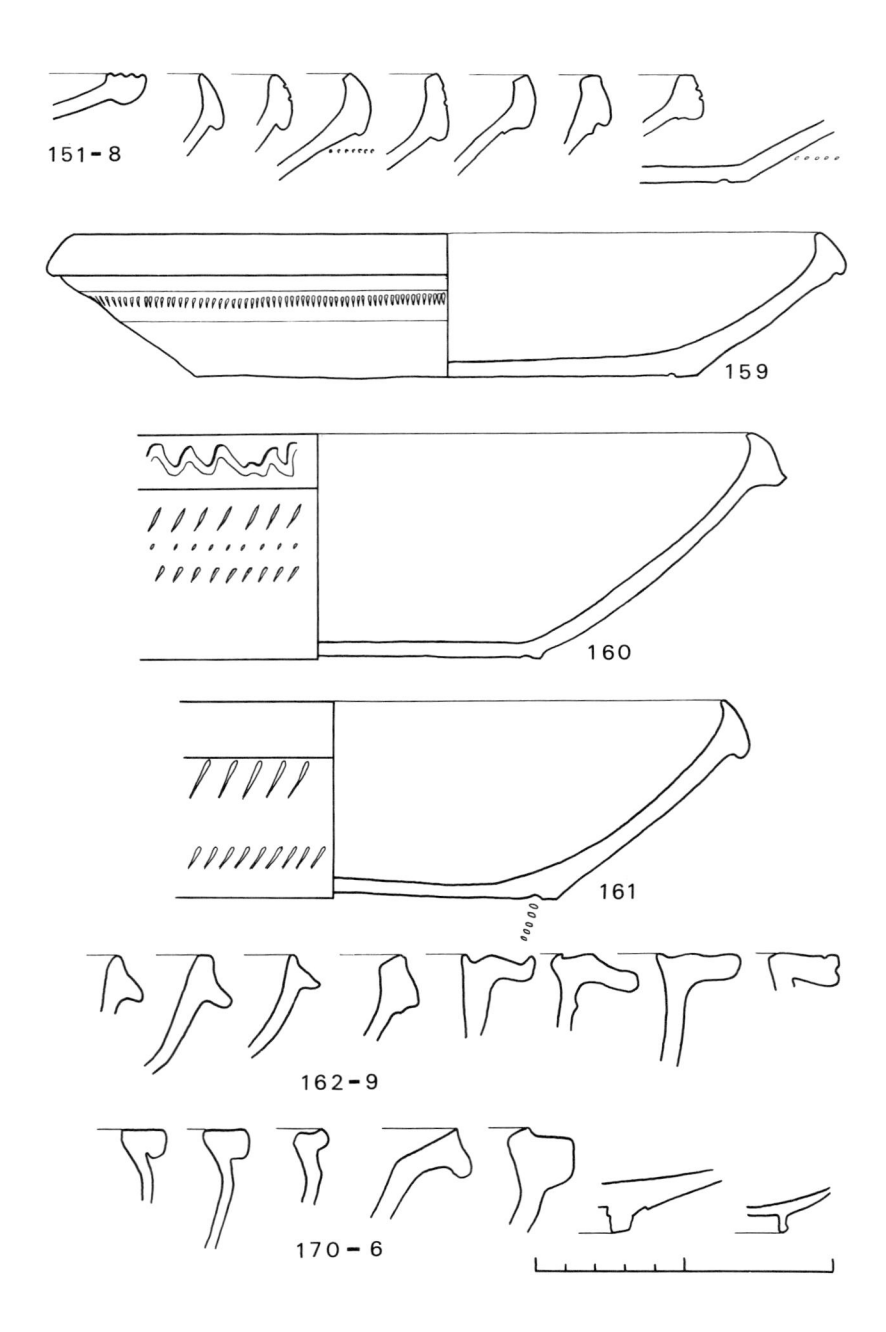

FIG. 31.

3. THE FINDS

to support this date though all three complete examples are from the fortress floor, so rouletting must have persisted on this class long after it was abandoned on the rims of Phocaean.

152. FIG. 31. Rim. Diam. 34.0. Fort × 2.
153. FIG. 31. Rim. Diam. 30.0. Fort × 3; Bas.
154. FIG. 31. Rim. Diam. 28.0. Fort × 3; one with dot rouletting below rim.
155. FIG. 31. Rim. Diam. 30.0. Bas × 2.
156. FIG. 31. Rim. Diam. 32.0. Fort × 2; Bas × 7; SS.
157. FIG. 31. Rim. Diam. 32.0. Bas; SS × 3.
158. FIG. 31. Base. Diam. 16.0. SS.
159. FIG. 31. Complete bowl. Diam. 26.6. LRP Form 9, 9, fig. 82. Fortress floor, NW Tower.
160. FIG. 31. Complete bowl. Diam. 31.2. LRP Form 9, 10, fig. 82. Fortress floor, Room IX.
161. FIG. 31. Complete bowl. Diam. 27.8. LRP Form 9, 11, fig. 82. Fortress floor, Room IX.

Other Fabrics

A dark brown micaceous clay was noted for 42, 46, and recurs in rims 162–5, more readily distinguished in profile from the types which they copy. The rims are formed by folding over the lip of the vase and not by rolling it in — the normal practice for Phocaean of this date. Rouletting appears below the rim on 163, 165. The date may be around the turn of the fifth and sixth centuries. A soft pink clay, fired far less well than Phocaean has been noted in the usual shapes and may represent an imitation (local?): see 22, 33, 35, 40, 43, 51, 75, 89, 93, 97, 101.

162. FIG. 31. Rim. SS × 2. One with graffito, FIG. 44 (i).
163. FIG. 31; PLATE 21. Rim. Fort × 2; SS; one with rouletting below rim.
164. FIG. 31. Rim. SS.
165. FIG. 31. Rim. SS; rouletting below rim.

Some bowl rims are in a pale micaceous clay, buff to pinkish-buff, one noted in a Phocaean shape (29). Most (166–169) are bowls with a flat, slightly overhanging rim whose top is usually grooved and sometimes decorated with incised zigzag or crosses (168). The shape as Waage nos. 856–9; *LRP* African red slip ware, 145–8, Form 93, late fifth to early sixth century. Some show clear signs of a brownish wash over the rim. The same fabric appears for some larger vases.

166. FIG. 31. Rim. Diam. 40.0. SS.
167. FIG. 31. Rim. Diam. 46.0. Fort × 3.
168. FIG. 31. Rim. Diam. 40.0. Fort × 2; SS.
169. FIG. 31. Rim. Diam. 40.0. Bas × 2.
170. FIG. 31. Rim. Diam. 30.0. Fort × 4.
171. FIG. 31. Rim. Diam. 30.0. SS.
172. FIG. 31. Rim. Diam. 20.0. The top of the lip with wavy incised lines. Fort.
173. FIG. 31. Rim. Diam. 32.0. Somewhat redder clay and dull cream slip. Cf. Waage no. 871. SS.
174. FIG. 31. Rim. Diam. 40.0. SS.
175. FIG. 31. Base. Diam. 20.0. Fort.
176. FIG. 31. Base. Diam. 12.0. Fort.
177. PLATE 21. Base with impressed star and dots pattern within. Buff clay with brownish wash on part of underside. Cf. the Çandarli pattern, *AM* xxxvii (1912) 375, fig. 6, 3. Bas.

The Other Vases

Virtually all the complete vases published here are from the destruction level of the fortress and were therefore in use in the mid seventh century AD. The study of Late Roman plain wares has yet to match that of the finer pottery although there have recently been some valuable summaries of types, as by S. J. Keay (*Late Roman Amphorae in the Western Mediterranean*, 1984) and the general survey by D. P. S. Peacock and D. F. Williams (*Amphorae and the Roman Economy*, 1986). A few complexes of pottery and other finds come close to the Emporio Fortress destruction in date and yield comparable finds of plain pottery. I list some which are geographically not too distant, and one or two others for the quality or relevance of their finds:

> The Byzantine wreck at Yassi-Ada. G. F. Bass et al., *Yassi-Ada* I (1982). The latest datable coin is AD 625/6. There is close resemblance to Emporio in plain and fine pottery and other finds.
> Istanbul. J. Hayes in *Dumbarton Oaks Papers* xxii (1968) 203–16. Dated deposits of ca. AD 650–670 with fine ware and cooking pots.
> Samos. A deposit in the Eupalinos tunnel. AA 1975, 26–35. Fine and plain ware, lamps.
> Cyprus, Kornos Cave. H. W. Catling, *Levant* ii (1970) 37–62. Mid-seventh century. Fine and plain wares and metalwork.
> Anemurium (Cilicia Tracheia). C. Williams, *Anatolian Studies* xxvii (1977) 175–90. A well, with a coin of AD 631; the site abandoned in AD 660. Fine ware and lids.
> Argos (destroyed AD 585). *Etudes Argiennes* (*BCH* Suppl. 6, 1980). Fine and plain ware, lamps.
> Benghazi. J. A. Riley in *Sidi-Khrebish* II (1979) for plain ware; P. M. Kenrick in III.1 (1985) for fine ware.
> Carthage. J. Hayes in *Excavations at Carthage 1976; Michigan Univ.* IV (1978) 43–63. Deposits XXI–V. Arab capture in AD 698.

There is some variety of fabric in the vases listed here but they are presented by shape and detailed problems of source cannot be entered into. The few vases which belong to the ninth-century reoccupation are kept separate, and there are very few catalogued pieces which are earlier than the last period of occupation in the fortress. There are some notable overall differences between these vases and comparable material from the Greek mainland, which is true also of the lamps found at Emporio. This indicates the cultural rift in this period between mainland Greece, which was on the whole not enjoying great prosperity, and the Asia Minor coast and islands which profited from the active commerce in the eastern Mediterranean before the Arab invasions.

One-Handled Jugs

These are the commonest small vases from the destruction level. 178–184 have broad flat bases from which the walls rise at first almost vertically. 185–196 have narrower bases with swelling bodies; among them the high neck of 196 is noteworthy. 197 and 198 have exceptionally narrow bases and ribbed fusiform bodies. 199–202 are unusual in having impressed bases. Grooves on the shoulder and the occasional use of the comb is all that is found by way of decoration. Handles are all rather heavy straps with a slight finger-groove on the outside. They compare poorly with the bodies of the vases in construction. The fabric varies considerably and

FIG. 32.

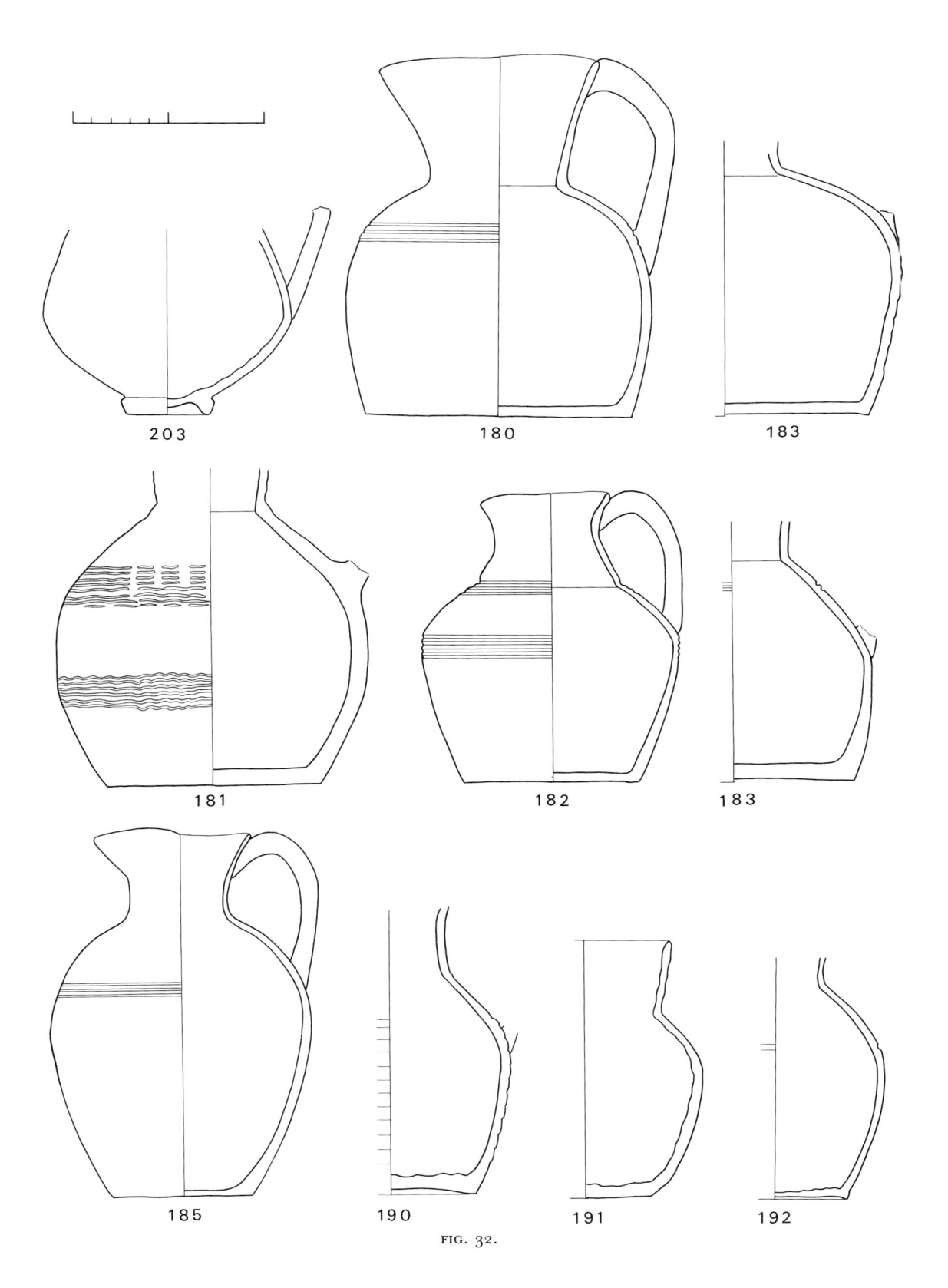

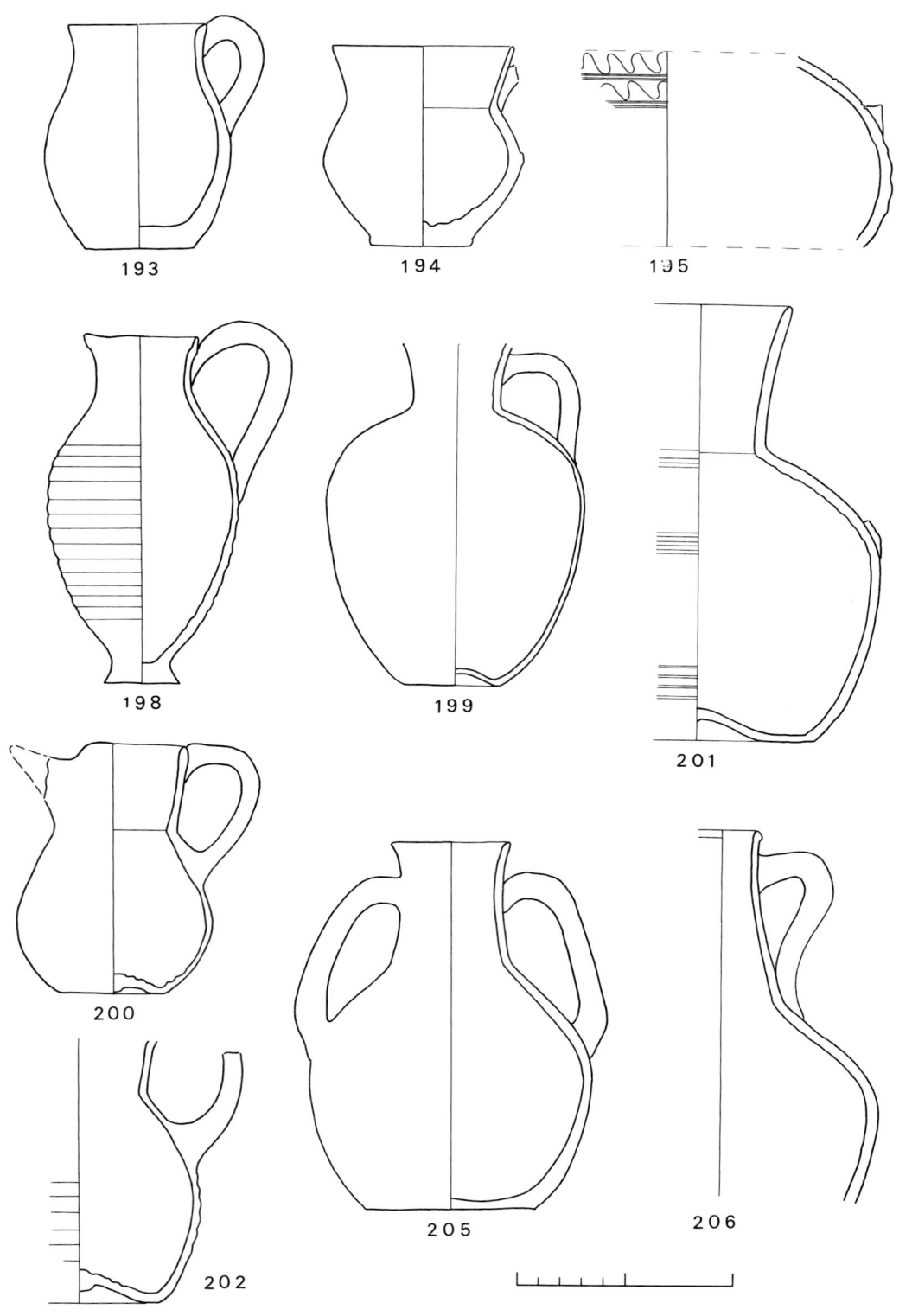

FIG. 33.

many must be imports. But for an occasional lumpy or carelessly fixed handle they are well-made vases. The trefoil lip is almost invariable.

There are close parallels for the flat-bottomed jugs 178–84 in *Yassi-Ada* I 168–72, P14–23, and with impressed bases, 199–202, ibid., P24–8, 32. Cf. also *Sidi-Khrebish* II 395–6 (flat bases); the Kornos Cave, *Levant* ii (1970) fig. 3. 5–10 (impressed bases); *Athenian Agora* V, pl. 35, N1–11.

178. PLATE 22. H. 21.0. Trefoil mouth; two grooves at shoulder; pale red clay. Fortress floor, Room XX.
179. PLATE 22. H. 20.01; neck missing. Three groups of wavy incised lines on body; pink micaceous clay. Fortress floor, Room XI.
180. FIG. 32. H. 19.5. Probably trefoil mouth; triple groove on body; pinkish grey clay. Fortress floor, Room XI. An identical jug from Room XX.
181. FIG. 32. Presd. H. 17.3; part of lip and handle missing. Two broad bands of wavy incised lines on body and graffito XAP on shoulder (FIG. 44, ix). Fortress floor, Room XI.
182. FIG. 32. H. 16.0; part of lip, probably trefoil, missing. Red brown clay. Fortress floor, Room XI.
183. FIG. 32. Presd. H. 15.0; neck missing. Pinkish grey clay. Fortress floor, Room XI.
184. FIG. 32. Presd. H. 14.4; lip, probably trefoil, and part of handle mssing. Double groove at shoulder; pinkish gray clay. Fortress floor, Room IX. An identical jug from Room XI.
185. FIG. 32; PLATE 22. H. 19.7; part of lip missing. Triple groove on body; pinkish buff clay. Fortress floor, Room I behind NW Tower. Similar jug from Room IX.
186. PLATE 22. H. 17.6. Trefoil mouth and narrow neck. Grooved lightly at neck; grey buff clay. Fortress floor, Room XX.
187. PLATE 23. H. 16.4. Trefoil mouth. Red grey clay. Fortress floor, Room IX.
188. PLATE 23. H. 15.0. Trefoil mouth. Pink-buff fabric. Fortress floor, Room XX.
189. PLATE 22. H. 24.0. Trefoil mouth. Body lightly grooved and deliberate light depressions in the wall of the vase around the shoulder; pale red clay. Fortress floor, Room IX.
190. FIG. 32. Presd. H. 15.8; lip missing, trefoil. Lightly ribbed body; gritty pink clay. Fortress floor, Room IX.
191. FIG. 32. H. 14.0. Presumably from a one-handler; pink clay. Fortress floor, NW Tower.
192. FIG. 32. Presd. H. 13.2. Narrow-necked, probably one-handler, neck missing. Fine pink-buff clay. Fortress, Cistern in Trench C, upper levels.
193. FIG. 33. H. 10.0. Round mouth; rather heavy walled; pinkish-grey clay. Fortress floor, Trench M.
194. FIG. 33. H. 9.6; part of handle and lip missing; pinkish buff clay. Fortress floor, Room XX.
195. FIG. 33. Fragment with incised wavy line decoration on shoulder. Fortress floor, Room IX.
196. PLATE 22. H. 18.5. Trefoil mouth, high neck. Grey-buff clay. Fortress floor, Room IX.
197. PLATE 22. H. 17.0. Lightly ribbed body. Fine grey clay. Removing Fortress wall, Room XII.
198. FIG. 33. H. 17.5. Lightly ribbed body. Buff-pink clay. Fortress floor, Room XI.
199. FIG. 33; PLATE 23. H. presd. 33.0; part of lip missing. Incised on the shoulder THEODOTOU (FIG. 44, iii). Fortress floor, Room IX.
200. FIG. 33; PLATE 23. H. 12.2. Trefoil mouth, rounded base, part of lip missing. Greyish red clay. Fortress floor, Room IX.
201. FIG. 33. H. 21.0. Flaring neck and cavity in base. Groups of grooves on body; part of lip and handle missing. Pinkish red clay. Fortress floor, NW Tower.
202. FIG. 33. Orig. H. ca. 14.4; part of neck missing. Trefoil mouth, rounded base. Pinkish grey clay. Fortress floor, Room XI.
203. FIG. 32. Presd. H. 11.3. Ring foot. Fine buff clay with slip. This may be appreciably earlier than the jugs from the fortress, the only one with a true ring foot. Bas. X, from patch of yellow sandy soil which may be same as section 6 level (5) FIG. 15.
204. Fragments from jugs with gouged patterns, vertical or slanting slashes running across the ribbed walls. In Athens this decoration is found on vases of the 4th to 6th centuries AD.

Two-Handled Jugs

205. FIG. 33; PLATE 23. H. 18.0. Pinkish grey clay. Cf. *Yassi-Ada* I 181–2 P70. Fortress floor, Trench M.
206. FIG. 33. Presd. H. 18.5; base missing. Flask with narrow neck and probably two handles; red clay. Fortress floor, Room IX.
207. PLATE 23. H. 21.0. Two grooves at shoulder. Pink grey clay. Fortress floor, Room IX.

FIG. 34.

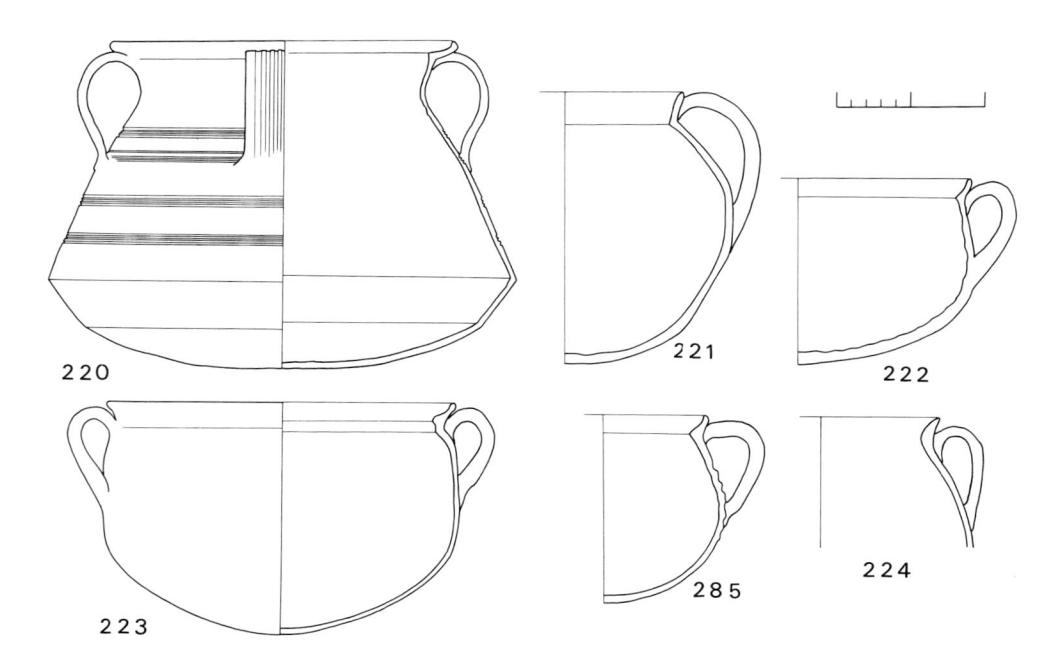

FIG. 35.

3. THE FINDS

Spouted Jugs

Only two specimens were found, one with two handles, one with one. They have the usual coarse strap handles and flat bases. Cf. *Yassi-Ada* I 173 P35–7.

208. PLATE 23. H. 17.3; end of spout missing. Two handles. Pinkish grey clay. Fortress floor, Room XXII.
209. PLATE 23. H. 14.5.; end of spout preserved. One handle. Coarse buff-pink clay. Fortress floor, Room IX.

Cups and Mugs

The thin-walled handleless cups, 210–2, were among the few smaller clay vases found. Their most distinctive feature is the hollow sinking within the foot. 213 has a single handle and is equally well made.

210. FIG. 34. H. 8.4. Thin, lightly grooved walls. Pink clay. Cf. *Yassi-Ada* I 171, 173, P34. Fortress floor, Room IX.
211. FIG. 34. Presd. H. 7.7. Upper half of handleless cup, as 210. Pinkish grey clay. Fortress floor, Room XII.
212. FIG. 34. Presd. H. 4.5. Base of handleless cup as 210 but larger. Pinkish grey clay. Fortress floor, beside Cistern, in Trench C.
213. FIG. 34. H. 7.0. Thin-walled. Fine pinkish grey clay. Fortress floor, NW Tower.

Open Jars and Dishes

These vary in size from the great basin in a familiar pale micaceous clay to small bowls and dishes for the table. Apart from the pithoi there were few open vessels and the finer red bowls probably served a considerable variety of purposes. Note that 217 antedates the fortress.

214. FIG. 34. H. 2.4. Small open bowl. Pinkish grey clay. Fortress floor, Room XVIII.
215. FIG. 34. H. 4.0. Small open bowl. Grooves below lip. Fine pink clay. Removing Fortress wall, Room XIX–XX.
216. FIG. 34. Diam. 28.0. Flat circular dish. Highly micaceous pink-buff clay. Fortress floor, Room IX.
217. FIG. 34. Diam. 46.0. Flat circular dish. Zigzag in low relief on underside. Pale pink micaceous clay. Below the fortress floor, Room XII.
218. FIG. 37. Presd. H. 22.0a. Open jar with incised wavy lines at neck. A scrap of the base shows that it was simple and flat but the diameter could not be determined. Good pink clay. Fortress floor, Room IX.
219. FIG. 38. Presd. H. 28.0, diam. at rim 56.0. Upper walls of a large basin. Highly micaceous pink-brown clay with a pale cream slip. Fortress floor, Room IX.

Cooking Pots

All have two handles and round bases but for the four-handled 220, which is a close imitation of a metal cauldron. Lip profiles vary, but only little, and size is fairly constant. The lumpy strap handles have a central finger groove. Many more fragments of these pots were recovered but the profiles were repetitive. As well as those catalogued, complete specimens were found on the fortress floor in Rooms IX (seven) and XI–XII (one). Cf. *Yassi-Ada* I 175–7.

220. FIG. 35; PLATE 24. Diam. at rim 23.6; H. 23.0. Red micaceous clay. The only four-handler and in a fabric superior to the others. Fortress floor, Room IX.
221. FIG. 35. H. 19.0, diam. at rim 16.0. Coarse grey clay. Fortress floor, NW Tower.
222. FIG. 35; PLATE 24. H. 13.0, diam. at rim 23.5. Gritty pink clay. Fortress floor, Room XII.
223. FIG. 35. H. 16.0, diam. at rim 23.0. Gritty pink clay. Fortress floor, Room IX.
224. FIG. 35. H. presd. 9.0, diam. at rim 16.0. Coarse red clay. Fortress floor, NW Tower.

Amphorae

The largest from the fortress period have cylindrical bodies with a knob foot (225–231). On the largest shown here (231) the foot knob is replaced by a simple blunt end. 231 has a simple rounded foot. 225 is the commonest type of tall amphora from Fortress destruction floors. Both 225 and 231 have their surfaces pared by vertical strokes of a knife which have left shallow striations or flutes, and on 225 at least the vase was subsequently coated with a pale cream slip. This scraping technique is met in various periods. It recurs in the class of smaller slim amphorae (232–5) which resemble nothing more than a rolled umbrella. The clay is different, pink or buff, and none seem to have been more than about half a metre high. That larger were made is shown by a specimen found in the sea, now in Chios Museum, 95.0 high and with the same scraped sides. The commonest type from the fortress floor is a broad jar with rounded base, its width nearly as great as its height (236–9). Representative examples are listed here. On these is found the characteristic incised pattern generally given the title 'combed ware', typical of Late Roman coarse pottery, though not always thought to have persisted as long as the Emporio finds suggest. The term is deceptive since close inspection shows that the decoration was effected with a single point held against the body of the vase and slowly raised in a continuous spiral while the vase was turned on the wheel. Subsequently some incisions were smoothed away above and below, leaving a band of ridges apparently applied with a comb. The spiral can be traced on complete specimens, and there is no evidence for a comb being placed on or lifted from the surface. The slightly irregular wavy effect is also found often to be inconsistent in adjacent rows. A wave effect could also be produced by lightly flattening the ridges in an upward or downward direction. The decoration preceded the fixing of the handles. Combs were used on other shapes, and appear on some of these broad amphorae but only to produce spaced groups of four or five parallel straight lines (238), and they could produce much more regular wave patterns than the single point. 240 is an example but unique in the finds.

Of the other amphorae 242 is unusual in having an impressed base and 241 looks forward to the type used in the reoccupation period (280–1). 243 is an import from Palestine as may be 226. Many of the others, except perhaps 240, could have been made on Chios, but the location of their origins requires an analysis and expertise to which the material has not as yet been subjected.

All are of types well familiar from other Late Roman sites. Cf. Peacock and Williams, Class 43 for 236–9; Class 44 (once thought Egyptian, probably Levantine) for predecessors of the reoccupation amphorae 280–1; Class 46 for the Palestinian 243 and compare 226 with Class 48/9 of the same probable origin; Class 51 for the slim 232–5; Class 54 for 241. At Yassi-Ada (I 155–60) Amphora Type 1 is the predecessor of our 280, and Type 2 closely matches our 236–40. At Sidi-Khrebish (II 226–7) there are examples of 233–5.

225. PLATE 24. H. 97.0. Coarse red clay with pale cream slip. The walls scraped vertically. Fortress floor, NW Tower.
226. FIG. 36. Presd. H. 90.0; neck missing and the handles appear unusually below the shoulder of the vase. Fortress floor, NW Tower.
227. FIG. 36. Neck and foot; H. of neck 22.0, of foot 12.0. Fine pale pink clay. Fortress floor, Room XX.
228. FIG. 38. Neck; presd. H. 21.0. Coarse red-grey clay. Graffito (FIG. 45, xvii). Fortress floor, Room XX.
229. FIG. 36. Rounded foot; presd. H. 11.4. Coarse grey clay. Fortress floor, Room XI.
230. FIG. 36. Toe of amphora; pink-grey clay. Graffito (FIG. 45, viii). Fortress floor, Room VIII.
231. FIG. 38; PLATE 24. H. 108.5. Pink-grey clay with white inclusions. Scraped, as 225. Fortress floor, NW Tower.
232. PLATE 25. Slim amphora. H. 41.0. Buff clay. The walls scraped vertically. Fortress floor, Room IX.
233. FIG. 37. Slim amphora, original H. ca. 52.0. Pale buff clay. Fortress floor, Room XI.

3. THE FINDS

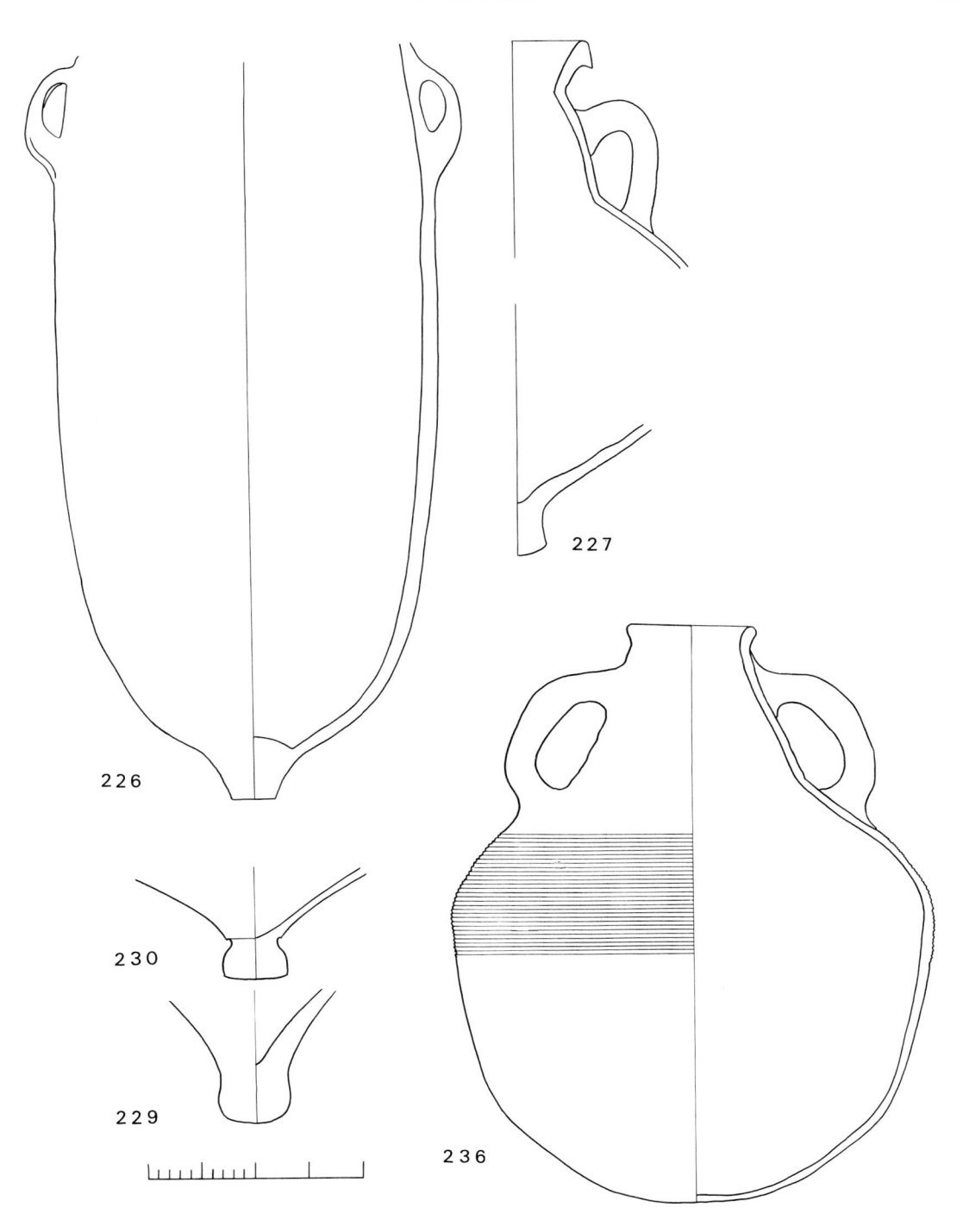

226

227

230

229

236

FIG. 36.

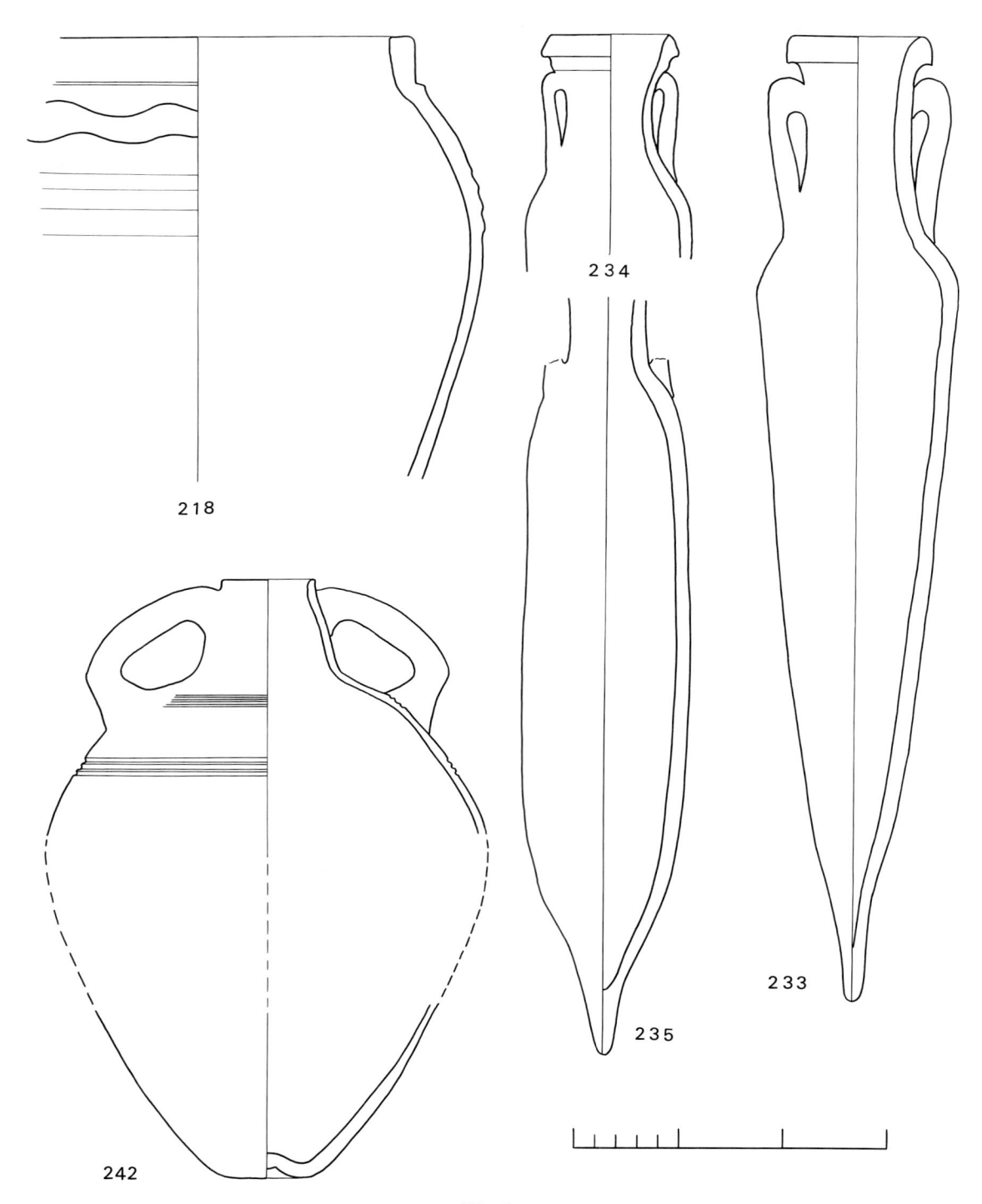

FIG. 37.

234. FIG. 37. Upper half of slim amphora, presd. H. 16.0. Very pale buff clay. Fortress floor, Room XII.
235. FIG. 37. Slim amphora, presd. H. 38.0; lip missing. Pinkish buff clay. Fortress floor.
236. FIG. 36; PLATE 24. H. 56.0. Broad amphora with broad band of incised wavy lines on body. Coarse orange red clay. Graffito (FIG. 45, xxiv). Fortress floor, NW Tower.
237. PLATE 24. H. 58.5. As the last but the decorated area is greater. Fortress floor. Another example is in a finer micaceous pink-buff clay: Bas. T sections 1 and 2 level (2a) DRAWING III (b) and FIG. 13.
238. PLATE 25. H. 48.5. Broad amphora with parallel groups of straight incised lines on the upper body. Pink-buff clay. Fortress floor, Room XII. Other examples with this decoration in Rooms IX (two), XIV, XVI and XI.
239. FIG. 38. Presd. H. 15.0; amphora neck. Reddish grey clay. Fortress floor, Room XXII.
240. PLATE 25. H. 46.0. Broad amphora with broad bands of comb-incised straight and wavy lines on upper body. Pale red clay. Graffito KOC on shoulder (FIG. 44, x). Fortress floor, Room IX.
241. PLATE 25. H. 45.0. Amphora with deep grooves on body. Pinkish buff clay. Fortress floor, Room IX. An identical example on the floor of the same room.
242. FIG. 37. Original H. ca. 30.0. Amphora with lightly impressed base; part of body missing. Parallel grooves at the shoulder. Flaky red clay. Fortress floor, Room XI.
243. PLATE 25. H. 46.0. Amphora with spiral ribbing at shoulder and grooved body. Pink-buff clay with pale cream slip. Fortress floor, Room IX.

Pithoi

Storage pithoi were found in almost all parts of the fortress, many near-complete, and scraps were found elsewhere on the site, especially near the Basilica. They were all stout, flat-bottomed jars without handles, most with a simple lip, roughly triangular in section. Sometimes ribs are found on the walls but the usual decoration is of incised wavy lines, single or multiple, applied with a comb, on the upper body and sometimes on the top of the lip. One only had painted decoration of irregular lines and loops (257). The clay is consistent, probably local: generally coarse, from pink to red-brown, sometimes with the grey core noted in earlier Chian wares. Exceptions are some with distinctive lip profiles having a heavy horizontal ledge on two (259, 261) and a heavily folded lip on another (258), and the highly micaceous pink-buff clay noted in some smaller vases. These may be imports. Only one pithos preserved evidence of its contents — 248, with burnt beans in its base. Some of the larger jars had been mended with simple lead clamps. The practice was common in antiquity and was mentioned by various writers (cf. *RE* s.v. 'Blei' 563).

244. FIG. 38. H. 46.0, diam. at rim 34.5. Wavy incised lines at shoulder and on top of lip. Gritty red-brown clay fired grey in core. Fortress floor, Room IX.
245. FIG. 38. Rim, diam. 64.0. Wavy incised lines below lip and grooves on its top. Coarse red clay. Fortress floor, Room I behind NW Tower.
246. FIG. 38. Rim, diam. 52.0. Lightly incised wavy lines between shallow grooves on top of lip. Fortress floor, Room I behind NW Tower. Similar decoration on fragments from Room XIX.
247. FIG. 38. H. 72.0, diam. at rim 54.0. Wavy incised lines on shoulder above a light ridge. Coarse pink clay. Fortress floor, NW Tower.
248. FIG. 38. Fragments from lip, body and base. Diam. at rim 48.0. Coarse pink clay. About one kilo of burnt beans found within. Fortress floor, Trench M.
249. FIG. 38. Upper part of pithos, diam. at rim 48.0. Lightly incised arcades on shoulder and on either side of two incised lines enclosing a rope pattern formed by transverse strokes. Fortress floor, Trench M.
250. FIG. 39. Upper part of pithos, diam. at rim ca. 55.0. Wavy incised lines on shoulder above a flat applied band. Coarse red clay. Fortress floor, Room VIII. Similar fragments from Room XIX.
251. FIG. 39. Fragments of lip and base, diam. at rim ca. 40.0. On shoulder ribs and wavy incised lines. Coarse red-brown clay, pink at surface. Fortress floor, Room XIX. Cf., the lid 272.
252. FIG. 38. Fragments of lip, body and foot, diam. at rim 54.0. Wavy incised lines at intervals of about 4.0 apparently over the whole of the body. Pink clay. Fortress floor, Room VIII.
253. FIG. 39. Rim, diam. 48.0. Coarse red clay. Fortress floor, Room XX. Two other examples of similar profile from same floor and Room XIX (one rim diam. 42.5)

254. FIG. 39. H. 58.0, diam. at rim 33.2. Gritty red clay. Graffiti (FIG. 45, xxvi). Fortress floor, Room XI.
255. FIG. 39. Base missing; presd. H. 61.0, diam. at rim 40.0. Three groups of four incised lines on upper body. Micaceous pinkish buff clay. Fortress floor, Room XII.
256. FIG. 39. Upper part of pithos, diam. at rim 37.2. Wavy incised lines at shoulder. Coarse brown clay, grey at core. Fortress floor, Room XX. A similar example from Room I behind NW Tower (diam. at rim ca. 40.0)
257. Fragments of a pithos bearing irregular painted decoration of red lines and loops. No lip or base preserved. Fortress floor, Room I behind NW Tower.
258. FIG. 39. Rim, diam. 80.0 (the flat base of either this or 261 had a diam. 36.0). Micaceous pink-buff clay. Fortress floor, Room I behind NW Tower.
259. FIG. 39. Rim, diam. 64.0. Traces of paint in angle above projecting ledge of rim: the edge of this projecting member bears an isolated group of eleven incised strokes, perhaps a tally of the jar's contents. Micaceous pink-buff clay. Fortress floor, Room I behind NW Tower.
260. FIG. 39. Upper part of pithos, diam. at rim 50.0. Incised wavy and straight lines on shoulder with light rib bearing a rope pattern of transverse notches. Micaceous pink clay. Fortress floor, Trench M.
261. FIG. 39. Rim and base of pithos, diam. at rim 60.6. Micaceous pink-buff clay. Bas. MM section 3 level (6) FIG. 13.

Lids and Stoppers

The commonest stopper for small-mouthed jars was a disc cut roughly from the wall of a broken amphora or pithos. Thirty of these were found in the fortress and five in the Basilica. Their size varies from a diameter of 5.0 to 18.0, the smaller being predominant. In only two cases was a hole cut in the disc near its edge, and these may have been weights of some sort. (Cf. *Yassi-Ada* I 160–1 for similar stoppers.) A few worn amphora stumps of fourth-century BC type were found in Roman levels and may have been similarly employed since their shapes lent themselves well to this purpose. Two specimens are shown in PLATE 25 A (diams. 6.2 and 3.8; the whirligig of notches was for the attachment of the conical toe to the body). Other lids range from small well-made concave discs with knob handles to great and coarse pithos lids up to 76.0 in diameter. Finger patterns and incised lines are the only decoration and incised lines are the only decoration but for an occasional graffito and the unique incised birds on 278. Handles are either central knobs or a simple loop. The clay is that of the pithoi, a coarse pink or red, often fired grey at the core, except for 262–4, of better levigated red clay.

262. FIG. 40. With knob handle. Diam. 16.0. Fortress floor, Room I behind NW Tower.
263. FIG. 40. With knob handle. Diam. 15.0. Fortress floor, NW Tower.
264. FIG. 40. With knob handle. Diam. 14.6. Fortress floor, Room III.
265. FIG. 41. With narrow knob handle. Diam. 15.6. Decorated with four 'spokes' of thumb-nail impressions. Fortress floor, NW Tower.
266. FIG. 42. With knob handle. Diam. 24.0. Graffiti. Fortress floor, Room IX.
267. FIG. 41. Fragment with knob handle. Spoke decoration of double rows of impressed points. Fortress, Room XIV–XV surface.
268. FIG. 41. Fragment of lid with knob handle. Impressed finger-tip decoration.
269. FIG. 42. With loop handle. Diam. 22.5. Irregularly decorated with small impressed circles.
270. FIG. 41. Fragment with stump of loop handle. Concentric lines of impressed 'pips'.
271. FIG. 42. With loop handle. Diam. 32.8. Concentric grooves and wavy line. Fortress floor, Room IX.
272. FIG. 42. With loop handle. Diam. 40.0. Triple grooves in spokes and arcs. Fortress floor, Room XIX. With pithos 253 (rim diam. ca. 40.0).
273. FIG. 41. With loop handle. Diam. 19.0. Crude incised tree pattern. Micaceous gritty pink clay. Fortress floor, Room XII.
274. FIG. 42. With stump of loop handle. Diam. 59.2. Parallel impressed wavy lines and graffito (FIG. 44, viii). Fortress floor, NW Tower.
275. FIG. 41. Fragment with irregular decoration of impressed circles and cross pattern. (Cf. *Hesperia* iii (1934) 293 no. 283)

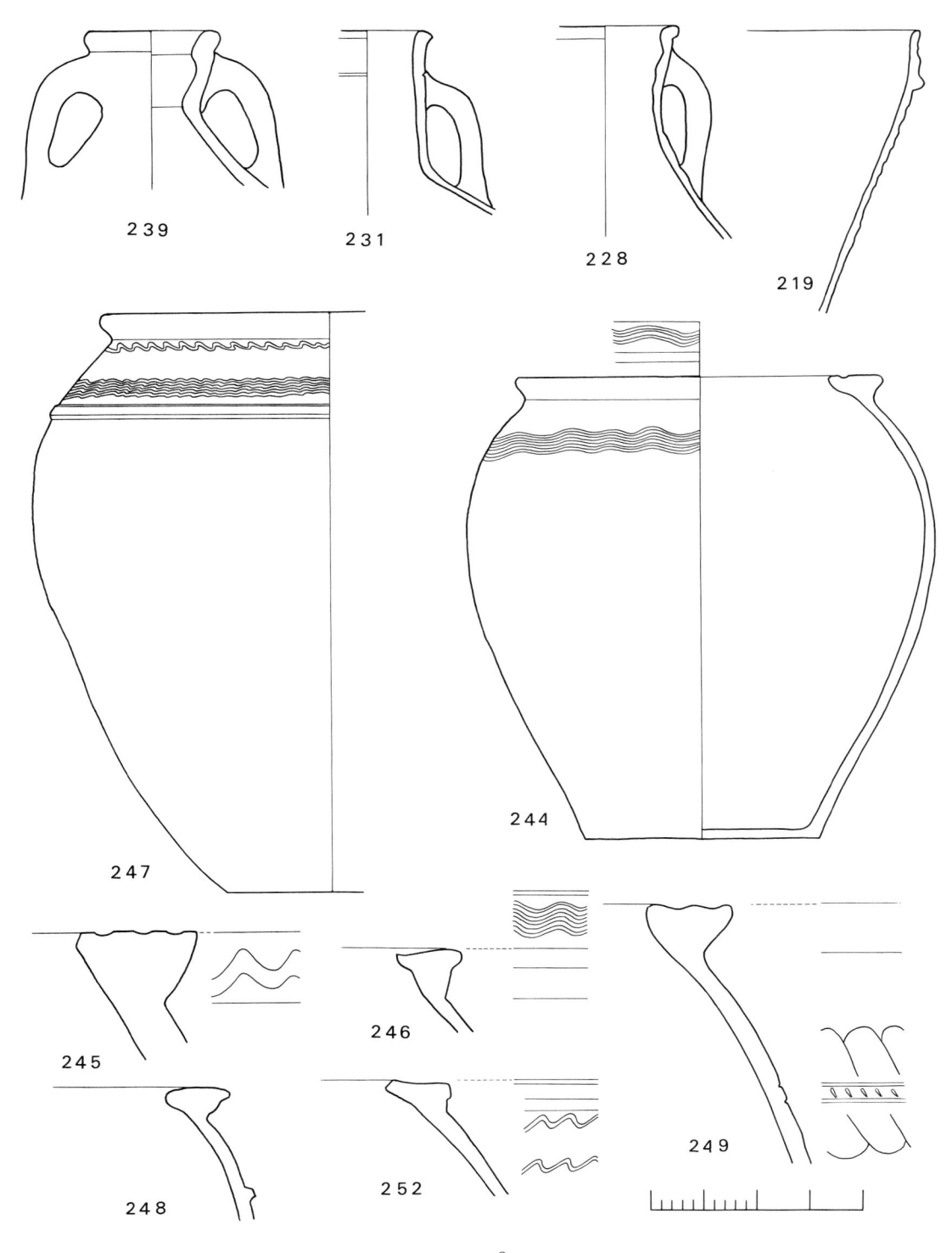

FIG. 38.

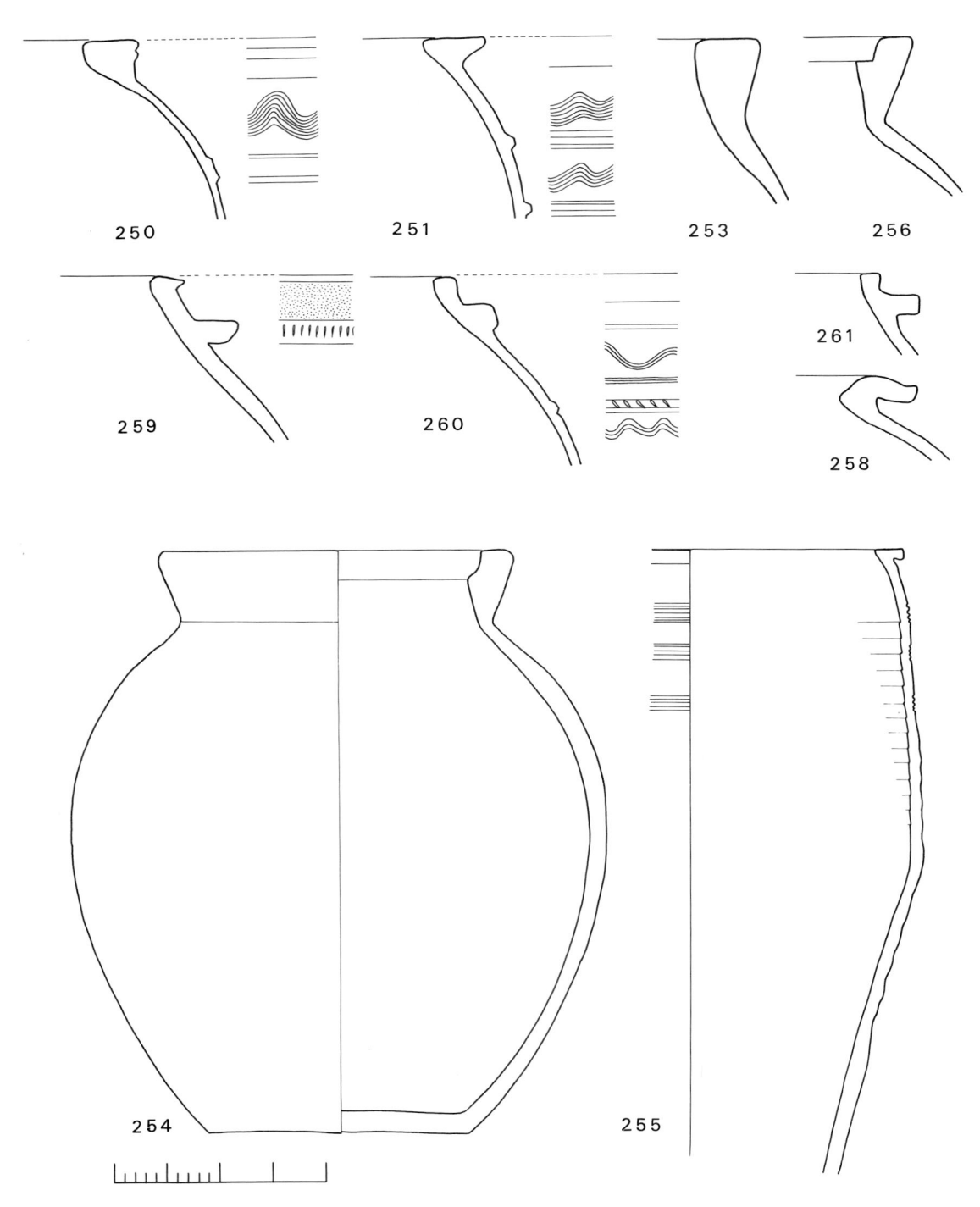

FIG. 39.

3. THE FINDS 113

276. FIG. 41. Fragment with concentric lines of impressed circles.
277. FIG. 42. Fragment, diam. 22.0; handle missing. Parallel incised wavy lines. Fortress floor, Room XX.
278. FIG. 42. Fragments, diam. 76.0. Irregular incised decoration of wavy lines and three birds. Pale clay. Fortress floor, Room III. Many other fragments of undecorated lids of this type were found, not deserving individual attention. Eight with loop handles from the fortress floors have diameters from 15.0 to 26.0, and one larger (diam. 52.0) with a loop handle in a rather pale buff clay. Two with knob handles have diameters 30.0 and 34.0.

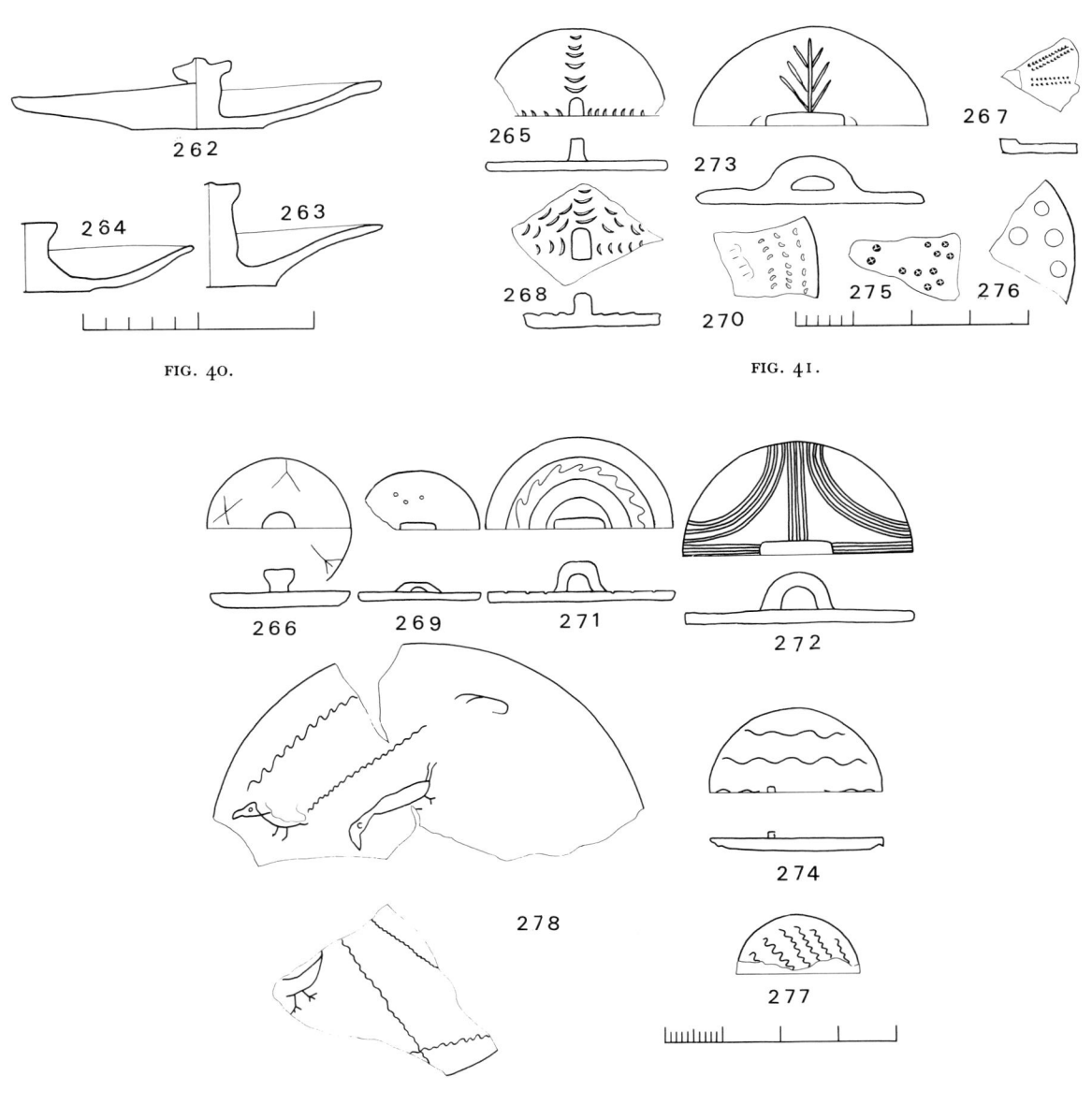

FIG. 40.

FIG. 41.

FIG. 42.

Brazier

279. PLATE 26. H. 13.0, diam. at base 19.0, walls ca. 2.0 thick. Five semicircular openings at the sides and a circular one at the top. Coarse pale red clay; no signs of burning. Fortress floor, Room IX.

Reoccupation Period Vases

The following are the only distinctive shapes associated with the reoccupation of the fortress in the ninth century AD, a date indicated by coins on the floors with the vases. Similar vases attest reoccupation also in the Basilica. The commonest shape is the round-bottomed amphora whose profile changed little since the seventh century though the lower body is narrower and pinched and the walls irregularly grooved, 280–1 (for these see the discussion of the Fortress period amphorae, above). The only storage jar (282) is unlike its predecessors in having a pointed foot. Cooking pots (284–5) have changed little. The jug 286 is included for the grooved walls, like the amphorae; it was associated with reoccupation levels but not from a floor.

280. FIG. 43; PLATE 25. H. 44.0. Amphora with lightly grooved body. Burned to a grey throughout; the lip rather squashed by the setting of the handles. Graffito (FIG. 45, xxvii). Fortress reoccupation floor, Room IX.
281. FIG. 43. H. 48.5. Amphora with lightly grooved body. Pink clay. Fortress reoccupation floor, Room XIV.
282. FIG. 43. H. 74.8. Pithos with pointed base. Highly micaceous coarse red clay. Fortress reoccupation floor, Room XV.
283. FIG. 43; PLATE 26. H. Presd. 35.4. Handled jar. Micaceous red clay. Fortress reoccupation floor, Room XII.
284. FIG. 43. Presd. H. 12.5, diam. at rim 15.0; base missing. Two-handled cooking pot. Micaceous red clay, burned grey in parts. Fortress reoccupation floor, Room IX.
285. FIG. 35; PLATE 25. H. 13.0, diam. at rim 14.0. Cooking pot. Coarse red clay fired grey in places. Basilica reocccupation floor. Bas. FF, above reoccupation (Period II) floor in NW corner of Anteroom to Baptistry. Cf. 287.
286. FIG. 43. Presd. H. 12.5. Upper part of jug, probably one-handled. Deeply rippled walls. Reddish clay fired grey at core. Fortress reoccupation floor, Room III.
287. PLATE 25. H. 9.5. Mug. Coarse red clay. Basilica reoccupation floor. Context as 285.

Glazed Ware

288–90 are from a Tomb III within the Chapel in the fortress. The church was built long after the fortress and the pottery is the only evidence for its date. The tomb had been plundered but the decorated vases were probably part of its original furnishing. The decoration of 288–9 and the shapes of all can be paralleled in a group of vases from a cistern in the Athenian Agora, published by Alison Frantz in *Hesperia* vii (1938) 431ff. (Group A, Period II), suggesting a date in the eleventh century, probably in the first half. 291 may be an example of a local ware.

288. FIG. 43; PLATE 26. Presd. H. 10.0. Part of one-handled jug. Black and a slightly lustrous dark green on a dull white ground. Good red clay. This is the 'Black and Green Painted Ware' described by Frantz, op. cit., 430; for the shape cf. ibid., 441, fig. 4, A21, and the spiral decoration, 442, fig. 5, A18. From the Fortress Chapel Tomb III.
289. PLATE 26. From the lip of an open bowl. Mottled grey decoration on a pale cream ground within. Outside, cream stripes only. Good red clay. From the Fortress Chapel Tomb III.
290. PLATE 26. From a flat dish with upturned rim. Yellow-white and a greenish brown glaze. Outside, glaze stripes. Good red clay. 'Slip-painted Ware'; Frantz, op. cit. 431; for the pattern cf. *Hesperia* iii (1934) 324 fig. 18a,b. From the Fortress Chapel Tomb III.
291. FIG. 43; PLATE 26. From the rim of an upright-walled bowl. Dull black paint on pale greenish white slip. No paint within. Impure red-brown clay. A slight thickening at the bottom of the sherd may suggest the proximity of a handle. Fortress, Trench V, south.

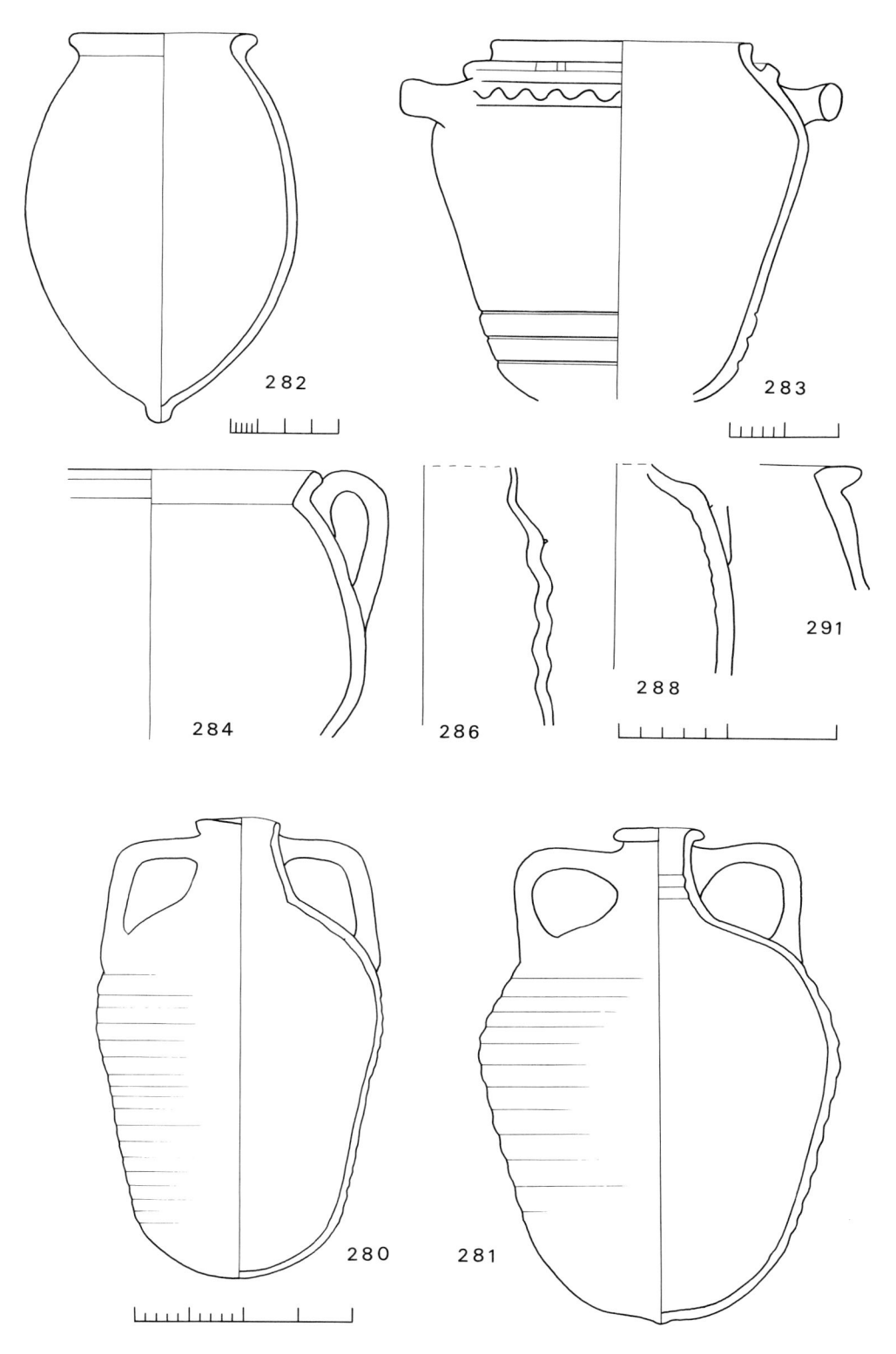

FIG. 43.

Graffiti

Of the many graffiti on pottery few preserve as much as one complete letter or symbol and of these only a small proportion is intelligible. On the early Roman vases there is only one (i). Most are on pottery of the fortress period. John the Boatswain clearly asserts his ownership of a pithos (ii) while Theodotos writes his whole name on a jug (iii) and only his initials on two amphorae (vi, vii) and two bowls (iv, v). He may have been a retailer since a pithos lid with the initials was found in the fortress tower storeroom (viii) and the room in which his other vases were found seems to have been uncommonly well stocked with pottery. XAP on a jug (ix) is the abbreviated XAPIC of so many potters' stamps, or of XAPA. KOC on x is probably an abbreviation. xi–xv are symbols, some of them variations on the familiar Christian monogram, and others have letters or groups of letters which may be parts of names, record commodities or quantities, or be mere caprices. See FIGS. 44, 45 for all except (iii).

 i. On the rim of the bowl 162: CIX.
 ii. On the shoulder of pithos (diam. at rim 42.5; coarse red-brown clay) as 244: ΙΩΑΝΝΟΥ ΚΕΛΕΥΣΤΟΥ. Fortress floor, Room XIX–XX.
 iii. PLATE 23. On the shoulder of jug 199: ΘΕΟΔΟΤΟΥ.
 iv. On the base of a bowl: Θ; on its outer wall: Θ and other letters.
 v. On the base of a bowl: Θ.
 vi. On the shoulder of an amphora as 238: ΘΕ.
 vii. On the shoulder of an amphora as 238: ΘΕ.
 viii. On pithos lid 274: ΘΕ.
 ix. On the shoulder of jug 181: XAP.
 x. On the shoulder of amphora 240: KOC.
 xi. On the neck of a broad amphora: KO. Fortress, Room XI–XII.
 xii. On the shoulder of a jug: +PTO. Fortress, Trench E.
 xiii. On the shoulder of an amphora as 237: cross monogram. Fortress floor, Room XI.
 xiv. On the shoulder of an amphora: pattern or letters impressed before firing. Bas. CC, from ruin debris high above floor.
 xv. On the foot of amphora 230: B.
 xvi. On the shoulder of an amphora as 238: apparently a name: ΟΛΥΓΡΕΑ. Fortress floor, Room XI.
 xvii. On the neck of amphora 228: ..ΚΕΨ.., ..ΙΒ.., etc.
 xviii. On the shoulder of an amphora: CIAC. Fortress floor, NW Tower.
 xix. On the shoulder of an amphora: ANA... Fortress floor, Room XI.
 xx. On the shoulder of an amphora as 237: ΟΛΙ. Fortress floor, Room XI–XII.
 xxi. On the shoulder of a pithos: ΑΠΖ. Fortress floor, NW Tower.
 xxii. On the shoulder of an amphora: ..CΘΕΩ. North of Basilica.
 xxiii. On the shoulder of an amphora: +ΩΙ.
 xxiv. On the shoulder of amphora 236: AN.
 xxv. On the underside of bowl: F, Ψ, Σ.
 xxvi. On pithos 254; on the body Δ; ΩΙ.
 xxvii. On the shoulder of amphora 280 (reoccupation period): B
 xxviii. On the shoulder of an amphora (reoccupation period): monogram? Fortress, Room IX.
 xxix. On the shoulder of amphora : Δ.
 xxx. On the shoulder of amphora: HB. Fortress floor, NW Tower.

3. THE FINDS

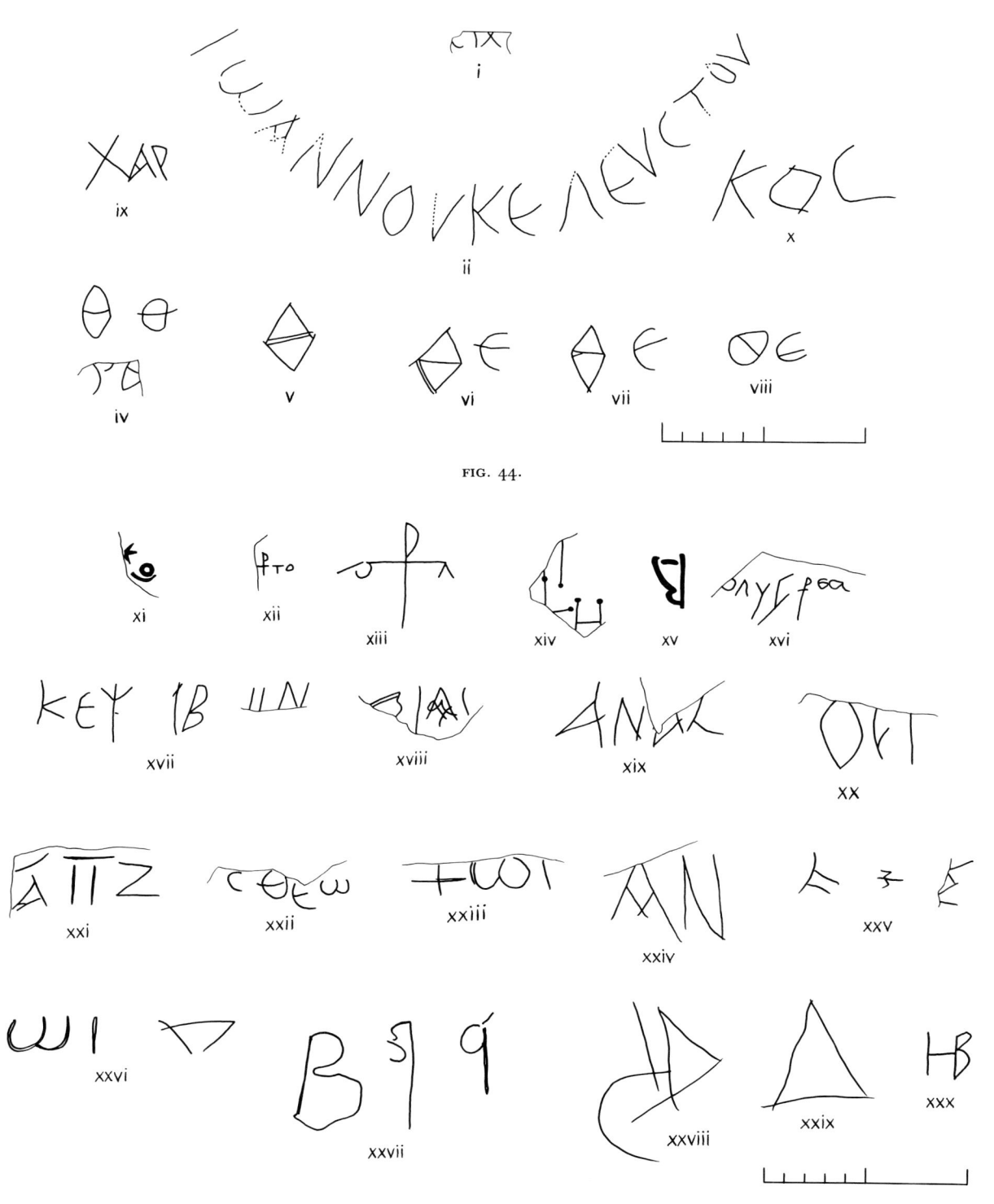

FIG. 44.

FIG. 45.

Lamps

As with the other pottery, there are two major groups, early Roman of the early centuries AD (292–307) and late Roman of the fifth to seventh centuries (314–342). A number of scraps (308–313) seem to date from the intervening years.

Of the earlier pieces a small group (292–6, 309) is from fill beneath the Basilica apse with pottery of the second century AD (5–11). Eastern and Asia Minor types predominate, notably 'Ephesian'.

The most important of the later lamps were recovered complete on the Fortress floor (315, 317–9, 321, 329–31, 334–6). 314–28 are a familiar class of Byzantine lamps, of Asia Minor origin (cf. H. Menzel, *Antike Lampen, Mainz* (1954) 99f.). Several were found on the fortress floor, which demonstrates their continued use to the mid-seventh century. The clay of the Emporio examples is pink, mainly micaceous, and all may be of local manufacture, from moulds derived from mainland models. The African lamps (329–33; see *LRP* 310–14) seem also to have survived in use to the mid-seventh century. Only 329 is in the distinctive fabric; the others are in a softer red (or grey) clay, imitative of the main class. Of other finds on the Fortress floor 335 has the late characteristic of the retraction of the spout within the outline of the body of the lamp and 336 seems an import from Palestine, as may be the fragment 342 (cf. the amphora 243). 337–45 are lamps and fragments from other parts of the site which must be dated to the main late Roman period of occupation. No complete or near-complete lamps were recovered from levels of the reoccupation period.

292. Small fragments with tongue decoration of *Corinth* IV.2 Types XXIII, XXIV. Bas. From fill in apse, section 8 level (7) FIG. 16.
293. Small fragments with double or triple grooves round the disc and pierced handles with double longitudinal ridges. Brownish or pink clay painted orange-red over a white slip. Profile of shoulder as *Corinth* IV.2 74, fig. 34.7. Ephesian? Second century AD. Bas. Context as 292.
294. PLATE 26. Fragment from shoulder. Pinkish buff clay. Part of cable pattern? Bas. Context as 292.
295. PLATE 26. Fragment from spout. Pinkish buff clay with little mica. Bas. Context as 292.
296. FIG. 46; PLATE 26. Fragment of Ephesian lamp. Grey, slightly micaceous clay. Three holes pierced in the disc as well as the central one. Shoulder decorated with tongues, dots and tassels. Cf. *Corinth* IV.2 Type XIX fig. 29. 55. First century. Bas. Context as 292.
297. PLATE 26. Fragment from shoulder, Ephesian lamp. Grey clay. False maeander and dot pattern; cf. ibid., fig. 29, 36. Bas. B section 9 level (2) FIG. 16.
298. PLATE 26. Fragment from shoulder of Ephesian lamp. Grey clay. Chevrons and dot pattern; cf. ibid., fig. 29, 25–7. Bas. From surface in sounding AA south of NN.
299. Fragment from squared spout of Ephesian lamp. Grey clay. Bas.
300. PLATE 26. Fragment from shoulder of lamp with immense plastic volute beside the spout and tongues and ovolo on disc and shoulder. Pink-buff clay with a red wash. Cf. *Corinth* IV.2 Type XXI. The size of the volute is notable. First century AD. Bas. VV section 1 level (12) DRAWING III (b).
301. PLATE 26. Fragment from shoulder. Red clay. Ovolo. Bas.
302. Fragment of handle, clay and slip as 293. Bas.
303. PLATE 27. Fragment from disc. Red-brown clay. Heart-shaped petals and dots. Cf. *Corinth* IV.2 Type XXVII no. 700. First/second century. Bas.
304. PLATE 27. Fragment from disc. Buff clay. Floral with bell-shaped flowers. Bas.
305. PLATE 27. Fragment from disc. Buff clay. Ovolo, and a quadrilateral object decorated with a branch, perhaps a gladiator's rectangular shield seen from the side; cf. *RM* xxxii (1917) 163, fig. 17 and *JRS* xxv (1935) 65 for detached gladiators' shields on Samian ware. Bas.
306. FIG. 47. Fragment from base. Red clay. An alpha in low relief within base ring. Cf. *Corinth* IV.2 Type XX; Ivanyi, *Pannonische Lampen* 71, no. 521, pl. 75.?9. Bas. Below floor of Narthex in N, section 10 level (6) FIG. 17.
307. PLATE 27. Fragment with scalloped edge, possibly from handle attachment. Pinkish-buff clay. Bas. Below floor of narthex in N, section 10 level (5) FIG. 17.
308. PLATE 27. Fragment from handle and rim. Pink-grey clay with brown paint. Volute and tongues in relief. Bas.

3. THE FINDS

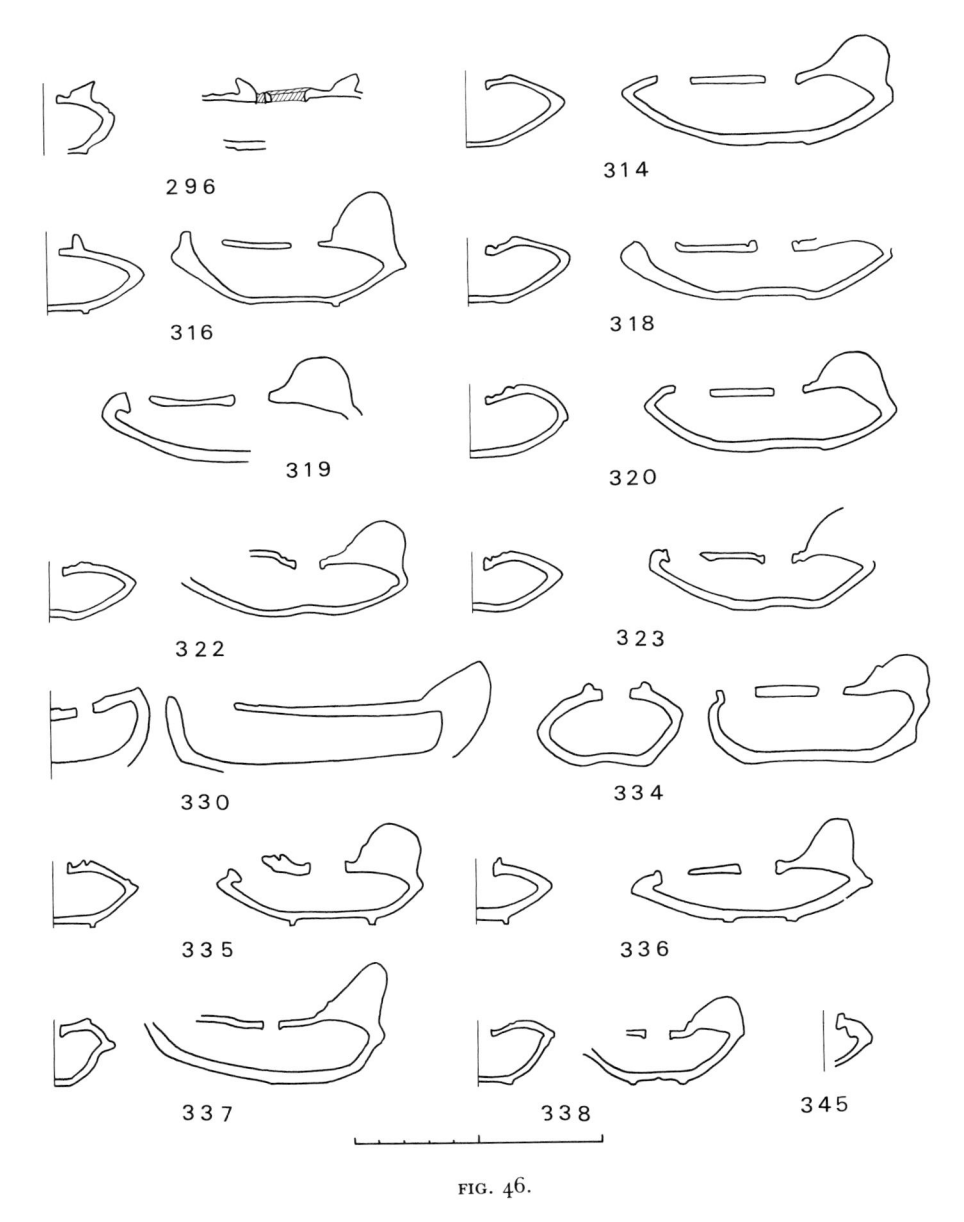

FIG. 46.

309. Fragment from shoulder. Pinkish buff clay with dull brown wash. Chevrons and tongues. Cf. *Corinth* IV.2 Type XXVII. Bas. From fill in apse, section 8 level (7) FIG. 16.
310. PLATE 27. Anthemion handle with herringbone pattern. Pink clay. Cf. *Ephesus* IV.2 pl. 5, 953–4; *Agora* VII no. 351. Foot ring double and a short double ridge from it towards the handle. Fourth century AD. Bas. RR, from surface deposit as section 8 level (2) FIG. 16.
311. PLATE 27. Fragment of disc and handle stump. Pinkish-buff clay. The scene in relief is not clear but seems more probably erotic than martial. Fourth century or later. Bas.
312. PLATE 27. Fragment from disc. Buff clay. A tree. Third/fourth century. Bas. From east part of UU, in angle behind Diakonikon apse to SW above stone paving there. Cf. 313.

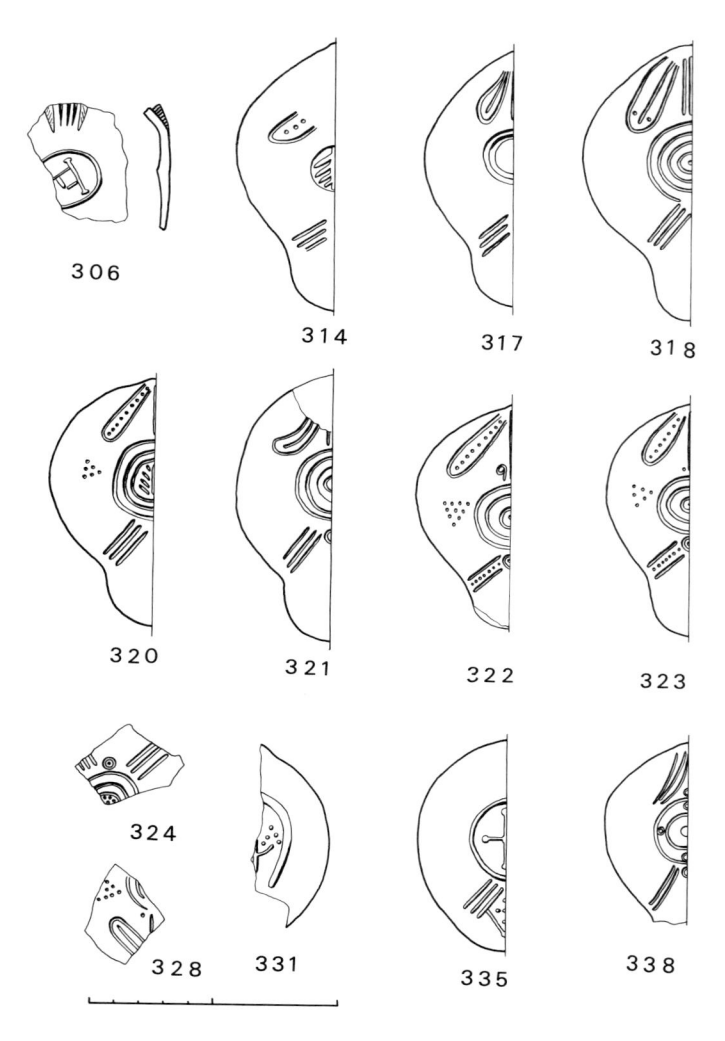

FIG. 47.

313. PLATE 27. Fragment from shoulder and disc. Pinkish buff clay. An animal, probably a bear, rearing on its hind legs before an upright structure. Probably a bear before the *cochlea*, a device like a revolving door from behind which the gladiator or *lustrarius*? could dodge the animal's attacks in the arena. The *cochlea* is usually central. Cf. Walters, *Catalogue* 160f. fig. 218, no. 1068 and references. Third/fourth century. Bas. From same context as 312.
314. FIGS. 46, 47; PLATE 27. Lamp with solid handle. L. 11.5. Pale grey burned clay, some mica. Tongue pattern on shoulder. Fort, Bas.
315. PLATE 27. Lamp with solid handle. L. 11.1. Tongue pattern on shoulder. Micaceous pink clay. Tongues. Fortress floor, Room IX.
316. FIG. 46; PLATE 27. Lamp with solid handle. L. 10.01. Dark grey burnt clay. Tongues on shoulder. Slightly raised ring base opening horseshoe-like towards the spout. Fort × 3 (two in pink clay), floor in Trench M.
317. FIG. 47; PLATE 27. Lamp with solid handle. L. 10.03. Pinkish grey micaceous clay. Concentric circles on shoulder. Fortress floor, Room IX.

318. FIGS. 46, 47; PLATE 27. Lamp with broken handle. L. 11.1. Pink micaceous clay. Concentric circles on shoulder divided by bars and double dots; one of the circles embellished with dots, as is the ring round the central hole. Cf. *Ephesus* IV.2 pl. 10, 1878. Fortress floor, Room IX.

319. FIG. 46; PLATE 27. Lamp with solid handle. L. 10.6. Pink micaceous clay. Concentric circles divided by bars on the shoulder. Most of base missing. Fortress floor, Room III. Fort x 2, Bas.

320. FIGS. 46, 47; PLATE 27. Lamp with a solid handle. L. 10.4. Greyish pink micaceous clay. Cable pattern on shoulder. Fort x 4, Bas x 3.

321. FIG. 47; PLATE 27. Lamp with solid handle. L. 10.9. Pink clay. Vine scroll with grape bunches. Fortress floor, Room IX.

322. FIGS. 46, 47; PLATE 28. Lamp with solid handle. L. presd. 9.9. Pink micaceous clay. Stylised vine scroll with grape bunches. Bas. T, section 2 level (5c) FIG. 13. Two fragments from same mould from Fort.

323. FIGS. 46, 47; PLATE 28. Lamp with solid handle. L. 9.8. Buff-pink micaceous clay. Dotted fish and circles on shoulder. Bas. From same context as 322. Similar, Bas. B, section 9 level (2) FIG. 16.

324. FIG. 47. Fragment from base. Pink clay. Fort.

325. PLATE 28. Fragment from solid handle and shoulder. Pink clay. Tongues on shoulder, cf. 314. Bas. From ruin debris between 1.00–1.50m above mosaic floor of Narthex in EE.

326. PLATE 28. Fragment from shoulder. Pink clay. Concentric circles divided by tongues, cf.318–9. Bas. Similar fragment from Fort.

327. PLATE 28. Fragment of solid handle and shoulder. Pink micaceous clay. Tail of fish from shoulder?, cf. 323. Fort.

328. FIG. 47. Fragment from base. Pink clay. Bas.

329. PLATE 28. Spout. Hard bright orange clay. Foot of a cross. African fabric. Fortress floor, NW Tower.

330. FIG. 46; PLATE 28. Complete lamp, base worn. L. 13.2. Red clay. Ivy-leaf pattern enclosing chi-rho monogram. Fortress floor, Room XX.

331. FIG. 47; PLATE 28. Fragment of lamp with solid semicircular handle. Grey clay. Ivy-leaf pattern enclosing a chi-rho monogram. Base pattern in relief. As last. Fortress floor, Room III.

332. PLATE 28. Back of lamp, profile as 330. Red clay. Ivy-leaf pattern enclosing forepart of running dog. Cf. Cardaillac, *Lampes antiques découvertes dans l'Afrique du Nord* 118 figs. 154, 158, and especially, Brants, op. cit., pl. 8, 1157 (Tunis). Fort.

333. PLATE 29. Fragment from side and shoulder. Red clay. Herringbone pattern. Cf. *Corinth* IV.2 no. 1456. Bas.

334. FIG. 46; PLATE 29. Lamp with solid handle. L. 9.4. Pinkish grey clay. Raised arcs; no decoration on lower half which seems not moulded. Akin to 314–328 but different clay. Fortress floor, Room IX.

335. FIGS. 46, 47; PLATE 29. Lamp with solid handle. L. 8.7. Grey clay. Tongues on shoulder. Low relief on base. Fortress floor, Room XI.

336. FIG. 46; PLATE 29. Lamp with small solid handle. L. 9.8. Gritty ochre clay. Oval base ring. Palestinian. Fortress floor, Room XII.

337. FIG. 46; PLATE 29. Lamp with solid handle. L. 9.9. Pinkish red clay. Tongues and circles. Cf. *Pergamum* I.2 Beil. 59,7. Bas. From 0.85m below surface in C outside basilica, in angle between east wall and north side of apse.

338. FIGS. 46, 47; PLATE 28. Lamp with spout and handle missing. Presd. L. 7.4. Pinkish-brown clay. A fragment from a similar lamp shows that it had a solid handle. Bobble decoration and hatching round central hole. Cf. Brants, op. cit. pl. 8, 1123; *Agora* VII no. ,349. Probably fifth century. Bas. MM, section 3 level (6) FIG. 13.

339. PLATE 29. Fragment from front of lamp. Pinkish-red clay. Tongues on shoulder and spout bridge; on disc an eight-pointed star. Cf. *Pergamum* I.2 Beibl. 59,6 and Walters, op. cit. 201 fig. 301 no. 1339 (Sardis). Sixth century, cf. 340. Bas. V, section 1 level (5b) DRAWING III (b), at 1.73m below surface.

340. PLATE 29. Fragment of lamp with solid handle. Clay and shape as last. Tongues on shoulder and disc. Bas.

341. PLATE 29. Fragment of body and handle. Brown clay. Vine leaves and grape clusters on shoulder and disc. Probably fifth century. Bas, and fragments of a similar lamp.

342. PLATE 29. Fragment from shoulder. Hard brown-grey clay. Scroll with rosette and grape cluster. Palestinian? Fortress, Trench E.

343. PLATE 29. Fragment from shoulder and disc. Buff clay. May be fifth century. Bas.

344. PLATE 29. Fragment from front of lamp. Pink-orange clay. Branch on shoulder. Fort.

345. FIG. 46; PLATE 29. Fragment of miniature undecorated lamp. L. presd. 4.0. Pink clay. Bas. Trench L, surface.

3. Other Materials

Introduction

The minor objects of stone, glass and metal bring a site to life far more readily than does its pottery. Nearly all the Roman objects from Emporio are from the floors or debris of the fortress which was destroyed in the 660s AD. There seems to have been little subsequent plundering, though floors seem to have remained exposed for some time, and the preserved parts of furnishings, ornaments, implements and even games help towards a vivid appreciation of the appearance, and even a little of the atmosphere of that Christian community that lived and worked under the constant threat of extinction at the hands of the Arab invaders. The Basilica church was, it seems, more thoroughly robbed by the later occupants and builders on the site so that we are left little to suggest its furnishing. But churches, like temples, change little and are always better known than the homes of the people who worshipped within them, so we may count ourselves lucky in the variety of the finds in the fortress. It must be remembered that it was as much a fortified town as a military camp in its last years. Earlier Roman finds, and later mediaeval ones are few.

As we might expect, fishing tackle is much in evidence, lead net weights, fish hooks, and sail hoops; and John the Boatswain's store-jar (graffito, FIG. 44, ii) reminds us of one of the major occupations of the townsfolk. Farming too must have been important then. Chian wine and mastic were certainly still assured a market, probably even in the west, but it is the mills that serve home consumption that we find in the town, with the steelyards, balances and weights for the retail trade. The iron axe heads, pruning hooks and saws are exactly like those in use today, and in the collection of modern Chian implements and their names, compiled by P. P. Argenti and H. J. Rose in their *Folk Lore of Chios* (1949) it is easy to find ready parallels with the past.

The distaff side is aptly represented by the spindle hooks, thimbles and needles (some of them tough enough to use on sailcloth), though by little else, and the military character of the fortress is also poorly represented by a few spear heads. Jewellery is scarce with but one gem, one small cameo, a pendant and occasional bronze rings. The black and white bone counters suggest that *tavli* was as popular in the seventh century as it is in *kapheneia* today.

Ornate hinges from chests or the doors of cupboards help to fill in some of the details of house interiors but there seems to have been little pretentious furnishing in the small rooms with their earth floors and narrow gravel or cobbled streets outside. Light was provided by both clay and glass lamps which were suspended from bronze hooks, chains and rods. The tiles with circular apertures may also have helped lighten the interiors since no pane glass for windows was found like that employed in the Basilica.

The contents of Theodotos' store (Room IX) are perhaps worth detailing since it is a remarkable collection. It seems to have been a *pantopoleion* in true Greek style, with the emphasis on hardware, though carpenter and fisherman were also served, as well as the bric-à-brac hunter. The amount of pottery is phenomenal: at least three pithoi, eight amphorae, ten cooking pots and eight jugs, as well as bowls, lamps (which show no signs of use) and a brazier. Two great marble dishes around a metre in diameter lay one above the other in a corner. A dozen fish hooks and a host of lead net weights were at hand for the fisherman; knives, a saw and whetstone for the carpenter; bronze and lead weights for the counter scales and steelyard; a needle for the housewife and cheap gems for the curious. And from his own furniture hinges, lamphangers and locks. His neighbour in Room XI–XII, was similarly, though less fully stocked.

In the publication of these objects I have closely followed Gladys R. Davidson's (Mrs Saul Weinberg) arrangement in her publication of the Minor Objects in Corinth (*Corinth* XII, 1952). The measure of my indebtedness to this book may be judged from the numerous references to it. As with the plain pottery, an important complex for comparisons has proved to be the Byzantine wreck at Yassi-Ada which seems to have been well stocked with domestic appliances and furniture.

The objects are grouped according to their purpose rather than their material.

1. Vessels and Furniture

Circular Marble Table Tops or Dishes

These are all of coarse-grained greyish-white marble, probably either Ephesian or Proconnesian. Surface and rim are invariably carefully polished with the underside roughly clawed. All have a shallow plain footing. A flat-topped rim seems to have been the rule except for F5.

F1. FIG. 48. Fragments of the rim. Diam. ca. 72.5; H. of rim 2.4. Fortress floor, Room III.
F2. FIG. 48. Diam. 109.0; H. of rim 2.2. Fortress floor, Room IX, beneath F3.
F3. FIG. 48; PLATE 16b. Diam. 90.4; H. of rim 5.8. See F2.
F4. FIG. 48. Fragment of rim. Diam. over 60.0; H. of rim 5.6. Fortress, Room I behind NW Tower.
F5. FIG. 48. Fragments. Diam. ca. 100.0; H. of rim 5.0. The largest fragment was on the floor of Room XI but other fragments were found in higher levels at hand and help complete the profile.

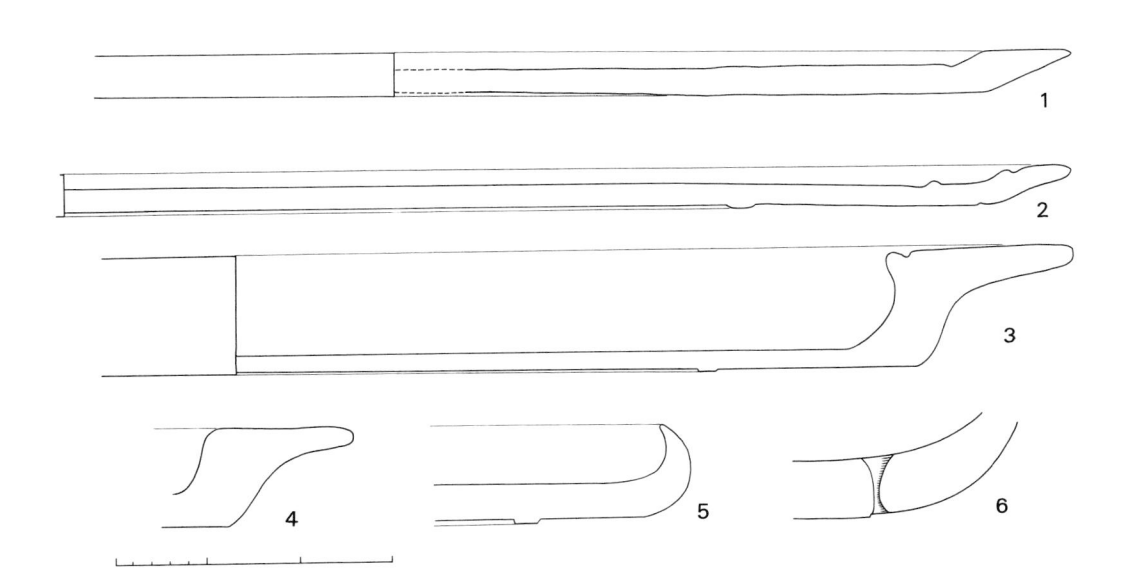

FIG. 48.

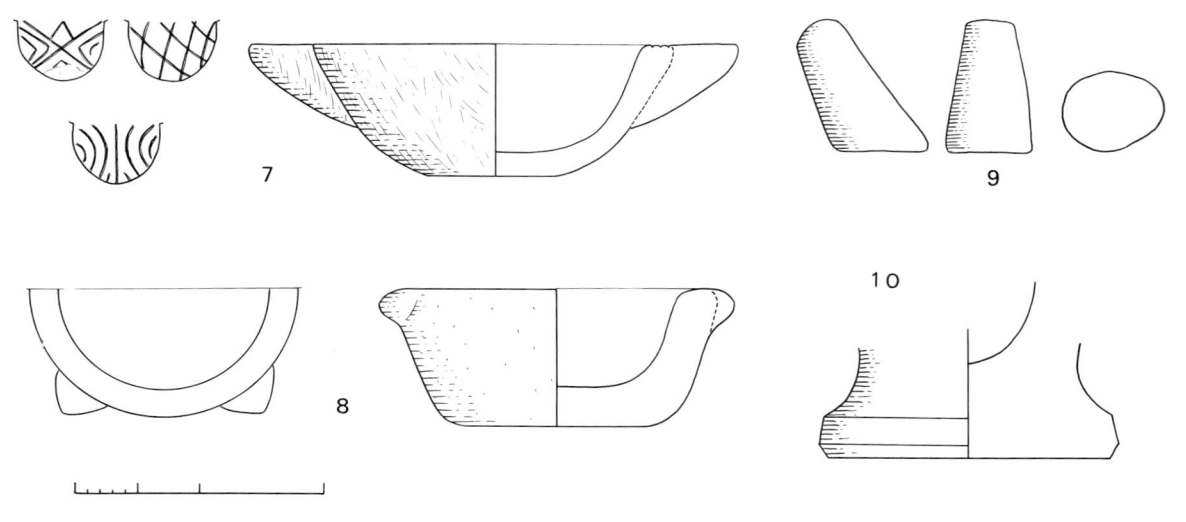

FIG. 49.

Stone Basins and Mortars

See *Corinth* XII 122f. F8 is certainly a mortar and the pestle F9 might have gone with it since it was found nearby.

F6.   FIG. 48. Fragment of the wall and foot of a bowl. Diam. of foot ca. 100.0; thickness 2–3.0. Fine grain white marble. A hole cut just outside the footring. Bas. U, from 0.65m below surface in SE corner of trench, apparently from section 7 level (3) FIG. 15.

F7.   FIG. 49. Fragments of bowl of coarse grained white marble. Diam. 19.6; H. 11.0. Three of four false spouts preserved, each with a different linear pattern. Interior well smoothed, outside rough-clawed. Cf. *Yassi-Ada* I 290–1, MF 54 for a very similar piece; and *Corinth* XII pl. 61. 827. Fortress floor, Room III.

F8.   FIG. 49. Fragments of a basalt mortar. Diam. 21.6; H. 11.6. Three of the four solid lugs are preserved. Fortress floor, Room XIX.

F9.   FIG. 49. Basalt pestle. H. 11.0. Cf. *Corinth* XII 189f. pl. 86. 1438. Fortress floor, Room XIX.

F10. FIG. 49. Fragment of standed bowl or mortar. Diam. at base 24.0; presd. H. 14.0. White marble with bluish stains, perhaps Proconnesian. Inside smooth, outside decorated with band of vertical grooves. Cf. *EADélos* XVIII 105f. Fortress, west of N Tower.

Glass Vessels

The only datable contexts are on the fortress floor. All pieces were shattered although it was clear that two types, of generally uniform shape, predominated: goblets with short stems and lamps. The former have a long life and similar examples at Corinth are dated to the tenth and eleventh century AD, some four centuries later than these (*Corinth* XII 108 fig. 12 nos. 711–18). The lamps are of canonical late Roman, Byzantine, mediaeval, even modern type, with long 'test-tube' bases. They have been discussed by E. M. Crowfoot and D. B. Harden in *JEA* xvii (1931) 196ff. The bronze lamp-hangers and chains must have been used for them. With the goblets and lamps were a few cups and bowls and three miniature unguentaria from the fortress floor. The preserved fragments are so small that they are treated together and the most characteristic pieces are illustrated. The house at Pindakas yielded the nearest complete profile (F15e).

3. THE FINDS

The Basilica area yielded a number of pieces which can be dated early Roman, and, with the few lamps, coins and vases of the first and second centuries, might be associated with the building that preceded the Basilica church. Unfortunately they are not stratified. Finally, an assortment of handles probably belong to vases of the last period of the fortress, cups, bowls and lamps.

No glass whatever was found in the 9th-century reoccupation levels in the fortress but it is more than likely that some of the unstratified pieces, particularly from the Basilica area where later chapels were erected, are mediaeval. For other objects in glass see F128–30.

In surface levels beside the harbour at Emporio were found several lumps of fused matter which indicate the presence of a glass kiln nearby. The structure itself was not located; indeed it is probably not preserved since in this area the topmost levels are generally prehistoric. They might belong to the fortress period or may indicate a temporary industry supplying glass for the Basilica building.

F11. FIG. 50. H. 3.1. Fragment of cut glass bowl. Colourless. For the type and parallels see *Corinth* XII 93–5 fig. 6 no. 592. 2nd century AD. Bas.

F12. FIG. 50. H. 1.7. Fragment from the rim of a plate. Crystalline white. Early Roman. Bas.

F13. FIG. 50. Diam. 5.2. Fragment from foot of a bowl or cup. Crystalline white. Early Roman. Bas.

F14. FIG. 50. Fragments of goblets with short stems. Colourless. (a)–(e) are a selection of bases and stems from the floors of fortress rooms. They are made in varying techniques; see *Corinth* XII 85f. for the later goblets from Corinth and D. B. Harden, *Roman Glass from Karanis* (1936) 167ff. Various fragments of rims and straight or slightly incurving walls probably go with them. The two fragments combined (e) seem certainly from the same vase and may be restored after a vase at Corinth. (a) Stem and part of base. H. 3.4. (b) Stem and base. Diam. 4.3. T 13 (c) Base. Diam. 4.5. (d) Base. Diam. 5.5. T 15. (e) Stem, base and rim restored after *Corinth* XII 108 fig. 12 no. 718. Restored H. 11.1.

F15. FIG. 50. Fragments from bowls and cups. Colourless, and pale green. (a)–(d) resemble fragments of others found on fortress floors. Various straight and curved walls and plain rims may belong, as well as the smaller handles. (e) is the only glass vessel from Pindakas (6th cent. AD) (a) Wall. H. 6.5. (b) Base. Diam. 6.4. (c) Base. Diam. 4.9. (d) Base. Diam. 6.0. (e) Cup fragments. Restored H. 6.0. From the floor of a room in the late Roman houses on the lower terrace at Pindakas (*BSA* liii/iv (1958/9) 297).

F16. FIG. 50 a, b. Fragments of lamps. Pale green. Typical of fragments from the fortress floors. Many fragments of straight walls and handles may be attributed to the same type. The profile is generally more angular than those illustrated in *JEA* xvii (1931) pl. 29. 21–6. Another fragment is from a solid base with an irregular outline.

F17. FIG. 50; PLATE 30. Handles are grouped together though they must be from various shapes which can only be guessed. Plain handles (a,b) should be from cups or bowls. Others, with plain trailers hanging from them, may be from the straight (c) or curved walls of lamps (d). Serpentine trails (e,f) are an elaboration of the same type. The lug (g) is notable. All, except (c), (e) and (g) are from the fortress floors; (e) and (g) were not stratified, and (c) is the only antiquity post-dating the 4th century BC found at the temple site on Prophetes Elias (*Greek Emporio* 22).
(a) Pale green. (b) Pale green. (c) PLATE 30. Three handles (two shown), all from one vessel. Clear green. From the surface in the Archaic temple of Athena on Prophetes Elias. (d) Pale green. (e) PLATE 30. Dark blue. (f) PLATE 30. Pale green. (g) PLATE 30. Dark blue.

F18. PLATE 30. Unguentarium. Pale green. H. 4.4. Fortress floor, Room IX.

F19. PLATE 30. Unguentarium; lip broken away and body slightly flattened. Pale green. H. 3.9. Fortress floor, Room IV.

F20. PLATE 30. Unguentarium. Pale green. H. 4.6. Fortress floor, Room IX.

F21. FIG. 50; PLATE 30. H. presd. 5.5. Fragments of bottle with shallow, oblique ribbing. Colourless. A less regular and probably earlier version of the type familiar in the mediaeval glass factory at Corinth, cf. *Corinth* XII 118f. no. 782 fig. 17 pl. 59 (dated 11th to mid-12th century AD). Mrs Weinberg has seen the fragments and commented on the similarity in fabric and decoration. Fort, surface.

F22. PLATE 30. Fragment of mould-blown vessel. Blue. Probably 7th cent. AD or later.

F23. PLATE 30. Fragment of bowl. Pale blue and white horizontal streaks. Bas, surface.

F24. FIG. 50. H. presd. 7.3. Fragment from wall of bottle. Pale green. Fortress floor.

Metal Vessels

F25. FIG. 51. Fragment of silver saucer or dish. 3.5 × 3.5; thickness 0.1. Original profile uncertain. Fortress floor, Room XV.

F26. FIG. 51. Fragment of bronze saucer or dish. 5.7 × 2.5. Bas. U, from SE corner of trench apparently from section 7 level (1) FIG. 15.

F27. FIG. 51. Fragment of bronze sheet, folded and with a slight curve. L. 25.0. This seems to have been folded and crimped onto a hoop-like object, perhaps of wood, and may have served as the rim of a vessel. Fortress floor, Room IX. A similar smaller fragment from Fortress floor, Room XIX–XX.

F28. FIG. 51; PLATE 30. Bronze pan handle. L. 9.5. Fortress wall (reoccupation period), Room XII.

Lids and Stoppers

For the clay stoppers and pithos lids see 262–78.

F29. FIG. 51. Stone stopper. Diam. ca. 4.0; thickness 0.5–0.7. Cut from greenish slate. Fortress floor, Room XI–XII.

F30. PLATE 31. Bone stopper. H. 1.8. A knob of bone has been thrust into the core of a larger, hollowed section of bone and the ends subsequently smoothed. Cf. *Corinth* XII pl. 64.875 (ours is not pierced or otherwise cut, so cannot be a hinge, as those discussed ibid., 129). Fortress, Cistern in Trench C.

Bronze Hinges

See *Corinth* XII 131f. These are from chests or perhaps cupboard doors. All are decorated more or less neatly with incised circles but for F39 which has punched dots. The similar decoration and dimensions of hinges found on the floor of some rooms indicates that they are from the same piece of furniture (F33, 35, 36).

F31. PLATE 30. L. 18.0. Line of incised concentric circles. Fortress floor, Room IX.

F32. PLATE 30. L. 9.0. Incised lines and irregularly placed circles. A bronze pin in the loop of one hinge. Fortress floor, Room XII.

F33. PLATE 30. L. 10.7. Incised concentric circles. In the pierced end-disc part of a bronze nail with spherical head. Fortress floor, Room XXII.

F34. PLATE 30. L. 8.2. Incised concentric circles. In a hole near the joint a bronze nail with spherical head (L. 4.0; diam. 0.03) and in the loop of the hinge part of an iron nail. Fortress floor, Room IX.

F35. PLATE 30. L. 9.0. Incised concentric circles. In each hole by the joint a bronze nail and part of a bronze pin in the loop of the hinge. Fortress floor, Room XXII.

F36. PLATE 30. Fragment. L. 4.0. Incised concentric circles. In the disc a bronze nail. Fortress floor, Room XXII.

F37. FIG. 51. L. 7.4. Small incised circles. Fortress floor, Room IX.

F38. FIG. 51. L. 10.4. Incised strokes and circles. Fortress floor, Room XXIV.

F39. FIG. 51. Fragment. L. 10.6. Lightly impressed or punched dots. Fortress floor, Room IV.

F40. FIG. 51. Fragments. Bas. L, from debris above destroyed floor of Nave.

F41. FIG. 51. Fragment. W. 3.0. Incised circles. Fortress floor, Room XI–XII.

Locks?

A number of iron box-shaped objects from the fortress floor are all so poorly preserved that little more than their dimensions could be recovered. They may be locks; cf. *Corinth* XII 137f.; J. C. Waldbaum, *Metalwork from Sardis* (1983) 69–76. No keys were found.

F42. 10.1 × 8.0 × 3.5. Hopelessly corroded. Firmly attached, at least by corrosion, to two of the corners, are two iron rings, one 6.0 in diameter and 2.0 thick, the other 7.0 in diameter and 2.0 thick. Fortress floor, Room IX.

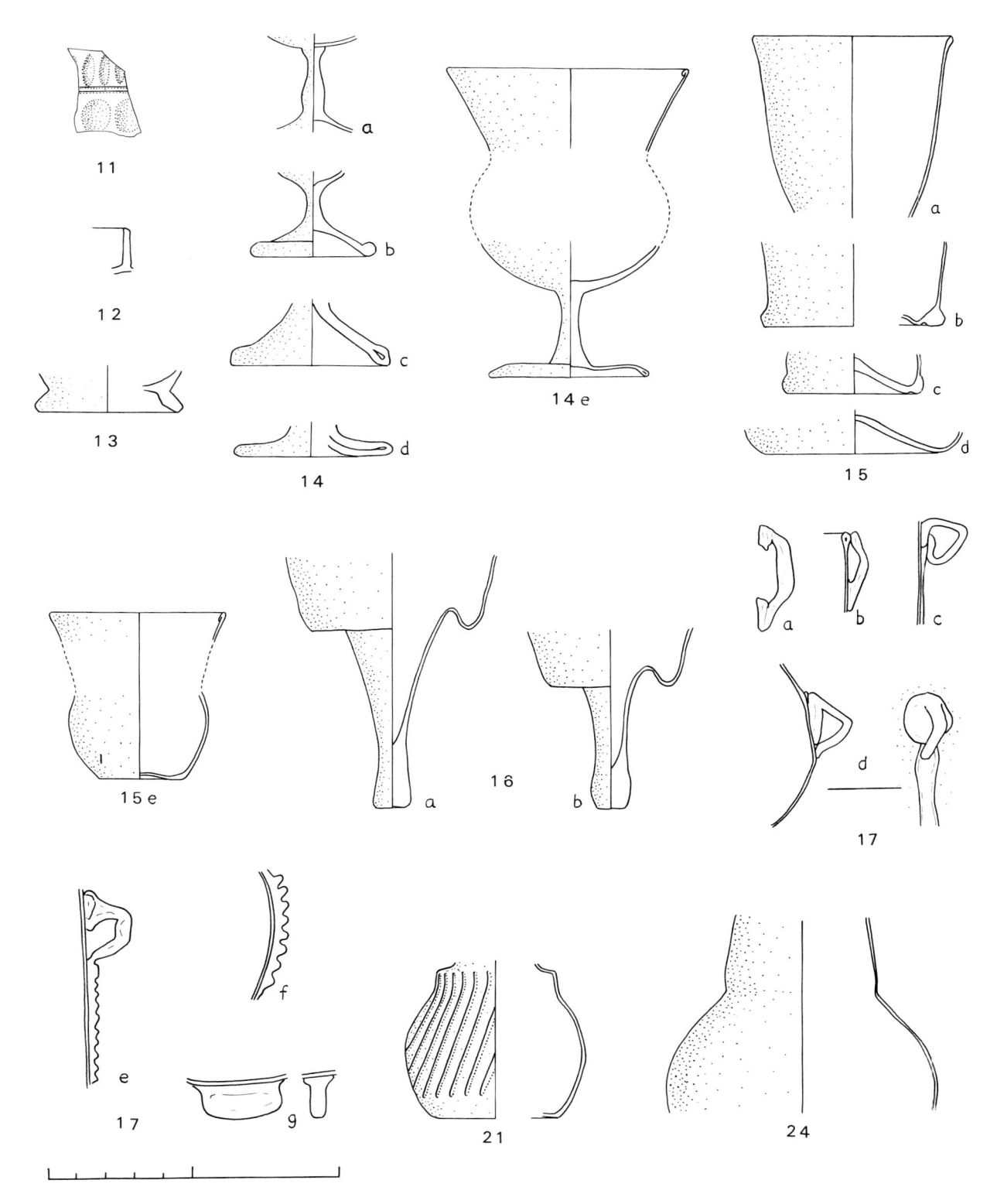

FIG. 50.

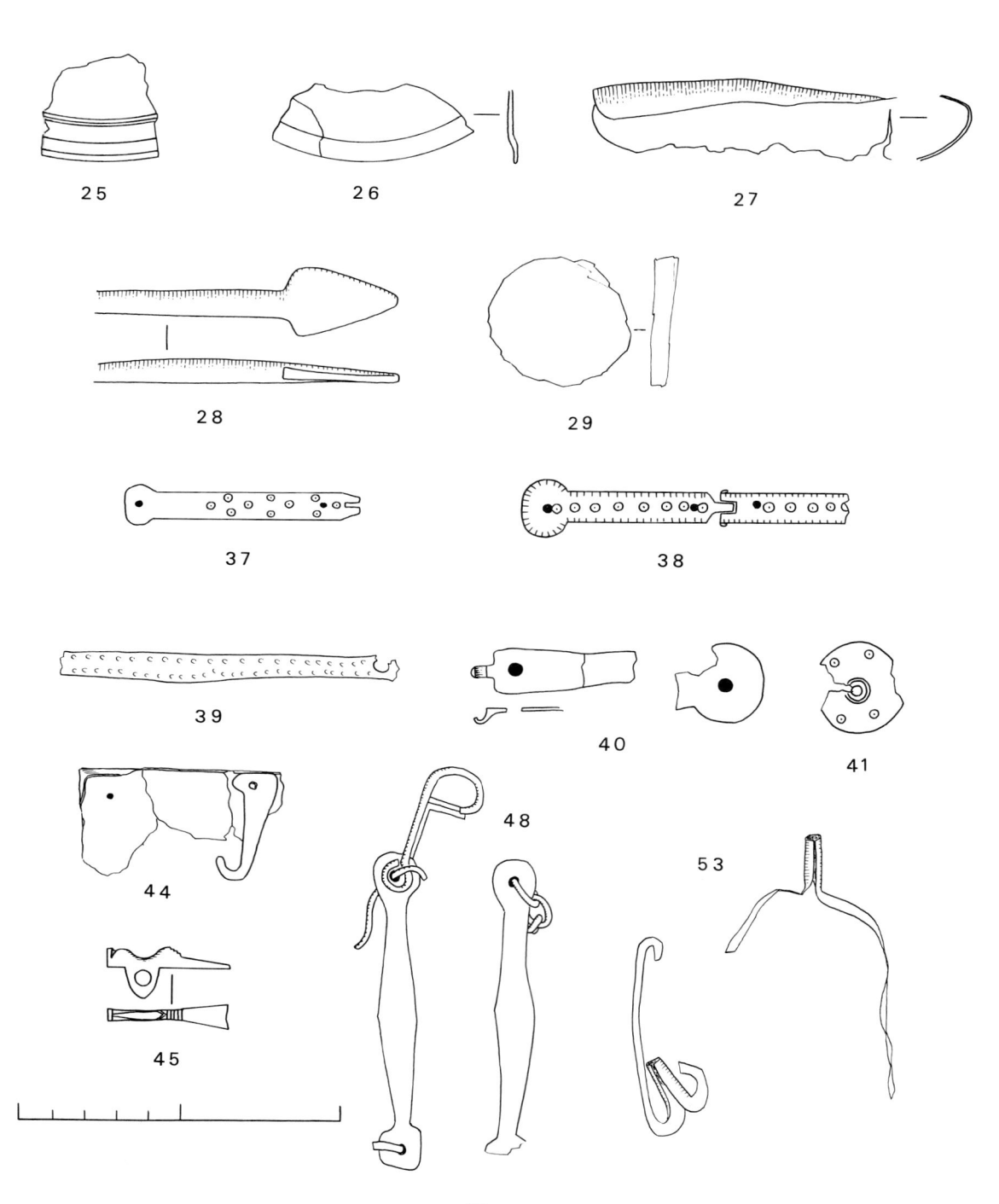

FIG. 51.

F43. Open on one side. 13.0 × 6.0 × 2.0. Corroded onto one of the short ends is an iron nail 8.0 long. Fortress floor, Room IX.
F44. FIG. 51. Fragment with internal hooked member fastened by bronze. 6.4 × 3.6. Fortress floor, Room XIX.
F45. FIG. 51; PLATE 30. Moving part from a lock? Bronze. L. 3.8. Fortress floor, Room XXII.

Lamp-Hangers and Chains

See *Corinth* XII 126; *EADélos* XVIII 141. The pendants for glass lamps or *polykandela* seem to have been either simple flexible chains, or made of rigid members with links at either end. The rigid part could be either a bronze rod or a bronze strip in the shape of an elongated diamond and it is the latter type which is most common. Since no *polykandela* were found we may assume that these pendants were for glass lamps, of which there are many fragments (F16). Similar pendants were found in the 6th-century church of Ag. Titos in Gortyn, published by Orlandos in *Epet. Et. Byz. Spoudon* iii (1926) 322 fig. 21, now in the Historical Museum at Heraklion; and in the Kornos Cave in Cyprus, *Levant* ii (1970) 50, fig. 5, 18. Others from an early 8th-century synagogue in Jericho are published by Baramki in *QDAP* vi (19) 75 pl. 22; and cf. *Metropolitan Museum Bronzes* (1915) 240 no. 685, from Cyprus.

All are bronze unless otherwise stated.

F46. PLATE 31. Overall L. 23.4. Fortress floor, Room XI.
F47. PLATE 31. L. of hook with fragment of strip 15.05. Fortress floor, Room IX.
F48. FIG. 51. Fragments; L. of hook with strip 13.4. Fortress floor, Room IX.
F49. PLATE 31. Overall L. 17.5. Fortress floor, Room XII.
F50. PLATE 30. Link and staple. L. 3.5. Fortress floor, Room IX.
F51. Other fragments of hooks and strips from pendants like 46 were found as follows: three in Fortress Room IX, one each in Rooms XIX–XX, III, VIII, the Cistern in Trench C.
F52. Links and short lengths of bronze chain from pendants, or possibly weighing instruments, were found in Fortress Rooms IX, XIV–XV. Bas. JJa outside north wall of basilica 1.20–1.60m below surface.
F53. FIG. 51. Lead strips; 0.3–0.6 wide and L. up to 10.5. Some are split or bent into a U section to grip lamp wicks. They stood, or lay in the glass lamps and supported the wick overhanging the rim of the lamp. Found in profusion on fortress floors, particularly the 'shops'.

Iron Rings, Hoops, etc.

F54. Rings. Most are poorly preserved but the following dimensions were determined:
(a) Diam. 7.0; thickness 1.1. Fortress floor, NW Tower. (b) Diam. 6.0; thickness 1.0. Fortress floor, Room III. (c) Diam. 4.4; thickness 1.7. Bas. EE, from 1.00m below surface high above floor at south end of Narthex. (d) Diam. 5.0; thickness 0.8. Fortress floor, Room IX. (e) Diam. ca. 11.5; thickness 2.0. Fortress floor, Room IX.
F55. Hoop fragments. Diam. 6.0; W. of hoop 4.0; thickness 0.8. Fortress floor, NW Tower.
F56. Hoop fragment. Diam. uncertain; W. of hoop ca. 3.0; thickness 0.8. Fortress floor, Room IX.
F57. FIG. 53. Pierced iron disc or washer. Diam. 3.8. Bas.
F58. FIG. 52 (isometric). Fragment of iron casing for a rectangular beam or support (table leg?). L. 9.0; W. 5.5; H. 6.0. Three nail holes along one edge. Fortress floor, Room IV.
F59. Iron spit? L. 52.0; square section 1.5 × 1.5. Fortress floor, Room IX.

Nails

F60. Bronze nails. 20 nails or fragments were found in late Roman levels, most from the fortress. The small number alone suggests that they were not commonly employed, particularly when compared with the iron examples. The heads are invariably rounded and the pins square in section. Typical examples appear in FIG. 53.

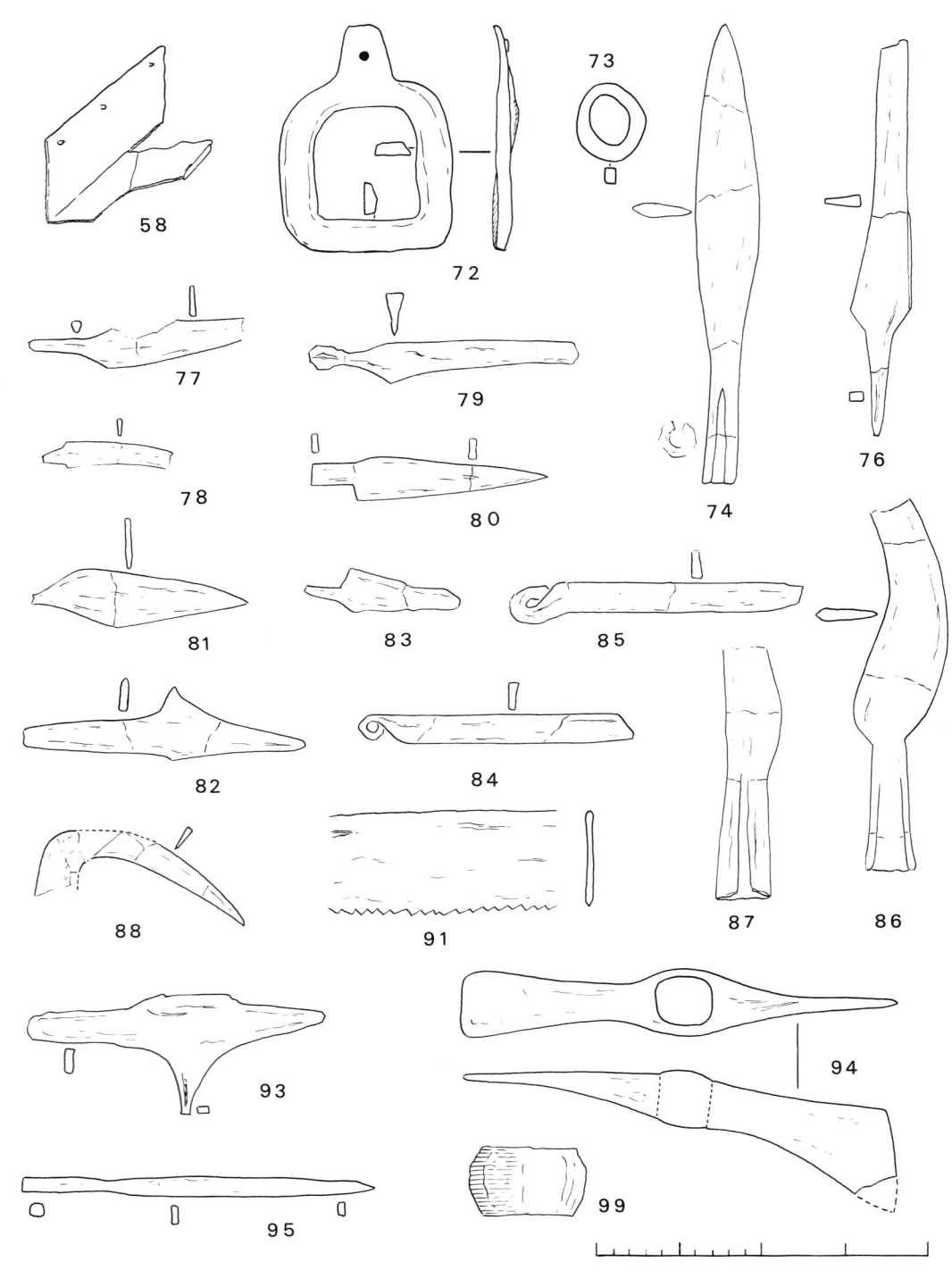

FIG. 52.

F61. Iron nails. Every room in the fortress yielded its harvest of the iron nails used in the timbering of its roof or furniture. The normal type has a square head and is square in section. Lengths range from 18.0 to 7.0 and the heads from 3.0 across to 1.5. The commonest size was 9.0 long with 2.0 square heads. A typical example is shown in FIG. 53(a); (b) and (c) are unusual for their shortness and circular section.

2. Implements and Instruments

Spinning and Sewing

F62. FIG. 53. Bronze spindle hook. L. 3.8. Traces of wood in the socket. Cf. *Corinth* XII 173, pl. 78. 1223–8. Fortress floor, Room IV.

F63. FIG. 53. Bronze spindle hook. L. 3.7. Fort. Similar examples were found in Bas. U or R surface, section 8 level (2) or (3), and B section 9 level (2) FIG. 16.

F64. PLATE 31. Fragments of bronze thimble. H. 1.6. Cf. *Corinth* XII 175, pl. 79.1285–98. Fortress, Cistern in Trench C.

F65. PLATE 31. Bronze needle. L. 9.3. The eye has been bent into a hoop. Roughly circular section. For bronze needles and their manufacture see *Corinth* XII 173, pl. 78. Fortress floor, Room XI.

F66. PLATE 31. Bronze needle. L. 9.4. Circular section. Fortress, Room XI.

F67. PLATE 31. Bronze needle, broken, with two circular eyes in its flattened head. Cf. *EADélos* XVIII pl. 82. 2–4 etc. The section is square and its stoutness suggests that it may have been used with twine, possibly on sailcloth. Fortress floor, Room IX.

F68. Broken tip of a bronze needle. L. presd. 5.0; diam. 0.2. Circular section. Fortress floor, Room XIX.

Fishery

The fish hooks and net weights are familiar from Roman and Byzantine seashore sites. Lead net-rings have been discussed by Benoit in *Rivista di Studi Liguri* xviii (1952) 274f. in connection with similar finds in wrecks of Marseilles: "fixés à la voile par des bandes de cuir, ils maintenaient en place les cordages servant à la manoeuvre de la voilure." Cf. *Olynthus* x pl. 90.160; *BSA* li (1956) 53f. no. 19, from Delphinion in Chios; and *Yassi-Ada* I 303–6.

F69. Bronze fish hooks. 20 of the simplest type were found in the fortress, all from the floors of two rooms (Theodotos' store and Room XI–XII). They range in length from 7.7 to 2.4, roughly circular in section with single barbs and flattened ends for attaching the twine. Cf. *Corinth* XII pl. 88.1447–8; *EADélos* XVIII pl. 69. 551, 553. (a)–(d) are from Room XI–XII; (e)–(q) from Room IX. (a) L. 7.7; W. 4.3. PLATE 31. (b) L. 2.9; W. 1.9. PLATE 31. (c) L. 5.5; W. 3.3. (d) Fragments of five broken hooks. (e) L. 4.3; W. 2.7. PLATE 31. (f) L. 3.3; W. 2.3. PLATE 31. (g) L. 3.0; W. 2.1. (h) L. 3.0; W. 1.8. (j) L. 2.9; W. 1.7. (k) L. 2.4; W. 1.5. PLATE 31. (l) L. 6.1; W. 4.3. (m) L. 4.5; W. 3.5. (n) L. 3.2; W. 2.5. (o) Badly twisted; L. ca. 5.0. (p) L. 7.1; W. 2.6. (q) Fragment.

F70. PLATE 32. Bronze fish hook and pin. Overall L. 13.0; L. of pin 7.4. The hook unusually terminates in a lop attached by another loop to a bronze rod. At the head of the rod is a knob holding a movable bronze loop. This is no doubt for bigger fish. The pin with loop head was found very close to the hook. Fortress floor, Room III.

F71. Lead net weights (*molybdis*). Rectangular lead strips folded lengthwise to grip the cord at the edge of the net. Cf. *Corinth* XII pl. 88.1449. They vary in length from 9.0 to 4.5, in width (folded) from 1.5 to 0.8 and their average thickness is 0.2. Nearly fifty were found in Room IX, Theodotos' store, and thirty in Room XI–XII. The other main source was Room III which yielded eleven, and others were recovered from Room IV (three). Three examples have relief patterns: (a) FIG. 53. L. 8.3. Herring bone pattern in relief. Fortress floor, Room IX. (b) FIG. 53. L. 8.0. Herring bone pattern in relief and the letters H, I I. Fortress floor, Room III. (c) FIG. 53. L. 8.0. Zigzag in relief.

F72. FIG. 52. Lead sail ring. W. 13.8. Irregular shape with pierced flange. Fortress floor, Room IX.

F73. FIG. 52. Lead sail ring. W. 4.5. Benoit, op. cit., records examples without pierced holes for cord or thongs. Fortress floor, Room III.

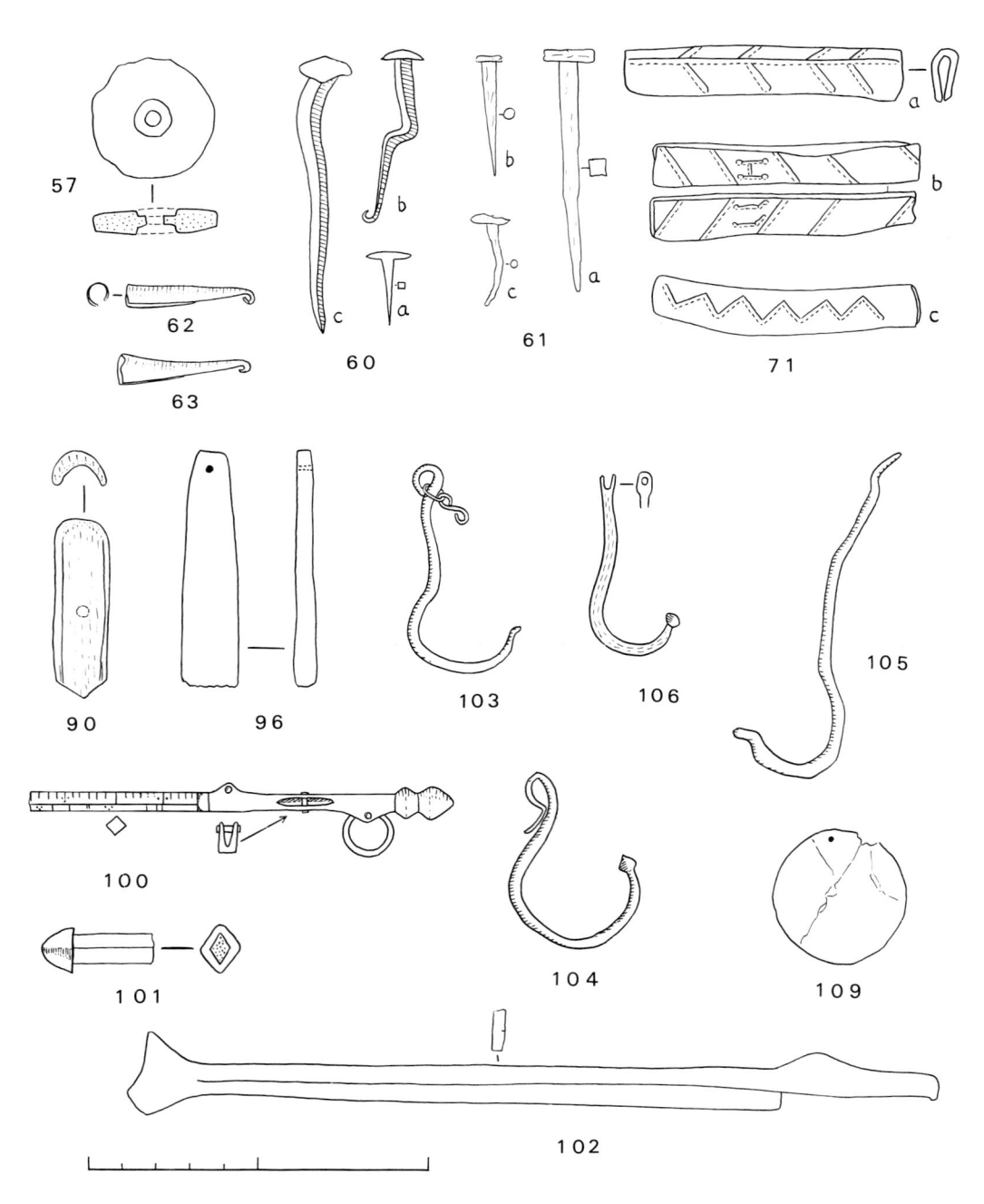

FIG. 53.

3. THE FINDS

Weapons

Other fragments of sockets and blades may be from spearheads.

F74. FIG. 52. Iron spearhead. L. 28.4; widest part of blade 4.0; diam. of socket 2.0. Fortress floor, Room IX.
F75. Iron spearhead. L. of blade 19.0; widest part 3.2; socket missing. Fortress floor, Room III.

Knives and other Implements

Compare the seventh-century knives in *Corinth* XII 199, pl. 93. 1567–8, where they are taken for weapons, probably from the graves of barbarian invaders. Our examples were probably for domestic use. The curved blades may be for pruning; cf. the bill hooks, *Yassi-Ada* I 234–7, and 237–9, Fe 12–3 for the axe-adze F94; also J. C. Waldbaum, *Metalwork from Sardis* (1983) pls. 10 (bill hooks), 11 (axe-adzes).

F76. FIG. 52. Iron knife blade and tang. L. 24.5; tip missing. Fortress, Room XI.
F77. FIG. 52. Iron knife blade and tang. L. 13.0; tip and part of cutting edge missing. Fortress floor, Room IX.
F78. FIG. 52. Iron knife blade and tang. L. 7.3; tip missing. Fortress floor, Room XIX.
F79. FIG. 52. Iron knife blade and tang. L. 16.2. Fortress floor, Room IV.
F80. FIG. 52. Triangular iron knife blade and tang. L. 14.0. Fortress floor, Room III.
F81. FIG. 52. Triangular iron knife blade and broken tang. L. 13.0. Fortress floor, Room IV.
F82. FIG. 52. Triangular iron knife blade with long tang. L. 17.0. Fortress floor, Room III.
F83. FIG. 52. Triangular iron knife blade with tang. L. 9.7. Fortress floor, Room III.
F84. FIG. 52. Iron blade with a loop (hinge?). L. 16.6. Probably shears; see the next. Fortress floor, Room XXII.
F85. FIG. 52. Iron blade with a loop. L. 17.6. See the last. Fortress floor, Room III.
F86. FIG. 52. Socketed iron pruning knife with curved blade. L. 23.0; tip missing. Fortress floor, NW Tower.
F87. FIG. 52. Socketed iron pruning knife with curved blade. L. 15.6; tip missing. Fortress floor, Room XIX–XX.
F88. FIG. 52. Crescent-shaped blade of an iron pruning knife. L. . Fortress floor, Room XXII.
F89. Part of crecent-shaped blade of an iron pruning knife. W. 4.5. Fortress floor, Room III.
F90. FIG. 53. Fragment of the bone handle plate of a knife (?). L. 5.5. One hole pierced for attachment. Fortress floor, Room IX.
F91. FIG. 52. Fragments of an iron saw. Overall L. of joining fragments 63.0; W. 6.0. A representative section is shown in FIG. 52. The teeth are poorly preserved but seem to be alternately inclined. Fortress floor, Room IX.
F92. Fragments of an iron saw, as the last. Overall L. of joining fragments 21.0; W. 5.8. Fortress floor, Room III.
F93. FIG. 52. Iron pick head (?) L. tip to tip 18.2. Fortress floor, Room III.
F94. FIG. 52. Head of an iron axe-adze. L. tip to tip 27.0. A carpenter's tool rather than a farmer's. Fortress, Room XXIV.
F95. FIG. 52. Iron chisel or gouge. L. 21.0. Fortress floor, Room XI–XII.

Whetstones

F96. FIG. 53. Fragment. Presd. L. 8.0; W. 3.5; thickness 2.0. Fine pale blue stone. Fortress floor, Room IX. (= *Prehistoric Emporio* II 652, no. 32, pl. 134)
F97. Fragment. Presd. L. 5.5; W. 3.3–3.5 (at break); thickness 0.7. Buff stone. Fortress floor, Room IV.

Mills

For the millstones and weights from an oil press in the late Roman houses at Pindakas see *BSA* liii/iv (1958/9) 304.

F98. FIG. 54. Stone hand mill. Diam. of upper part 48.5; of lower part 44.5. Cf. *EADélos* XVIII 131f. Fortress floor, NW Tower.
F99. FIG. 52. Stone rubber (?) Diam. 7.0; H. 4.4. Flattened, roughly circular. Fortress floor, Room XII.

9 8

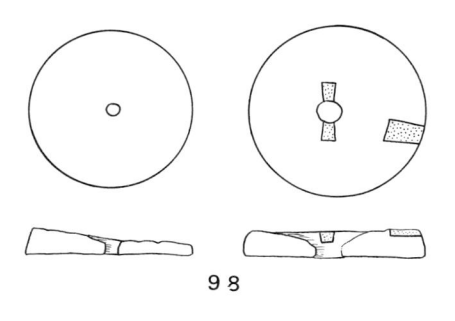

FIG. 54.

Weighing Machines

See *Corinth* XII 207f., 214f., pl. 98; *EADélos* XVIII 139ff. M. Bieber, *Skulpturen und Bronzen in Cassel* (1915) 83f. and pl. 50.341 illustrates a good complete example with hooks attached, and D. K. Hill discusses their use in *Archaeology* v (1952) 51ff.

F100. FIG. 53; PLATE 32. Bronze steelyard arm, broken at one end. L. 12.5. The upper register visible in the drawing records pounds, divided into halves, each of six ounces; the lower register (less clearly marked) whole pounds. Most similar are *EADélos* XVIII 140, fig. 164, B6723; *Corinth* XII pl. 98. 1661. Fortress floor, Room XII.

F101. FIG. 53. Bronze knob end of steelyard bar. L. 3.3. Fortress floor, Room IX.

F102. FIG. 53. Fragment of bronze balance (?) L. 24.0. Fortress floor, Room III.

F103. FIG. 53. Bronze hook and chain. H. of hook 6.4. Fortress floor, Room IX.

F104. FIG. 53. Bronze hook. H. 5.8; W. 4.2. From this type of hook the steelyard is suspended, cf. Bieber, op. cit., pl. 50. 341. Fortress floor, Room IX.

F105. FIG. 53. Bronze hook. H. 10.2. Bas. T, section 2, apparently from level (5) FIG. 13.

F106. FIG. 53. Bronze hook. H. 6.5; W. 2.5. Fortress, bottom of cistern in Trench C.

F107. PLATE 30. Bronze hook and chain. W. of hook 6.0. Fortress, Trench E.

F108. PLATE 30. Bronze steelyard hook with chains. Overall L. 10.3. Fortress floor, Room IX.

F109. FIG. 53. Bronze scale pan (?) Diam. 8.0. Badly preserved but at least one suspension hole is preserved. Fortress floor, Room IX. Small fragments of a similar object from the same floor suggest the pair.

F110. Fragments of hooks and arms of steelyards or scales were recovered from Rooms III (two), XI–XII (two).

Weights

See *Corinth* XII 208ff. pls. 94–5. The small circular or square bronze weights are inscribed with their value in ounces (*unciae*) with the symbol ΓΟ, or *solidi* (*nomismata*) with the letter N. These would have been used with scale balances while the heavier weights of lead encased in bronze were for larger weighing machines and steelyards. Weights F111, 120 and 121 were found in Room IX and might have belonged to one set; weights F115, 116, 117 and 119 are from Room III, perhaps from another set.

An important comparison for these weights may be made with the near-complete set of marked weights found in the (somewhat earlier?) Yassi-Ada wreck. These number eight, ranging from one *nomisma* to one pound. They are studied in detail by G. K. Sams in *Yassi-Ada* I chapter X. All examples that can be directly compared with the Emporio weights are markedly heavier. Sams deduces the use of a very light Byzantine pound of 285 grams, with a pound of fourteen ounces and an ounce of seven *nomismata*, rather than the usual earlier multiples of twelve and six. The highest weight for the ounce at Emporio is given by the three-ounce weight F115, with an ounce of 26.65 grams. Applying this to the other marked weights (see the Table) it can be seen that they all fit quite closely to this standard provided that six *nomismata* are taken to the ounce and not seven. That this is correct for Emporio is also suggested by the steelyard F100 where the pounds are marked in twelfths and the ounces must be presumed divisible into sixths. Only F113 seems a little underweight.

When the same standard is applied to the heavier, but unmarked weights (see Table) it appears that all fit easily into the standard in terms of whole (F119, 121), half (F116, 118) or three-quarter (F117) pounds. F120 is much battered and well below its true weight which may have been five pounds.

The standard gives a pound of at least 319.8 grams, which fits neatly into the range of 313–322 grams proposed by E. Schilbach (*Byzantinische Metrologie* (1970) 160–8; see Sams) for the sixth/seventh century AD; less, of course, than the Roman pound of 327.45 grams. The difference between the Emporio and Yassi-Ada standards should say something, if only negative, about the source of the equipment on the ship. For higher denominations of *nomismata* from Erythrae on the coast opposite Chios, see *AE* 1983, 256–7, nos. 5, 6, 9, 10.

Unbracketed numbers are 'real'. Bracketed are based on calculations from a pound of 319.8 grams; ounce of 26.65 grams; and *nomisma* of 4.44 grams.

Cat. no.	Value	Actual weight	Ideal weight
F111	3 nom.	11.7	(13.32)
F112	4 nom.	17.5	(17.76)
F113	2 oz.	47.7	(53.3)
F114	2 oz.	52.1	(53.3)
F115	3 oz.	79.95	(79.95)
F116	(1.5 lb.)	450	(499.7)
F117	(1.75 lb.)	545	(559.65)
F118	(2.5 lb.)	790	(799.5)
F119	(4 lb.)	1270	(1279.2)
F120	(?5 lb.)	1460	(1599)
F121	(8 lb.)	2530	(2558.4)

F111. FIG. 55; PLATE 32. Bronze weight. Diam. 2.4; weight 11.70 gms. Inscribed NΓ above rough curved lines. Three *nomismata*. Fortress floor, Room IX.

F112. FIG. 55; PLATE 32. Bronze weight. Diam. 2.5; weight 17.50 gms. Within a dotted circle the letters NΔ; above is a cross below an inverted triangle, and concentric circles around the centre hole. On the back concentric circles. Four *nomismata*. Fort.

F113. FIG. 55; PLATE 32. Bronze weight. Diam. 3.4; weight 47.70 gms. In a border of arcs and dots ΓOB with a cross above. Two ounces. Fortress floor, Room XI.

F114. PLATE 32. Bronze weight. Diam. 3.4; weight 52.10 gms. In a border of chevrons ΓOB with a cross between. Two ounces. Fortress floor, Room VIII.

F115. PLATE 32. Bronze weight. 3.2 × 3.2; weight 79.95 gms. In a border of chevrons and arcs ΓOΓ with a cross between. Three ounces. Fortress floor, Room III.

F116. FIG. 55. Lead weight with iron loop and bronze hook. Greatest diam. 4.6; weight 450 gms. Fortress floor, Room III.

F117. FIG. 55. Lead weight with iron loop and centre bar. Greatest diam. 4.6; weight 545 gms. Fortress floor, Room III.
F118. FIG. 55. Lead weight with iron loop, encased in two hemispherical bronze covers. Greatest diam. 5.6; weight 790 gms. Fortress floor, Room XIV.
F119. FIG. 55. Lead weight encased in bronze with two bronze links attached. H. of weight and loop 9.5; weight 1270 gms. Fortress floor, Room III.
F120. FIG. 55. Lead weight with fragment of iron loop; the lead encased in two hemispherical bronze covers. Greatest diam. 8.2; weight 1460 gms. Fortress floor, Room IX.
F121. FIG. 55. Bronze weight, probably with a lead core. Total H. 13.0; weight 2530 gms (30 gms less than the modern Greek 2 *okades*). Pairs of incised grooves on its surface. Fortress floor, Room IX.
F122. FIG. 55. Tapering cylindrical lead weight. H. 2.9. Fortress floor, Room XIV–XV.

3. Jewellery and Miscellaneous

Sundry Decorative

F123. FIG. 56; PLATE 32. Intaglio ringstone of pale sard. 1.7 × 1.3 × 0.15; bevelled edges. Asklepios with his stick and snake, holding an alabastron. The type is a common one (cf. *Lexicon Iconographicum* II s.v. 'Asklepios'; the alabastron is unusual but not surprising). Probably 2nd cent. AD. Fortress floor, Room IX.
F124. FIG. 57; PLATE 32. Fragment of onyx cameo. 1.2 × 1.15 × 0.1. Two youths (?). Fortress floor, Room IX.
F125. PLATE 32. Pendant in a bronze mount with broken loop. 2.6 × 1.8 × 0.7. The 'stone' is an *operculum* from a shell of the species Turbo, its smooth calcareous deposit being exposed here. The back of the pendant is closed with a bronze plate. Fortress floor, Room XI.
F126. FIG. 55. Boar's tusk pierced at one end; in the hole part of an iron pin. L. 5.2. Perhaps from a pendant. Fortress floor, Room XI. Cf. the similar pierced tusk, *Prehistoric Emporio* II 675, no. 55, pl. 142, which is from the archaic temple (i.e., also Basilica) area.
F127. FIG. 55; PLATE 33. Bone gaming counters. Average thickness 0.2, diam. 3.1. Fragments of sixteen were found, of which six were white, the others black; some of the white were burned. Cf. *Corinth* XII 217. Fortress floor, Room XII.
F128. PLATE 30. Glass bangles, fragments. Pale green and dark blue, twisted strips.
F129. Glass stud. Cf. *Corinth* XII 223, where it is suggested that such are inlays for jewellery. An example from Pindakas, *BSA* liii/iv (1958/9) 303 no. 14. Fort.
F130. FIG. 55. Glass disc. An inlay or gaming counter. Fort.
F131. FIG. 55. Lead cross-in-circle pendant. Diam. 3.0; thickness ca. 0.2. Cf. *Corinth* XII 256. 11th century or later. Found on the chest of the latest burial in Tomb I beside the chapel within the Fortress.
F132. FIG. 55. Bronze pin with a spherical head. Extended L. 9.0. Cf. *Corinth* XII 278. Bas. JJb, from 0.50–0.90m below surface outside north wall of basilica.
F133. Bronze pin with a spherical head. L. 5.3; the head W. 0.5. Bas. area.
F134. FIG. 55. Bronze pin with a looped head. L. 7.0. Fortress, Room XII.
F135. FIG. 55. Bronze ring. Diam. 2.1–2.3; thickness 0.1–0.2. Fortress floor, Room XIV–XV.
F136. FIG. 55. Pair of bronze earrings (?). 2.4 across. Bas. B, from eastern tomb in section 9 level (2a). FIG. 16. Probably mediaeval.
F137. PLATE 33. Lead statuette of the Virgin holding the Child. H. 6.6; slightly squashed. Pierced by four holes, at either side of the neck and legs. Bas. MM section 3 level (5) FIG. 13(a).
F138. FIG. 55. Bronze tweezers. L. 4.0. Bas.
F139. PLATE 33. Lead seal. W. 2.3. The monogram and legend are too poorly preserved to read. Cf. *Corinth* XII 312f. 9th cent. AD. Fortress, from a road of the reoccupation period beside Room IX.

Stones and Marbles

F140. Fragment of Chian breccia plaque, pink, yellow and grey. L. 6.0; thickness 1.5. SS. From surface level in sounding A, FIG. 1.
F141. Fragment of a plaque of lapis lacedaemonius. L. 3.6; thickness 0.4. Fort.

3. THE FINDS

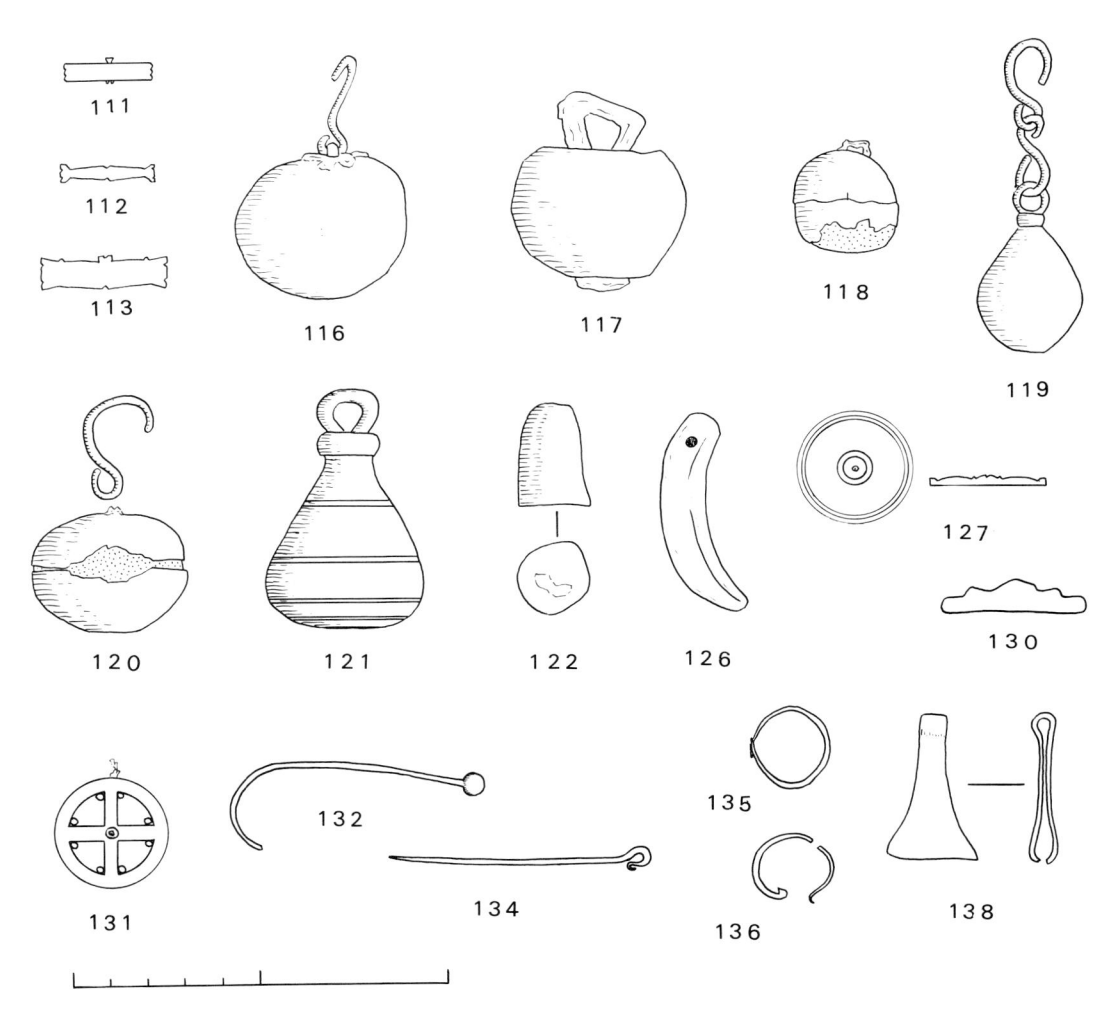

FIG. 55.

FIG. 56.

FIG. 57.

Miscellaneous

The purpose of most of these objects is not clear.

Bronze

F142. FIG. 58. Socket or band. L. 4.0; diam. 0.8. Fortress floor, NW Tower.
F143. FIG. 58. Socket or band. L. 6.7; diam. ca. 2.2. One end is plugged with cementlike material. Fortress floor, NW Tower.
F144. Disc, slightly convex. Diam. 4.2. No holes, so presumably not a scale pan. Fortress floor, Room III.
F145. FIG. 58. Disc fr. Diam. 4.5. Fortress floor, Room XIX–XX.
F146. FIG. 58. Strip with a lightly ridged edge. 5.0 × 1.6. Bas. JJa, from c. 1.00–1.25m below surface beyond north wall of basilica. Cf. coins C8, 9, 11, 14.
F147. FIG. 58. Perhaps from the lip of a vase. L. 3.3. Bas, VV section 1 level (12) DRAWING III G.
F148. Strip fr. L. 16.5, max.width 3.0, thickness 0.1. A slot cut near one end and a thin strip threaded through it. Fortress floor, Room XXII.

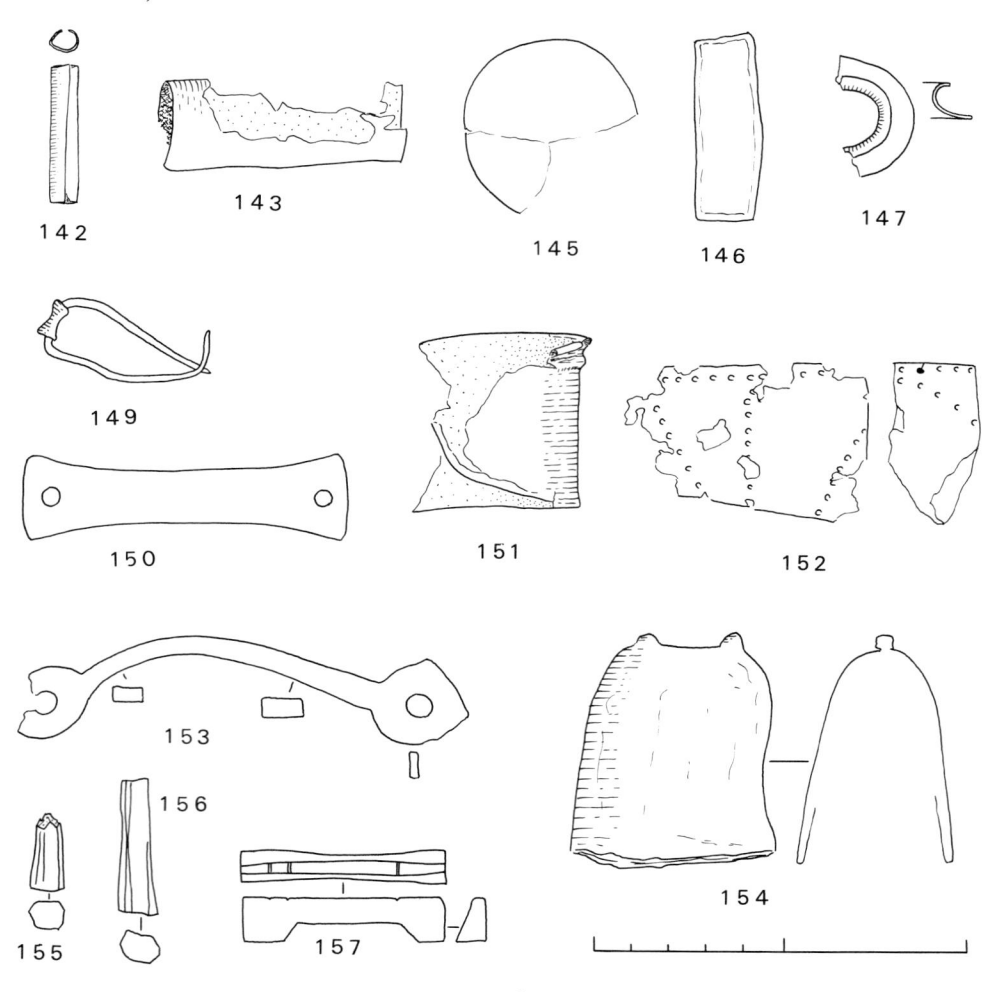

FIG. 58.

F149. FIG. 58. Bent rod with reel moulding; perhaps a handle. L. 4.5. Bas. From *Greek Emporio* 52, fig. 28 Trench E north of basilica apse.
F150. FIG. 58. L. 8.8; thickness 0.2. Bas. From *Greek Emporio* 52, fig. 28 Trench C SE of basilica.
F151. FIG. 58. Cylindrical container?; flattened. H. 4.7. A small pot or casing. Fortress floor, NW Tower.
F152. FIG. 58. Sheet frr. with impressed decoration. L. 6.5 and 4.4. Fortress, Room XIV–XV surface.

Iron

F153. FIG. 58. L. 12.0. Bas. B, section 9 level (3) or (4) FIG. 16.
F154. FIG. 58. Bell? H. 6.5. Fortress floor, Room III.

Bone

F155. FIG. 58. Peg? L. 2.3. Bas. From continuation of deposit of section 8 level (7) FIG. 16, in RR in northern half of apse.
F156. FIG. 58. Peg? L. 3.8. Bas. From same deposit as F155.
F157. FIG. 58. L. 5.4. Bas., B section 9 level (2) FIG. 16.

4. Coins

For Greek coins from the Fortress and the Basilica area see *Greek Emporio* 229, nos. 433–5, 437–42. Note that no. 437 (a 3rd-cent. BC coin of Erythrae) is from below the foundations of the north wall of the Basilica.

I am indebted to various scholars for help with these coins: Dr Philip Grierson, Dr Colin Kraay+, Dr Cathie King, Mrs V. Pennas, Dr Helen Brown, Dr Michael Metcalf.

All the coins listed are of bronze.

Roman

C1. Phaselis, Lycia. 1st cent. BC/AD. Diam. 19mm; wt. 4.58g.
   Obv. Athena Promachos, with thunderbolt and aegis; letters ΦΒ.
   Rev. Nike over prow.
   Cf. *BMC* Lycia 82, 19. Basilica foundations, under the archaic inscription, *Greek Emporio* 186, no. 22. G section 4, FIG. 14.
C2. Elaea, Aeolis. 1st cent. BC. Badly worn. Diam. 15mm; wt. 2.9g.
   Obv. Head of Persephone.
   Rev. ΕΛΑΙΤΩΝ and torch in wreath.
   Cf. *BMC* Troas 127, 20–7. Fortress debris, Room XI.
C3. Patrae, posthumous Augustus. 1st cent. AD. Diam. 26.5mm (clipped in half); wt. 5.05g.
   Obv. Augustus radiate. [DIVUS AUGUS]TUS PATER
   Rev. Colonist ploughing. [COL A A] PATRENS
   Bas. From continuation of deposit of section 8 level (7), FIG. 16, in RR in northern half of apse. Cf. C5.
C4. Eastern mint (Constantinople, Nikomedia, Kyzikos or Alexandria). Honorius — Theodosius II. AD 408–423. Diam. 14mm; wt. 2.15g.
   Obv. Head.
   Rev. Emperors hold globe between them. GLORIA ROMANORUM.
   Cf. R. A. G. Carson and J. P. C. Kent, *Late Roman Bronze Coinage* (1960) GLORIA ROMANORUM type 23.
   Bas. N, from section 10 level (4) FIG. 17, below mosaic floor of Narthex.

C5. Diadumenian, Ephesus. AD 217/8. Diam. 16mm; wt. 2.6gr.
Obv. Head of Diadumenian. ...] VMENIANOΣ.
Rev. Artemis beside tree, hand to head. ΕΦΕΣΙΩΝ.
Cf. *BMC* Ionia 90, 298(obv.), 299(rev.); *McClean Coll.* III no. 8135 (rev.). Bas. From same context as C3.

C6. Maximianus Herculius (286–305), Heraclea?. AD 292–5. Diam. 23mm; wt. 1.78gr.
Obv. Head with radiate crown, paludamentum. IMPCMAMAXIMIANUS P F AUG
Rev. Emperor receiving Victory from seated Jupiter. CONCORDIA MILITUM
Cf. *RIC* V.2 289, 595(obv.). Fortress surface.

C7. *vacat.*

Byzantine

DOC = A.R.Bellinger, *Catalogue of the Byzantine Coins in the Dumbarton Oaks Collection* (1960–)
MIB = W. Hahn, *Moneta Imperii Byzantini* (1973)

C8. Zeno (474–91), minimus. Diam. 8.5mm; wt. 0.8g. Cf. H. L. Adelson and G. L. Kustas, *ANSNotes and Monographs* 148 (1962). Bas. JJa, from 1.26m below surface beyond north wall of basilica. Cf. C9, 11, 14.

C9. Minimus, late 5th cent. AD. Diam. 10mm; wt. 1.25g. Those with a cross on the rev. are generally attributed to Theodosius II, AD 408–50. Bas. JJa, from 1.17m below surface beyond north wall of basilica. Cf. C8, 11, 14.

C10. Anastasius I (491–518), follis, large module. Diam. 32mm; wt. 16.6g. Constantinople; off. E. Dated 512–17 (*MIB* I 27), or 498–518 (*DOC* 23k3). Bas. MM section 3 level (6) FIG. 13, below later floor.

C11. Anastasius I, pentanummium. Diam. 12mm; wt. 1.85g. Constantinople. Dated as last. Bas. JJa, from 1.26m below surface beyond north wall of basilica. Cf. C8, 9, 14.

C12. Justin I (518–27), follis. Diam. 33mm. Constantinople; off. B. Dated 522–7 (*MIB* I 12), 518–27 (*DOC* 9b2). Pindakas,

C13. Justin I, half follis. Diam. 24mm; wt. 7.7g. Constantinople; off. Γ. Dated as last (*MIB* I 19; *DOC* 15c1). Bas. JJb, from 1.15m below surface beyond north wall of basilica. Cf. C16.

C14. Justin I, pentanummium. Diam. 12mm; wt. 1.65g. Constantinople; off. E. Dated as last (*MIB* I 33; *DOC* 22b2). Bas. JJa, from 1.22m below surface beyond north wall of basilica. Cf. C8, 9, 11.

C15. Justinian I (527–65), decanummium. Diam. 15mm; wt. 1.8g. Probably Nikomedia. Dated 564/5 (*MIB* I 118b; *DOC* 161.2). Bas. T section 2 level (9) FIG. 13, from 2.60m below surface.

C16. Justinian I, pentanummium. Diam. 13mm; wt. 2.32g. Constantinople. Dated 542/3–551/2 (*MIB* I 103b), 543–65 (*DOC* 97e1–10). Bas. JJb, from 1.15m below surface beyond north wall of basilica. Cf. C13.

C17. Justin II (565–78), follis. Diam. 30mm; wt. 10.5g. Constantinople. Dated 575/6 (*MIB* I 43a; *DOC* 40c). SS. From 1.96m below surface in Trench E level (7) FIG. 18.

C18. Justin II, half follis. Diam. 21mm; wt. 6.72g. Thessalonica. Dated 566/7? (*MIB* II 68b; *DOC* 62). Bas. VV section 1, DRAWING III (b). Recorded as from 2.87m below surface at bottom of level (13) but probably fallen from above.

C19. Similar? very decayed. Diam. 23mm; wt. 5.0g. Obv. bust. Regnal year 1 or 2? Bas. T section 2, FIG. 13. Apparently from 2.90m below surface in level (11a) with building debris from time of construction of basilica church complex.

C20. Similar, but obv. two seated figures; very worn, mint and date illegible. Diam. 22mm; wt. 4.75g. Bas. T section 2, FIG. 13, from 2.00m below surface in level (5c) with debris of Period I destruction. Cf. C30.

C21. Tiberius II (578–82), pentanummium, broken and worn. Diam. 14mm; wt. 0.55g. SS. From c. 0.75m below surface in Trench A, FIG. 1.

C22. 6th-cent. pentanummium, worn; Justinian or earlier? Diam. 11mm; wt. 1.15g. Bas. MM section 3, FIG. 13, from 2.04m below surface in level (7) which appears to be building debris from time of construction of basilica church complex.

C23. Phocas (602–10), follis. Diam. 31mm; wt. 11.2g. Constantinople? Dated 606/7 (*MIB* II 61c; *DOC* 29a–d). Fortress floor, Room VIII (make up of floor?).

C24. Heraclius (610–41), follis. Diam. 28mm; wt. 10.03g. Cyzicus; off. B. Dated 610/1 (*MIB* III 184; *DOC* 167b). Fortress, below floor Room XXII.

C25. PLATE 33. Heraclius, follis. Diam. 32mm; wt. 12.1g. Constantinople?; off. A. Dated 610–3 (*MIB* III 158; *DOC* 70d1). Official style? Fortress, Room IX below deposit raising level of road.

C26. Heraclius, half follis. Constantinople. Date 610–13? (*MIB* III 169a; *DOC* 72–3b). Basilica area. From *Greek Emporio* 52, fig. 28 Trench C, SE of basilica. Cf. C40, 47, 48.

C27. Heraclius and his son Heraclius Constantine, follis. Diam. 33mm; wt. 12.55g. Constantinople; off. E. Dated 613 (*MIB* III 159b; *DOC* 76e1–4). Fortress, Room XI.

C28. Heraclius and his son Heraclius Constantine, follis. Diam. 39mm; wt. 3.9g. Nikomedia; off. B. Dated 613/14? (*MIB* III 175a; *DOC* 159b.1–4). Fortress, makeup of road beside Room XII.

C29. Heraclius and his son Heraclius Constantine, follis, struck over a follis of Phocas from the mint of Nikomedia. Diam. 34mm; wt. 11.0gr. Constantinople; off. Γ. Dated 615/16 (*MIB* III 160; *DOC* 81b). Fortress floor, Room XXII.

C30. Heraclius, half follis, severely worn. Dated 614/15. Bas. T section 2, FIG. 13, from 2.00m below surface in level (5c) with debris of Period I destruction. Cf. C20.

C31. Heraclius, his son Heraclius Constantine and wife Martina, follis. Diam. 28mm; wt. 3.95g. Constantinople. Dated 616/17 (*MIB* III 161; *DOC* 90c). Fortress, Room XXII.

C32. Heraclius and his son Heraclius Constantine, half follis. Diam. 19mm.; wt. 4.4g. Thessalonica. Dated 618/19 (*MIB* III 228; *DOC* 144.1–4). Fresh condition. Fortress, Room VIa.

C33. Heraclius (three standing figures: Heraclius, his son and wife), follis. Diam. 25mm; wt. 7.55g. Thessalonica; off. B. Dated 624/5 (*MIB* III 221; *DOC* 147). Fortress debris, Room XXII.

C34. Heraclius (figures as last), half follis. Diam. 23mm; wt. 3.52g. Thessalonica. Dated 626/7 (*MIB* III 229; *DOC* 151). Bas. From 1.25m below surface in trial of 1953 in area of MM.

C35. PLATE 33. Heraclius (figures as last), follis. Diam. 27mm; wt. 7.15g. Thessalonica; off. B. Dated 627/8 (*MIB* III 221; *DOC* 148). Bas. CC, from 1.00m above pebble mosaic floor in SE corner of South Stoa of Atrium just south of doorway into Narthex.

C36. Heraclius (figures as last), half follis. Diam. 22mm; wt. 4.5g. Thessalonica. Dated 630/1 (*MIB* III 229; *DOC* 151). Fortress floor, Room XII.

C37. Heraclius (two standing figures of Heraclius and son), follis. Diam. 29mm; wt. 7.0g. Constantinople; off. B. Dated 632/3 (*MIB* III 164b; *DOC* 108b). Overstruck. Bas. CC (later UU), from 0.95m below surface (c. 0.50m above pebble mosaic floor) on east side of Anteroom to Baptistry.

C38. Heraclius (figures as last), half follis. Diam. 26mm; wt. 5.1g. Constantinople? After 629/30 (*MIB* III 171a; *DOC* 118–9). Fortress Chapel, below floor.

C39. Heraclius, half follis. Diam. 24mm. Badly worn. Thessalonica? Dated 635/6. Fortress, Trench DF.

C40. Constans II (641–8), follis. Constaninople; off. . Dated Year 2? (=642/3) (*MIB* III 162c; *DOC* 60b). Basilica area. From *Greek Emporio* 52, fig. 28 Trench C, SE of basilica.

C41. Constans II, follis. Diam. 24mm; wt. 5.35g. Constantinople; off. B? Dated Year 5? (=645/6) (*MIB* III 167). Fortress, cleaning floor in NW Tower.

C42. Similar type, badly worn, issued 642–8. Diam. 24mm; wt. 5.3g. Fortress debris, Room XXII.

C43. Similar type, badly worn. Diam. 23mm; wt. 4.96g. Fortress, Room XIII.

C44. Similar type, badly worn. Diam. 25mm; wt. 6.05g. Fortress floor, Room XXII.

C45. Constans II, follis. Diam. 23mm; wt. 4.7g. Constantinople; off. E? Dated 642/3 (*MIB* III 163a; *DOC* 61e1). SS. Trench E.

C46. Constans II, follis. Diam. 24mm; wt. 4.8g. Syracuse. Dated 642/3 (*MIB* III 204), 641 (*DOC* 9a–f under Heraclonas). Fortress floor, Room XXIV.

C47. Constans II, follis. Constantinople. Type issued 655/6–657/8 (*MIB* III 173c or d; *DOC* 77a–78b2). Basilica area. From *Greek Emporio* 52, fig. 28, Trench C, SE of basilica. Cf. C26, 40, 48.

C48. Constans II, follis. Constantinople. Dated 659/60 (*DOC* II,2 class 9). Basilica area. From *Greek Emporio* 52, fig. 28, Trench C, SE of basilica. Cf. C26, 40, 47.

C49. PLATE 33. Constantine IV (668–85), half follis. Diam. 29mm; wt. 9.2g. Constantinople; off. E. Dated 673? Similar to *MIB* III 83, *DOC* 35b, but here the emperor bears a shield on his left shoulder and holds a globe, not spear. SS. From c. 0.75m below surface in Trench C, FIG. 1.

C50. PLATE 33. Nikephoros I (803–11), follis. Diam. 23mm; wt. 4.6g. Cf. M.Metcalf, *Byzantion* 37 (1967) 279; *DOC* III,1 no. 5. Fortress, slab floor of reoccupation period, Room XX.

C51. PLATE 33. Leo V and his son Constantine. Diam. 19mm; wt. 2.5g. Sicily. Date 813–20. Fortress, reoccupation floor, Room IX.

Cyprus under the Venetians

C52. Pietro Loredan, 1567–70. AE Sixain. Diam. 19 mm; wt. 1.6 gr. Suspension hole, 1.5 mm diam.
Obv. [+SANCTVS MARCVS VENET] Lion of St Mark rampant.
Rev. [+PETR]VSL[AV]REDA [DUX] Cross, with lozenges in angles.
Cf. G. Schlumberger, *Numismatique de l'Orient latin* (1878–82) pl.8, 9. Basilica area. Found in dump.

C53. Similar. Diam. 20 mm; wt. 1.8 gr. Bas. From 1.33m below surface in equivalent of section 8 level (8) FIG. 16 in RR in northern half of apse. Probably from a later grave sunk into it.

Chios under the Genoese

C54. Battista Giustiniani Campi, podesta, 1487–8. Billion denomination. Diam. 20 mm; wt. 3.6 gr.
Obv. [CIVITAS.CHII] In the left half of the field, castle with three turrets, surmounted by crowned eagle; in right half, chatel tournois. Below, BI.
Rev. [CONRADVS REX ROMA. Cross potent]
Cf. Schlumberger, pl.15, 11. Bas. MM section 3 level (5) FIG. 13, from 1.62m below surface above late floor. Cf. C55.

C55. Domenico di Gio, Antonio Giustiniani Campi, Podesta, 1529. Diam. 19.5 mm; wt. 3.2 gr.
Obv. +CIVITAS CHII. Castle with three turrets, surmounted by crowned eagle. To left and right, D I.
Rev. +CONRADUS.REX.ROMA. Cross.
Cf. Schlumberger, pl.15, 13. Bas. MM section 3 level (5) FIG. 13, from 1.17m below surface north of wall A1.

C56. Similar. Diam. 18 mm; wt. 3.05 gr.
Only the I of D I is clearly visible, but the form of the cross in the rev. suggests that it is as Schlumberger, pl.15, 13, rather than 12, 14 or 15 on the same plate.
Bas. From 1.46m below surface in same context as C53.

C57. Similar? Poor condition. Diam. 19 mm. Disintegrated. Bas. From 1.50m below surface in GG just beyond north wall of basilica. Presumably from the later grave found here.

Chios under Turkish rule

C58. Cairo, Mustafa III, 1757–73. Diam 20 mm. Bas. J, from 0.99m below surface just outside main entrance into Narthex.

C59. Constantinople, Abdal-Majid, 1839–61. Diam. 14 mm. Bas. From dump.

C60. Constantinople, Abdal-Majid?. 1839–61. Diam. 21 mm. Bas. From above mosaic floor at east end of South Aisle.

Chapter 4
Tombs at Emporio and Dotia

Sinclair Hood

Tomb 2 in Area E at Emporio (FIG. 59. PLATE 34 (*a*), (*b*)).
The owner of the land told us about the existence of this grave low down on the north slope of the hill some metres to the west of the Mycenaean cist graves (tombs 3 and 4) (see *Prehistoric Emporio* i 86 fig. 47). The grave proved to be about 2.25m long by 0.85m wide, lined with roughly squared stones of various sizes, the joints between them being filled with cement. Two slabs about 0.18m wide projected a few centimetres from the sides at the east end of the grave at a height of about 0.60m above the floor (shown in Section A–B on FIG. 59). The slabs which covered the grave had been removed from it by the owner of the land before we came to excavate it. The grave contained the confused remains of three or four skeletons. We found nothing with them; but grave and burials are likely to date from the Early Christian period contemporary with the Basilica Church.

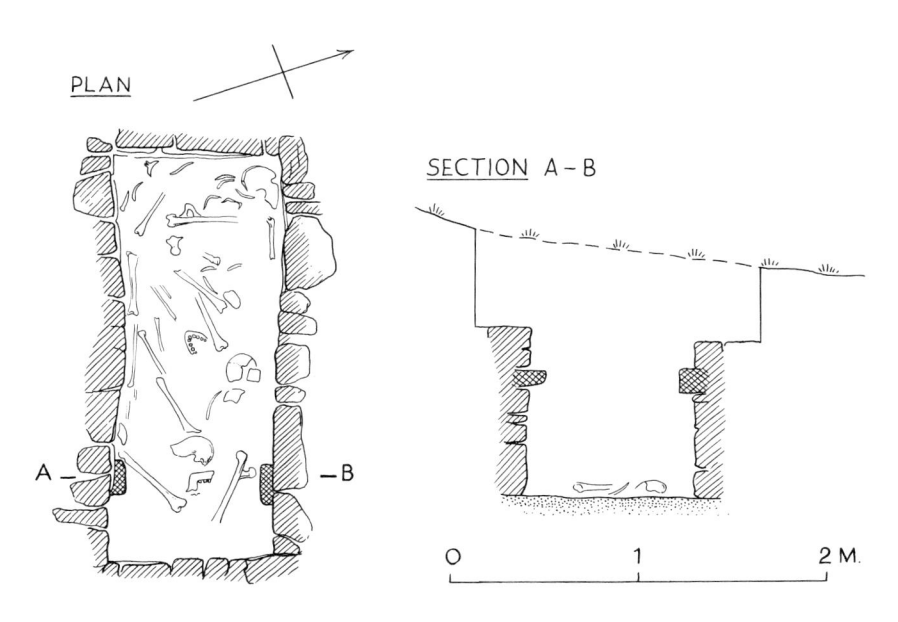

FIG. 59. Early Byzantine tomb at Emporio.

Roman tomb at Dotia (FIG. 60. PLATE 34 (*c*)–(*f*)).

This large stone-built tomb is romantically situated at the far western end of the plain of Dotia above the little bay of Vroulidhia a few kilometres south of Emporio (B on map, *Prehistoric Emporio* i 3 fig. 1). The rude construction of the chamber and its corbelled roof give it a venerable appearance, and the plan and elevation are reminiscent of the Isopata Royal Tomb at Knossos, although on a much smaller scale. This and the fine view from the site of the tomb across the waters of the Aegean no doubt gave rise to the suggestion that it might have been the burial-place of a Minoan sea-captain (*BSA* xli (1940–45) 38f.). The tomb, however, is certainly Roman or Early Byzantine, as I was able to establish during the course of investigations in the autumn of 1952 (see *JHS* lxxiii (1953) 124).

I was informed that the tomb had been discovered by Mikhaili Yiannakis about 1935. A modern hut or cottage was already it seems in existence beside it by the time of the Second World War (*BSA* xli (1940–45) 38). The chamber is underground and measures about two metres in length by 1.50m in width. It is lined with rectangular blocks of limestone set in courses. The exposed faces of these blocks have been roughly dressed. The joints, especially the horizontal ones between courses, tend to be wide, and in some cases at any rate small flat chips of stone have been inserted in them. The joints were filled with pink mortar, which overlapped generously onto the faces of the blocks where it was smoothed to give a flat surface. The existing earth floor of the chamber is nearly 0.10m below the bottoms of the walls (PLATE 34 (*c*)). The chamber may have been originally floored with stone slabs, but all traces of these had been removed before the time of my visit, if they had ever existed.

The upper three courses of masonry forming the side walls of the chamber are corbelled inwards; these courses are somewhat narrower than the lower three (PLATE 34 (*c*), (*d*)). The gap which remained across the top of the chamber was closed with three flat stone slabs; that on the west had also spanned the doorway and entrance of the tomb, but it had been broken (I was told) by Mikhaili Yiannakis in a search for treasure. The owner of the site at the time of my visit, Sidheros Yiannakis, also informed me that, when the tomb was discovered in the 1930's, the doorway was found blocked with a stone slab, and a single clay vase was recovered from the chamber.

The north wall of the entrance had been partly destroyed, and all traces of its south wall had been removed, by the time I saw the tomb in 1952. But remains of a floor of white cement were preserved in the entrance at a height of about 0.40m above the level of the existing earth floor in the chamber. The chamber may have been entered down a step or steps situated in the area occupied by the doorway.

In the autumn of 1952 I was able to clear away the soil over the roof of the chamber and expose the western end of it. The joints between the cover slabs and the area round their outer edges had been sealed with hard cement. A loose fill of quite small stones had been dumped into the spaces round the cover slabs on the north, south and east. The distance between the outer edges of this stone fill from north to south across the top of the tomb was about 2.95m.

The cover slabs are of some interest. That at the eastern end of the roof was about a metre long and some 0.75m wide. On the east side of it a kind of ridge about 0.06m wide could be distinguished through the cement which covered the joint here (see plan of top of tomb on FIG. 60). The fragment of another slab, which was lying in loose soil about 0.10m above the top of the chamber roof (FIG. 60 top left. PLATE 34 (*f*)), was 0.71m wide, and was preserved for a length of 0.98m with one end missing. Round the surviving end and two sides of this fragment were what seemed to be the broken stumps of walls *c.* 0.05–0.06m wide and only preserved to a height of 0.02m or less. At the time of the excavation this fragment and the slab incorporated in the roof of the tomb looked to me as if they might have formed part of the base of a limestone sarcophagus. A comparable fragment was visible in the 1950s built into the wall of a house at Anemonas north of Pindakas (see map, *Greek Emporio* xii fig. 1), and the man who found this fragment told us that it had come from a stone coffin.

Dr Stephen Hill has suggested to me, however, that the slabs from the tomb at Dotia might in fact be stone roofing slabs, intended for use like tiles on some monumental building such as a church. Roofing slabs of this kind according to Dr Hill are likely to date fom the fifth to seventh centuries AD, and a date in the fifth or sixth century is rather more probable for roofing slabs of the size of the slabs used to cover the tomb at Dotia.

A small fragment of flanged tile and a few nondescript sherds, including a twisted handle, were noted on the slopes immediately west of the tomb. Whether these might indicate the position of a house connected with the tomb remains uncertain. No other possible traces of a house or settlement of the Roman or Early Byzantine period were observed anywhere else in the area.

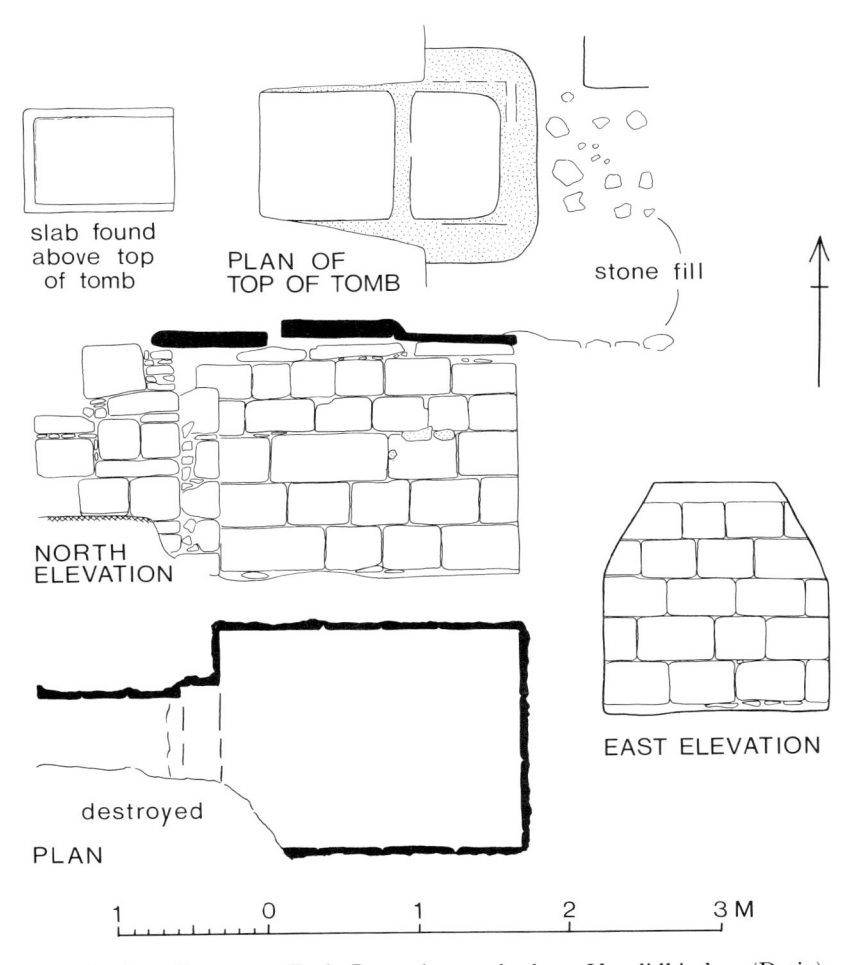

FIG. 60. Late Roman or Early Byzantine tomb above Vroulidhia bay (Dotia).

Plates

PLATE 1

(a) Excavations looking NW from Acropolis, Prehistoric trenches in foreground.

(b) Sea Shore Trials looking N from Acropolis.

(c) Emporio plain from NW, Acropolis in distance.

(d) Earlier column base reused in S stylobate.

(e, f) Earlier column bases (from Greek temple) reused in S stylobate.

GENERAL–BASILICA

PLATE 2

(a) Pavement of nave from NE, S stylobate beyond.

(b) S aisle from SE, S stylobate and nave beyond.

GENERAL–BASILICA

(a) W outside wall of nave from W, doorway from narthex on r.

(b) W outside wall of nave from SE, N stylobate on r.

GENERAL–BASILICA

PLATE 4

(a) Apse of Basilica church from W.

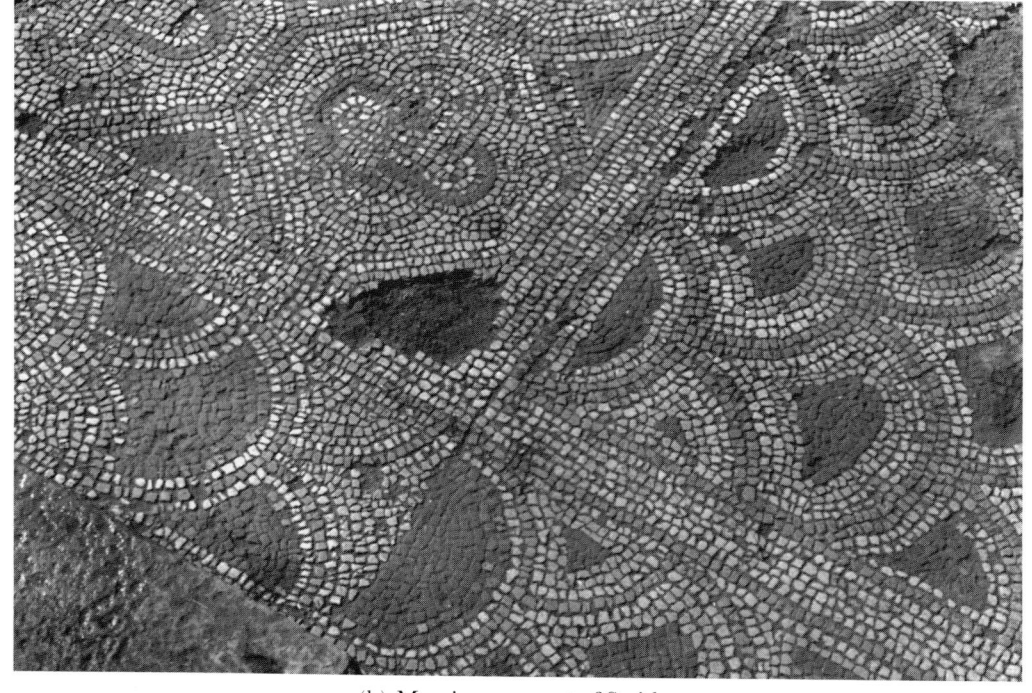

(b) Mosaic pavement of S aisle.

GENERAL–BASILICA

PLATE 5

(a) Reliquary at E end of nave, from S.

(b) Remains of bema rail at E end of nave, from N.

GENERAL–BASILICA

PLATE 6

(a) Column shaft from baptistry.

(b) Fragment of screen of white marble from baptistry.

(c) Dosseret block from S aisle.

GENERAL–BASILICA

PLATE 7

(a) Threshold of doorway between nave and narthex from SW.

(b) Layers below mosaic pavement in N aisle (trench G: Section 4), Archaic statue base in foreground, from N.

(c) Main entrance to church at N end of narthex, from SW.

GENERAL–BASILICA

PLATE 8

(a) Baptistry ante-room from SW, later floor (top l.) and door into S stoa of atrium (top r.).

(b) Baptistry ante-room from W, door into S stoa of atrium, and that from S stoa into narthex (top l.).

(c) Exedra (diakonikon) at S end of narthex.

(d) Mosaic pavement of narthex, from N.

GENERAL–BASILICA

PLATE 9

(a) Exedra (diakonikon) at S end of narthex, from N, steps to door into S stoa of atrium on r.

(b) S stoa of atrium with door into narthex, from W.

(d) Column shafts and capital in S stoa of atrium from E, door into ante-room of baptistry on l.

(c) Steps of door from narthex into S stoa of atrium, from SE.

(e) See (d).

(f) N outside wall of N stoa of atrium in Trench H, from N.

GENERAL–BASILICA

PLATE 10

(a) Baptistry with font and blocked S door, from NE.

(b) S arm of font from N.

(c) Lintel of original E entrance to baptistry.

(d) Wall in sounding E of Sea Shore Trials.

BASILICA–SEA SHORE

PLATE 11

(a, b) Painted plaster on W wall of baptsitry.

(c, d) Late mediaeval graves in area of apse of Greek temple E of Basilica.

(e, f) Acropolis from N and NW.

BASILICA–ACROPOLIS

PLATE 12

(a) W side of Acropolis from W.

(b) Main gate from N, jambs; outer threshold and possible Period I road surface.

(c) Main gate from S in trench T; jambs, inner threshold and Period I road surface.

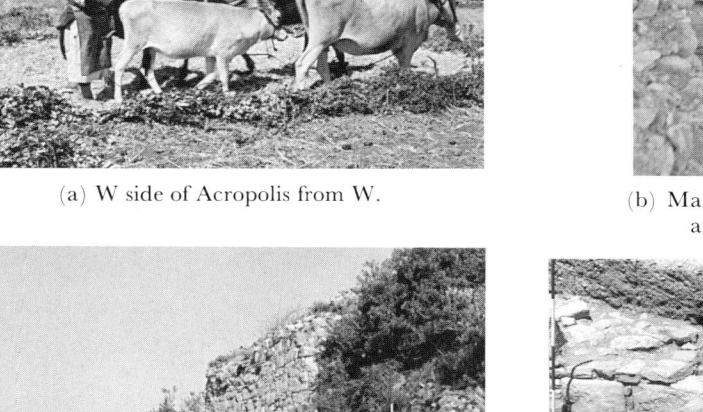

(d) N Tower from NW.

(e) N Tower from NW.

(f) N Tower from SW, interior partly excavated to Period I floor.

FORTRESS

PLATE 13

(a) Outer face of fortification wall on N side before excavation.

(b) As (a) in Trench L 1953.

(c) SW Tower, N wall and cobbled berm, from N.

(d) Junction of outer defence wall (r.) with main wall (at 19 on DRAWING IV) from SW.

(e) Postern by Chapel from NW, Period I cobbled passage, sleeper wall and post-hole.

(f) NW Tower (F 1953), interior from NW with approach passage at l.

FORTRESS

PLATE 14

(a) NW Tower (F1953), drain, doorway and approach passage in Period I, from SW.

(b) NW Tower, amphora and pithoi against S wall, from N.

(c) NW Tower, amphorae and quern (bottom l.) in SW corner, from W.

(d) Trench V 1953, outer face of fortification wall, from W.

(e) Ovens in angle between fortification wall (l.) and N wall of NW Tower, from N (scale in S oven).

(f) Trench T, Period I street paving flanked by walls 41 (l.) and 6, from NW.

FORTRESS

PLATE 15

(a, b) Outer defence wall by NW Tower, from SW; cross-wall and possible threshold of postern (r. of scale in (a), to l. in (b)).

(c) Trenches V, T and S 1953, from W.

(d) Trench V, tiles of Period I destruction, from NW.

(e) Trench S, Period I walls 7 and 8, from NW.

(f) Trenches F and E 1954 from N; period I doorway (with vertical slab) from Room IX into X, earliest Period I street level and wall 32 beyond.

FORTRESS

PLATE 16

(a, b) Period I destruction level Trench F 1954: group of jugs (a); marble dish (F 3) (b).

(c, d) Trench D 1954: (c) from SW, Period I floors and footings of wall 13; (d) from NW, Period I floor and doorway from Room XII into XIII (on r.), Period II wall 52 resting on Period I destruction level and remains of wall 14 (wall 51 of Period II removed).

(e) Trenches A and B 1954 from S, Rooms XXI in foreground, XXII and XX beyond, Period I floors and walls (top of wall 14/16 rebuilt in Period II).

(f) Trench B 1954 from SW; back of fortification wall below recent terrace, Period I floor removed to reveal pre-Roman stone strew.

FORTRESS

PLATE 17

(a) Trench J 1953 from N, Period I doorway in wall 16/18, Period II doorway above it.

(b) Trench J 1953 from SW, Room XIX in foreground and doorway into XVIII, Period I walls and floors (further wall 18 partly rebuilt in Period II).

(c) Trench J 1953 from SE, Period I walls and floors.

(d) Trench A 1954, E end of Room XX from N, Period I destruction level with pithos, jugs and tiles.

(e) Trench A 1954, Period I destruction tiles in room XXII.

(f) Trench C 1954, cistern and wall 26 from E after removal of Period I floor.

FORTRESS

PLATE 18

(a) Trench C 1954 from SE, wall 30 (r. foreground) and Period I slabs overlying edge of cistern.

(b) Cistern in Trench J 1954 from SE.

(c) Trench S 1953 from SW, Period I walls.

(d) Trench D 1954 from W, Period II walls of Room XII with steps up to street, Period I street level in r. foreground.

(e, f) Trench B 1954; (e) Room XIV from NW, Period II doorway with slabs of later Period II floor below, earlier Period II lime floor in foreground; (f) Room XV from NE with early Period II lime floor.

FORTRESS

PLATE 19

(a) Trench B 1954 from SW, Period II walls and door-slab emerging from stone strew.

(b) Trench J 1953 from NE, Period II walls and floors.

(c) Trench A 1954, W half of Room XX from N, Period II floor slabs and two vases (that beyond knife overlying coin C50).

(d) Chapel (A 1953) from E, Tomb I on r.

(e, f) Chapel, Tomb I; (e) from W with cover slabs in place; (f) from E showing burials.

FORTRESS

PLATE 20

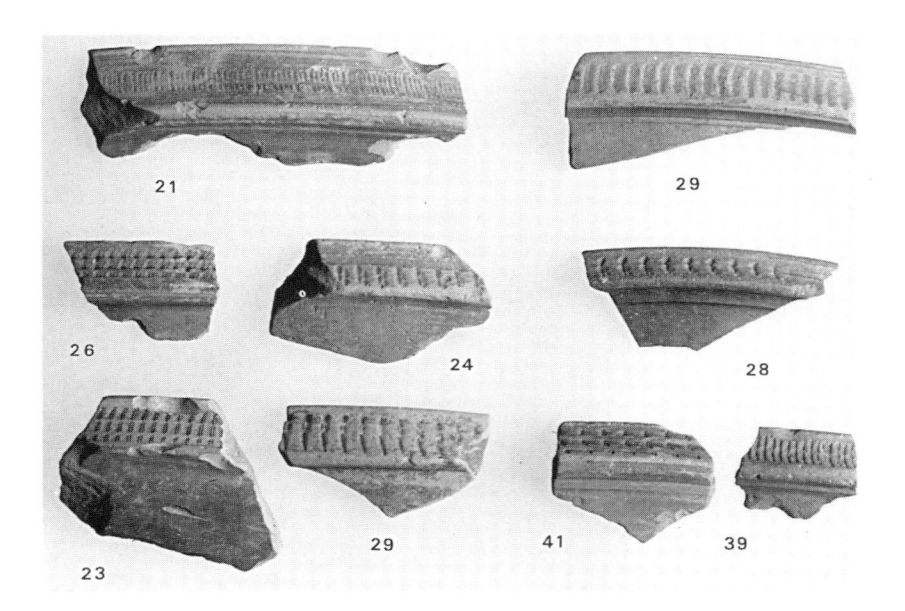

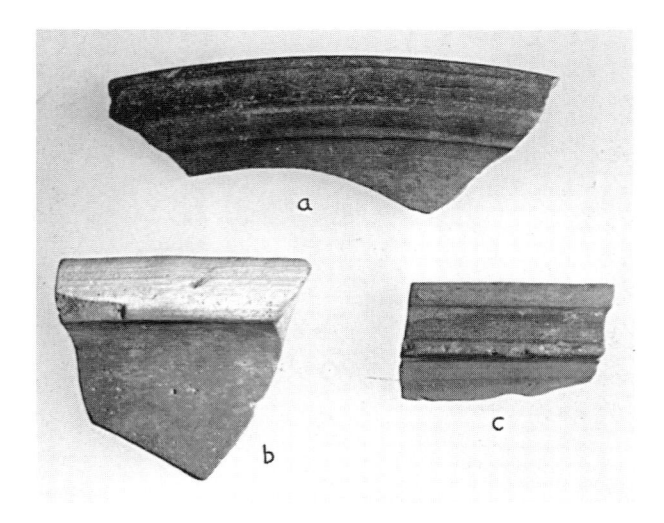

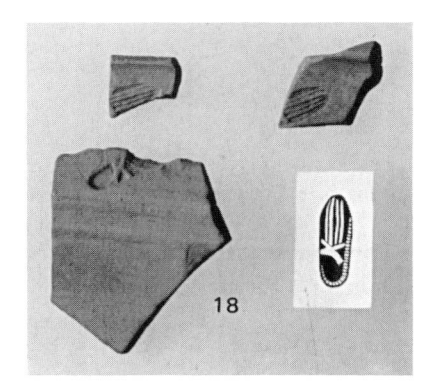

POTTERY

PLATE 21

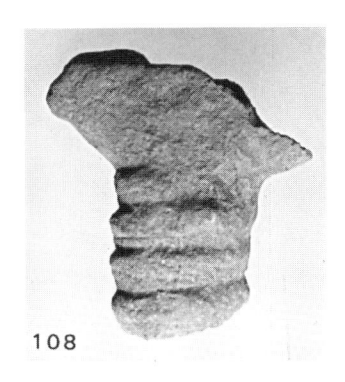

POTTERY

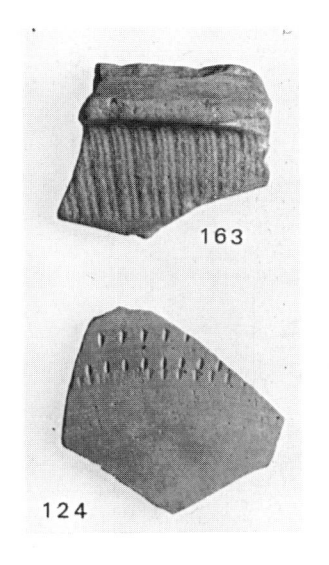

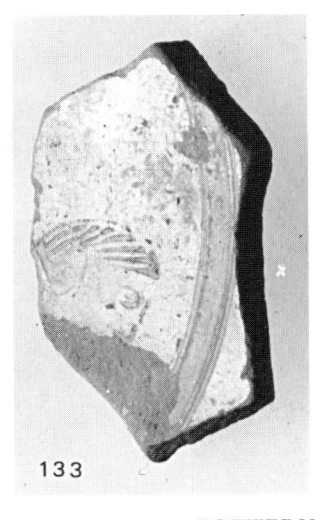

PLATE 22

POTTERY

PLATE 23

POTTERY

PLATE 24

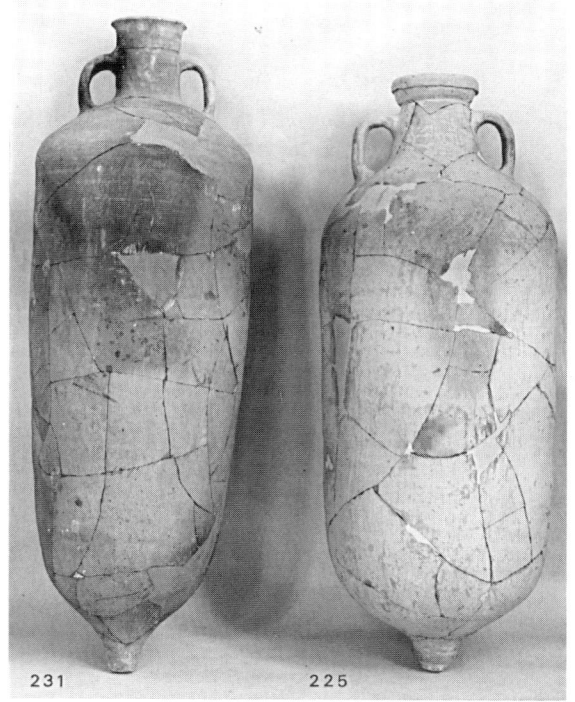

220

222

231   225

236

237

POTTERY

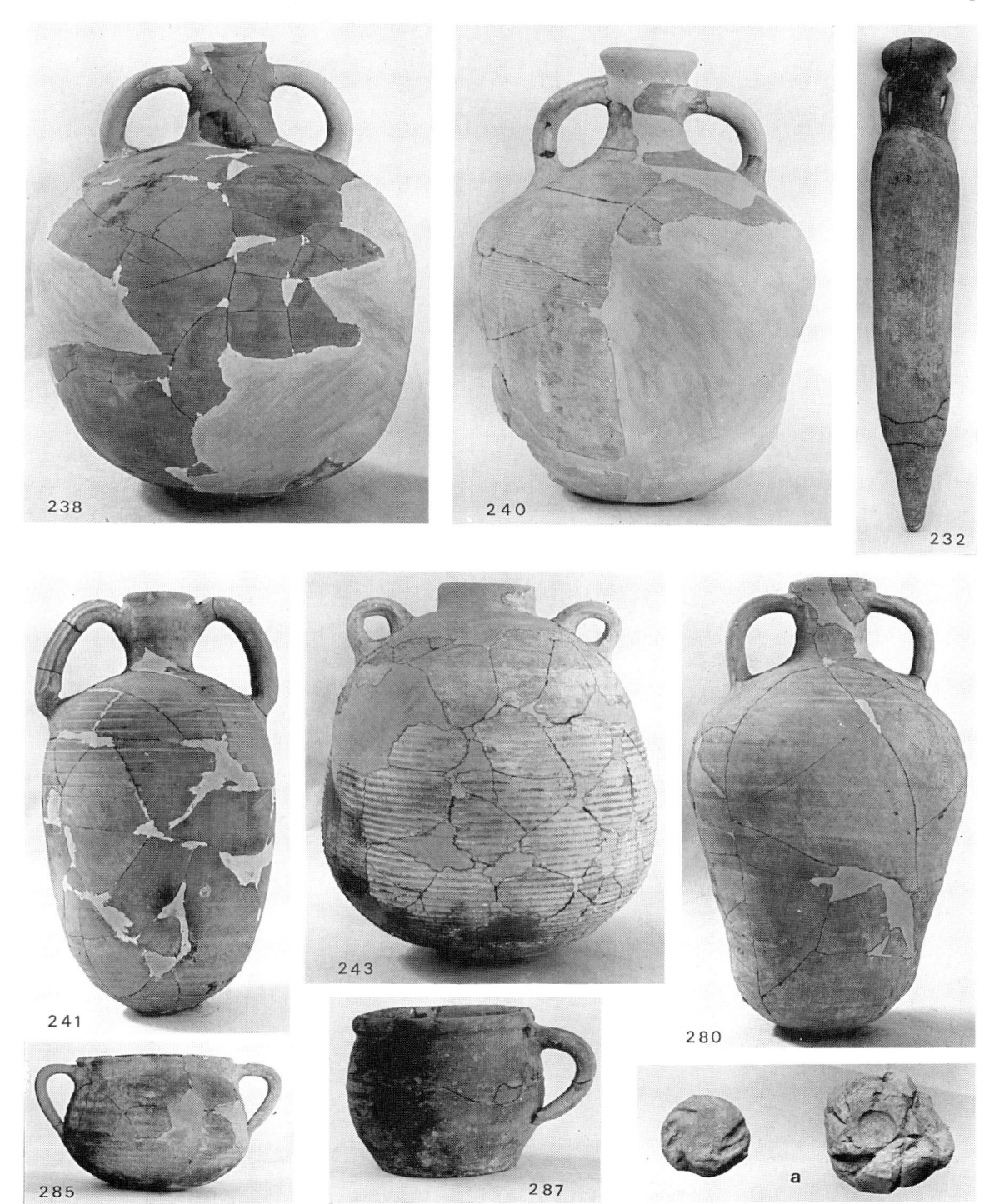

PLATE 25

POTTERY

PLATE 26

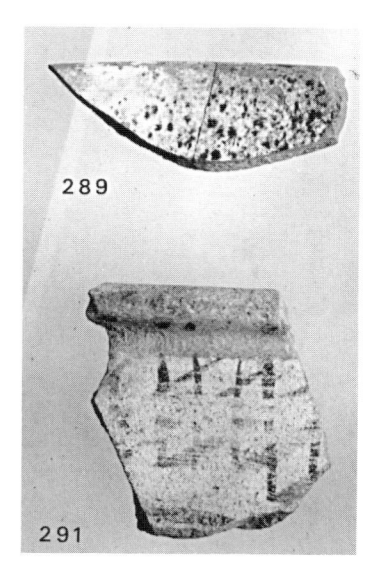

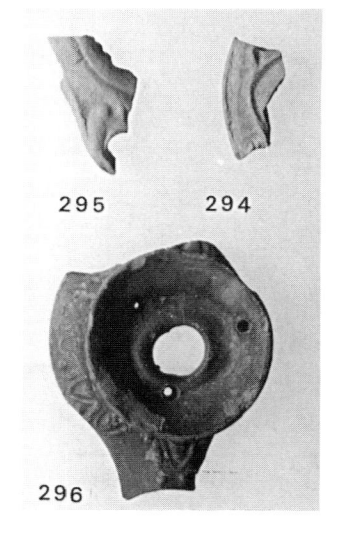

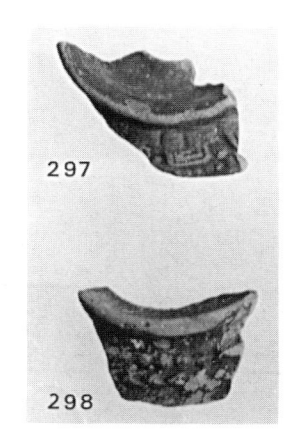

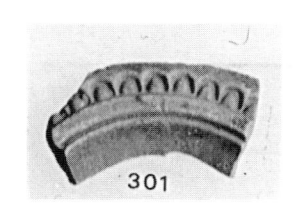

POTTERY—LAMPS

PLATE 27

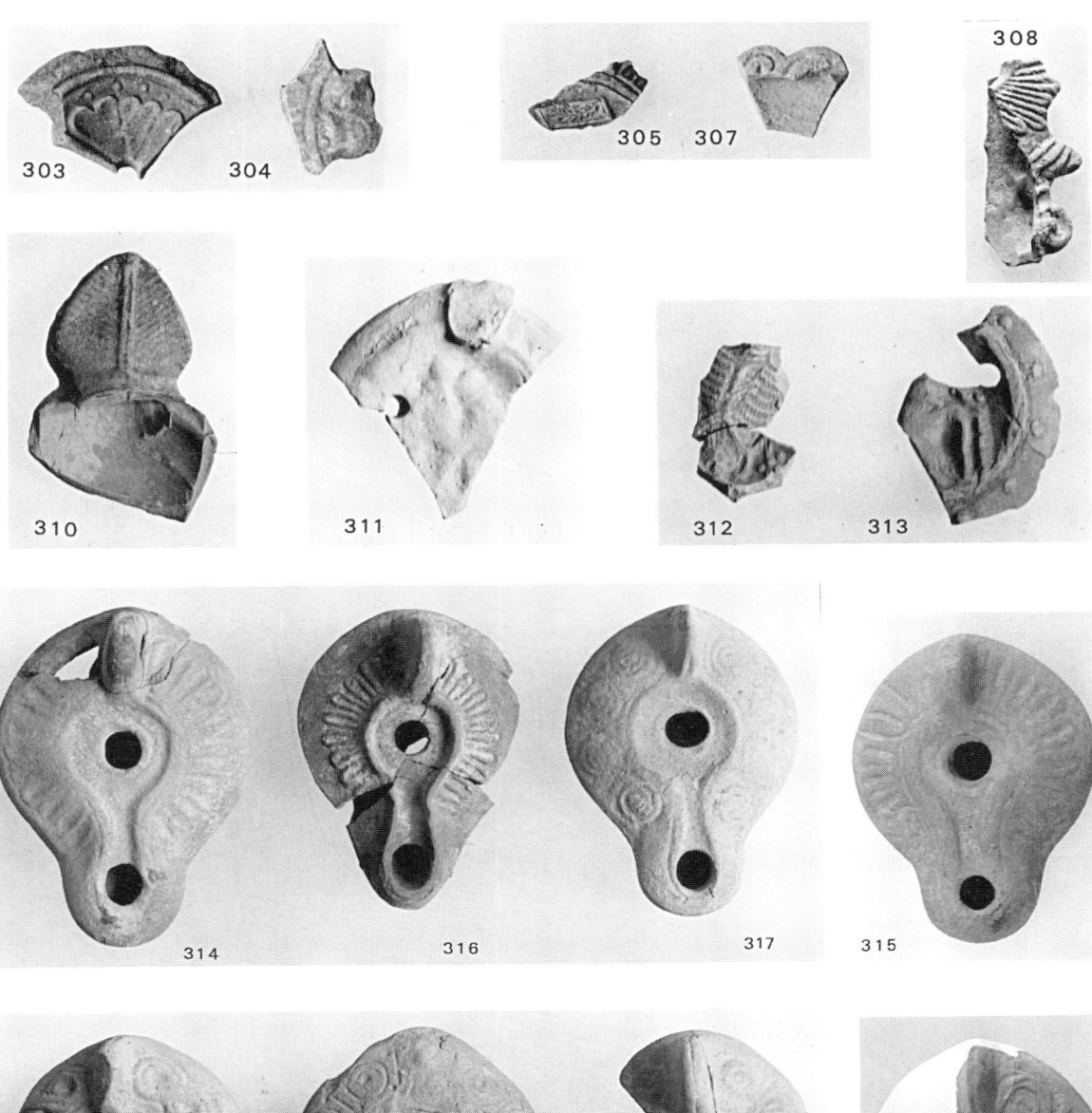

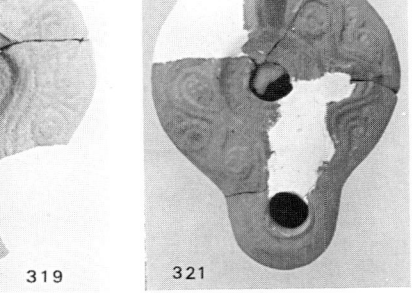

LAMPS

PLATE 28

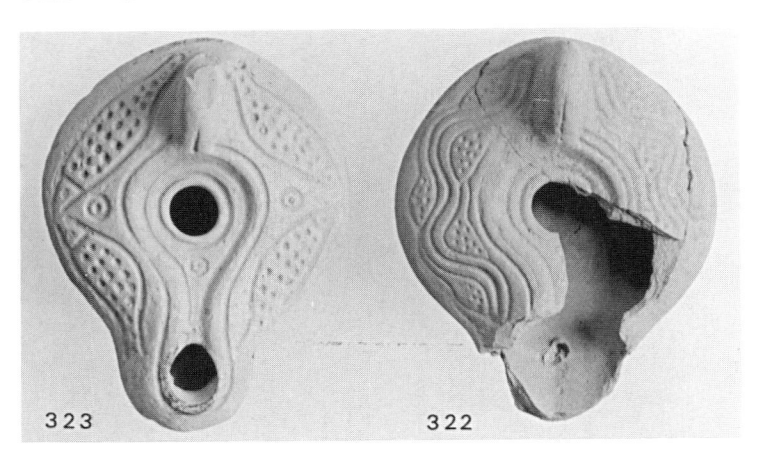

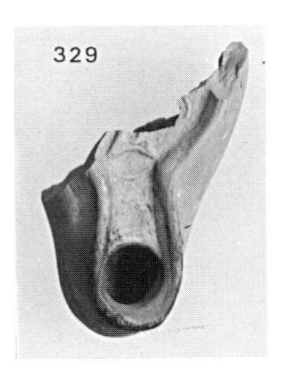

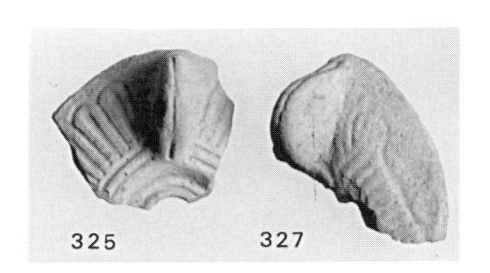

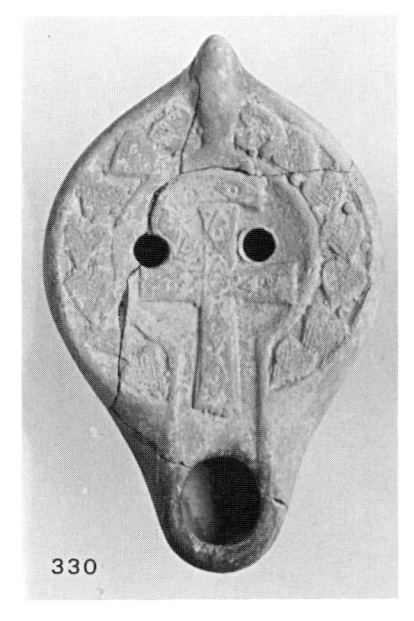

LAMPS

PLATE 29

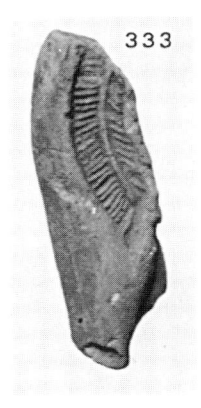

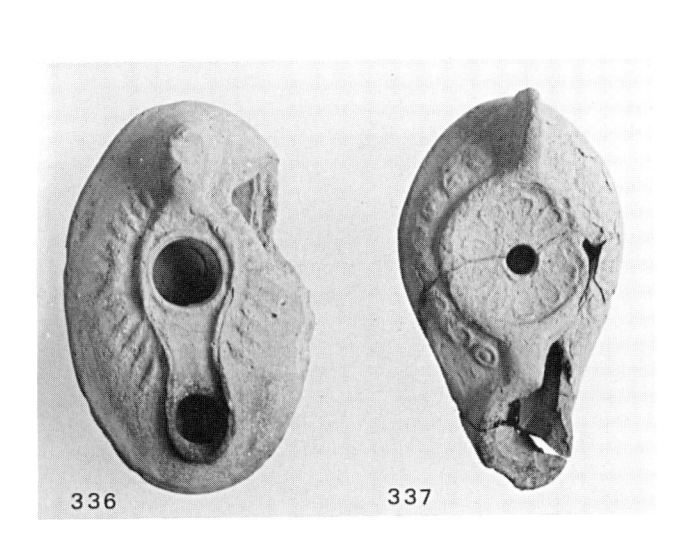

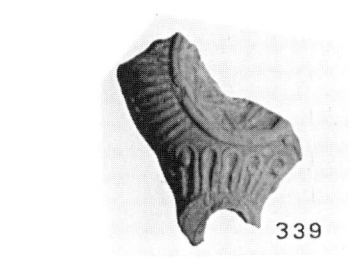

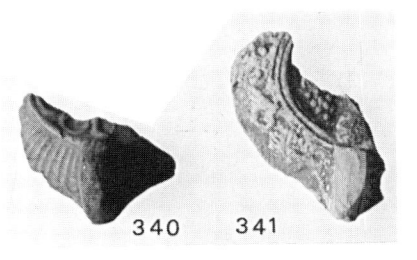

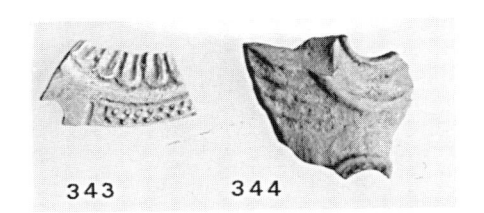

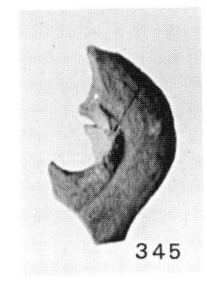

333
334
335
336
337
339
340
341
342
343
344
345

LAMPS

PLATE 30

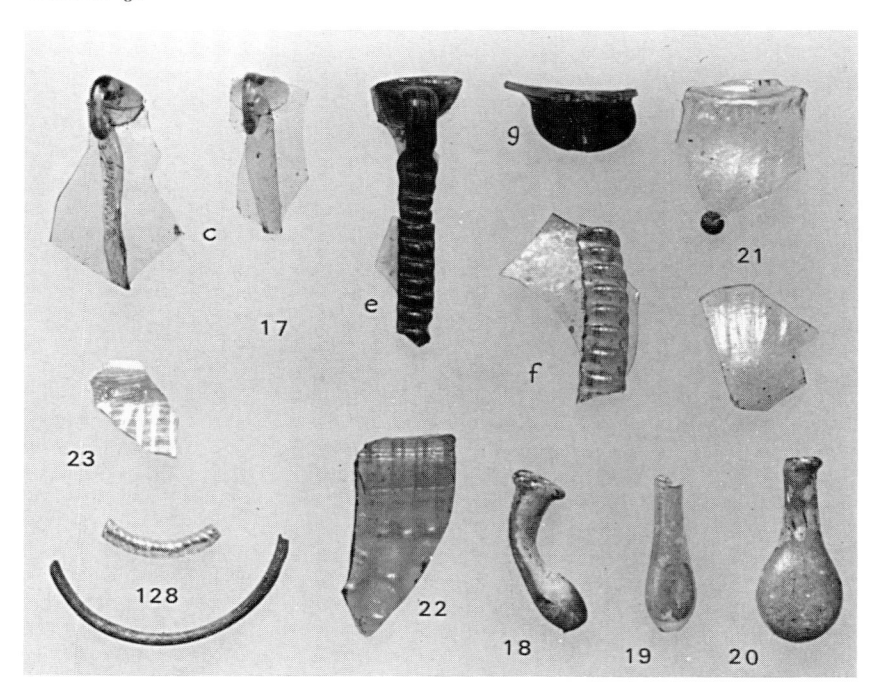

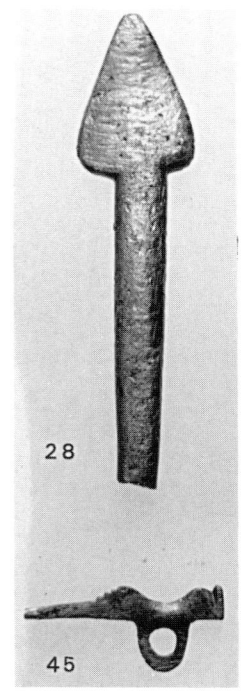

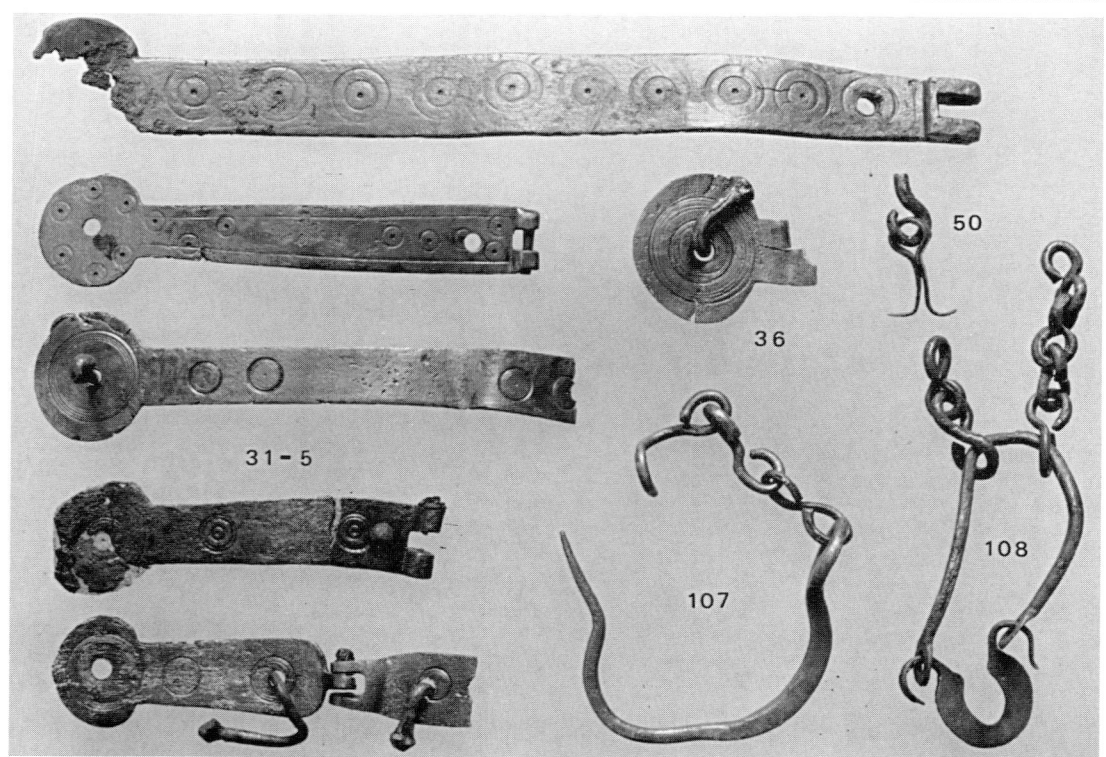

OTHER MATERIALS (F)

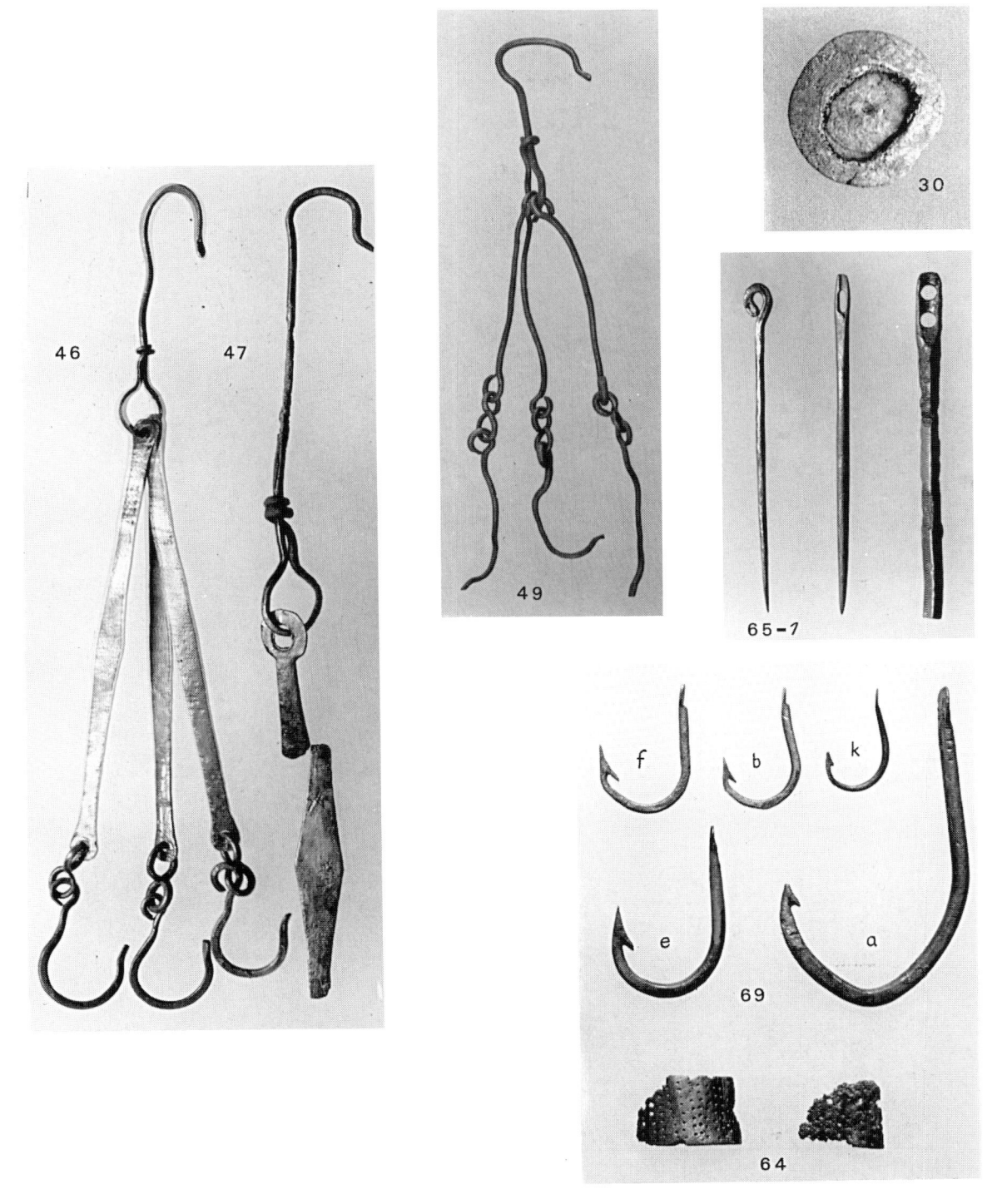

PLATE 31

OTHER MATERIALS (F)

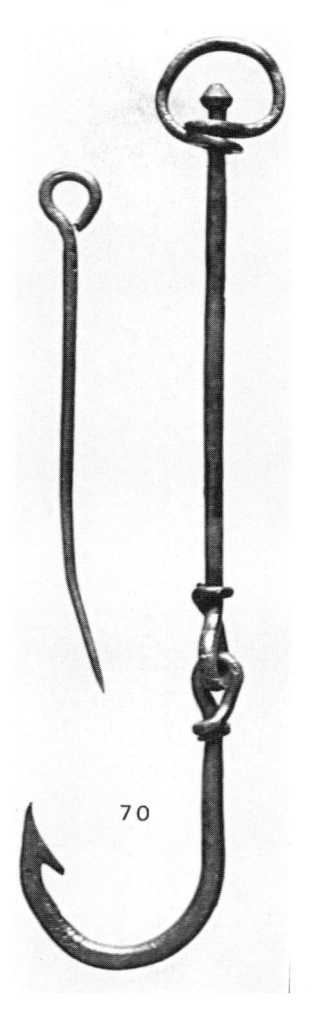

PLATE 32

70

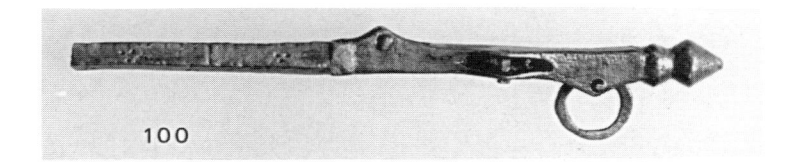

100

111 112

113

114  115

123

124  125

OTHER MATERIALS (F)

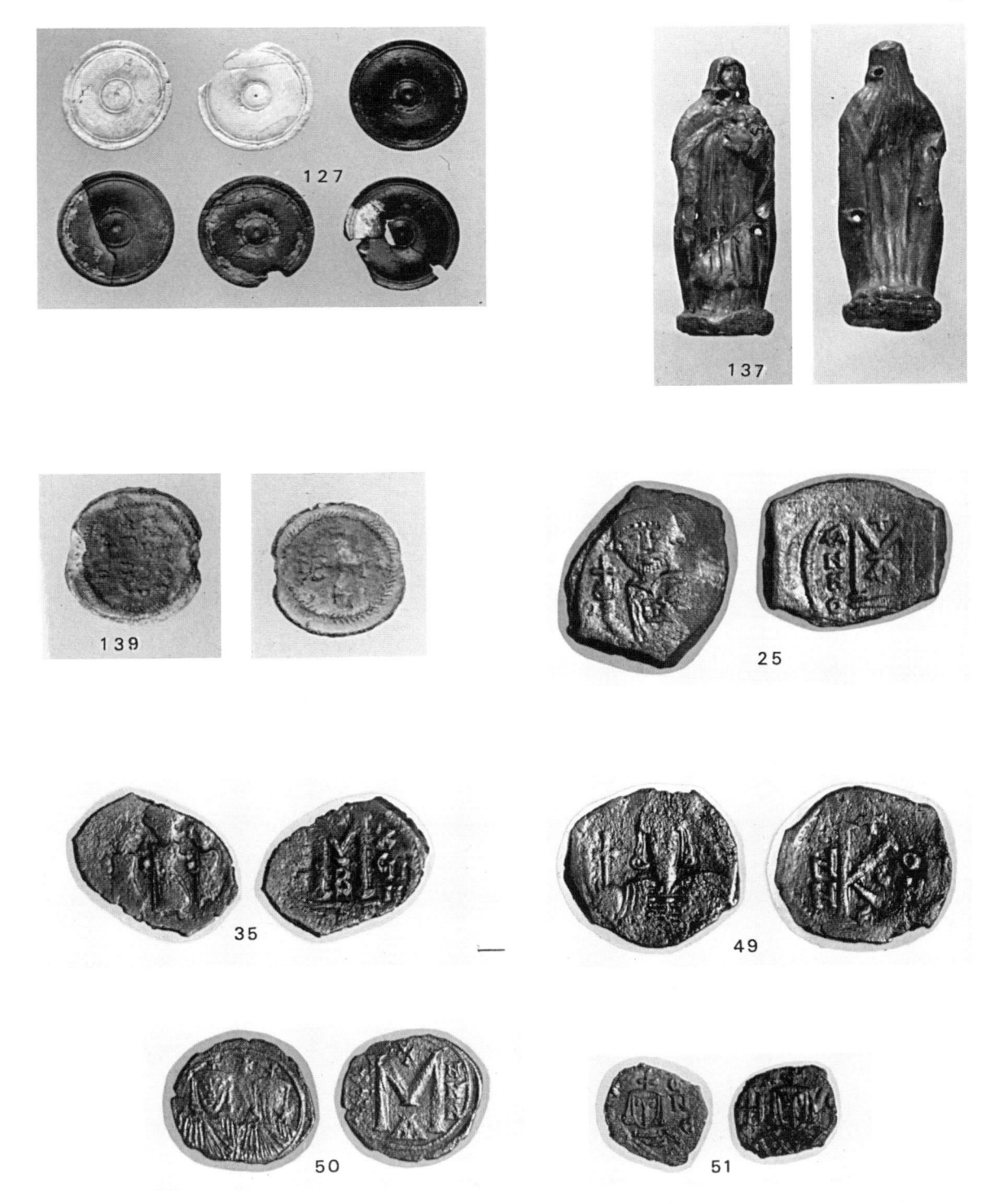

PLATE 33

OTHER MATERIALS (F)—COINS (C)

PLATE 34

(a, b) Tomb 2 at Emporio, (a) from SE, (b) from E

(c) Dotia, tomb above Vroulidhia bay, E end of chamber

(d) Dotia tomb, detail of NE corner of chamber

(e) Dotia tomb, entrance, N side

(f) Dotia tomb, stone tile used as roofing slab

TOMBS AT EMPORIO AND DOTIA